Who Is JESUS CHRIST?

And What Is His Purpose in Our Lives?

Evangelist Denlin J. Henry

Who Is Jesus Christ? And What Is His Purpose in Our Lives?
Copyright © 2024 by Evangelist Denlin J. Henry
All rights reserved • Third Edition

No part of this publication may be reproduced, stored in a retrieval system, or transmitted in any way by any means, electronic, mechanical, photocopy, recording or otherwise without the prior permission of the author except as provided by USA Copyright law.

Scripture quotations marked (NKJV) are taken from the New King James Version. Copyright © 1982 by Thomas Nelson, Inc. Used by permission. All rights reserved.

Scripture taken from the *Contemporary English Version*, Copyright © 1995 by American Bible Society. Used by permission.

Scripture taken from the New International Version. The Listener's Bible Copyright © 2012 by Bibilica, Inc.

Scripture taken from the Holy Bible, New Living Translation, Copyright © 1996 by Tyndale Charitable Trust

Hebrew references from The New Strong's Expanded Exhaustive Concordance of The Bible Red Letter Edition. Dictionary.com Copyright © 2015

Scripture taken from the Holy Bible, The Blue Letter Bible. Online Version. BlueLetterBible.org

New Webster's Dictionary Copyright © 1995 V. Nichols

Author's expression of the words *Soul Healing* was a revelation from God to Expected End Ministries. Used by permission from/representative of www.expectedendministries.com

For general information please contact: whoisjcministry4118@gmail.com

Integrity Publishing House want readers to prayerfully seek the divine council, guidance, advice and wisdom of the Holy Spirit, to lead them in their-individual spiritual growth, and relationship with God the Father and Son Jesus Christ. As the content of this book may be generalized and not specific to their individual personal spiritual needs.

Published by Integrity Publishing House

Edited by Michelle Murphy
Cover and Design by Deborah Ngoho-Toling

ISBN: 978-0-9888687-8-6 paperback
ISBN: 978-0-9888687-7-9 ebook

Biblical Studies / Covenant Living / Evangelism

Acknowledgment

I am grateful to God for giving me the divine supernatural ability to write the words concerning *Who is Jesus Christ? & what is His Purpose in our lives?* And to all my editors, designers and publisher who helped in the creation of this book.

"For I am not ashamed of the gospel of Christ, for it is the power of God unto salvation for everyone who believes…"

—Romans 1:16 NKJV

"Behold, I stand at the door and knock. If anyone hears My voice and opens the door, I will come in and dine with him and he with Me."

—Revelation 3:20 NKJV

Honor

In memory of my loving mother Icilda Henry (*Ms. Icy, Aunt Madam*) and father Hibbert Knibb Henry (*Mass Bert*).

Contents

Man's Beginning 1
The Result of Sin 9
The Plan of God 11
God Sent Jesus 13
The Use of the Blood During the Old Covenant 15
Jesus Christ Became the Curse 21
The Blood of Jesus Christ: The Blood of the New Covenant ... 23
Jesus Christ's Sacrifice 25
What Happened to Jesus Christ's Sacrifice? 27
Scriptures That Support Jesus Christ's Death Burial,
Resurrection, Ascension, and Seating in Heavenly Places 33
Those Who Hesitate to Receive Jesus Christ 35
Can God Receive a Horrible Sinner Like Me? 37
What Is Confessing the Word of God & Receiving Jesus Christ
(Yeshua) as Your Savior and Owner (Lord)? 41
What Does it Mean to Be Righteous? 49
How Do I Live a Righteous Life? 53
The Righteous and Sin's Price Tag 61
You Are Righteous, Not Unrighteous 65
Soul Restoration 67
The Ten Commandments The Old Covenant Era
of God's Judgment 81
The New Covenant Era of Grace: Mercy, Forgiveness,
Love, and Favor 85
Condemnation and Accusations 89

Massa Lad Accuser 91
Why Do You Take on the Name of Jesus Christ (Yeshua)? 97
Faith in God 101
Attitudes That May Hinder Your Faith 117
See Yourself as Christ Sees You 125
Very Important: Remember! Remember! Remember! 131
Prayer and Why Be Filled with the Holy Spirit? 137
Suggested Ways to Do Intercessory Prayer Meetings 149
The Importance of Intercessory Prayer and Praying in the Spirit 153
Watch and Pray 157
The Covenant Blessings of the Tenth 161
Praise and Worship 189
Who Is Jesus Christ (Yeshua)? What Was His Purpose on Earth? 195
Jesus Christ's (Yeshua) Statement 199
Featured Facts from the Bible 205
Lazarus and the Rich Man 207
The Soul of Man 209
Religions and Organizations 217
The Spirit of Man Versus the Soul of Man 221
Lust! Taking Fire to Your Bosom! 225
The Brazen Altar in the Old Testament and the Altar of
the Cross in the New Testament 229
The Lord's Coming for His Followers 231
Evil in the Earth: How Did This Come About? 233
Satan's Purpose on Earth 235
Hell 237
A View Into Hell 239
Telling Others the Good News, Your Mandate from Jesus Christ! .. 243
Glossary 245
Featured Scriptures from the Bible 251
Salvation Prayer 253

About the Author 255

Preface

In some societies, these questions are often asked: *Are you a Christian? Are you born again?* or *Are you saved?* The answers sometimes are, *I am a good person, I believe in God, I go to church sometimes, I am a religious person, I don't know if I am or not,* or *I am a Baptist* or *I am a Catholic.* These statements emphasize the denomination, institution, or a particular religious belief. However, one may not realize that being a Born-Again Believer is a spiritual, heavenly birth from above into the life of Jesus Christ, which is not a natural, physical birth in the earth. It means a life is taken from Satan's evil and death and placed into the everlasting life and love of Jesus Christ and God His Father. It is not having a relationship with an institution, denomination, or a particular religious belief. It is having a personal relationship with God the Father, God the Son Jesus Christ, and God the Holy Spirit. Some people already know that it is a relationship, but they tend to give excuses as to why they are not Born-Again Believers in Jesus Christ. They equate the Spiritual, Born-from-Above with their life experiences, whether good or bad: *I am too sinful, God can not forgive me,* or *I must clean myself up first.* Others equate Born-Again / Born-from-Above experience with their perception of other Believers in Christ: *The church is full of hypocrites* or *the preacher only wants my money.* For some people to develop a relationship with Jesus Christ, they need to know and understand the necessity or importance of inviting the Savior, whom they may not see but is written in the pages of a book called the Bible, into their private lives.

The book *Who Is Jesus Christ? And What Is His Purpose in Our Lives?* gives the reason why one should be Born Again, regardless of one's perceptions, excuses, experiences, prior knowledge, or ignorance about Jesus Christ.

One should also keep in mind that the Gospel does not necessarily have to be shared in a lengthy book because a transformed life can be a testimony to the delivering and saving power of Jesus Christ. Jesus Christ wants all of us to go and tell others of the great things He has done for us, like He told those in the Bible. Someone who was a drug addict or an alcoholic and is now free because of receiving Jesus Christ into their lives can share their testimony and bring others to Christ. No testimony is too small when shared with others.

Some people, after hearing the Gospel today, will reject Him and say, "Tomorrow I will become a Born-Again Believer in Jesus Christ," but one can never depend on tomorrow because tomorrow is not promised to anyone. The Bible says today is the day to receive Jesus. There are no genuine, legitimate, or truthful reasons for someone not to receive Jesus Christ as their Savior and Lord after they have heard the Gospel message, which tells them that eternal life with Him belongs to the whole world. This book was written to explain why it is necessary to surrender one's life to Jesus Christ, believe and confess that He is Lord, and thus experience an eternal transformation.

After one becomes a Born-Again Believer in Jesus Christ, growing up spiritually is a process. Believers in Christ are being birthed all over the world and for some new Believers, Bible-based churches may not exist. Therefore, feeding their spirits on the Gospel of Jesus Christ will more than likely have to be done using various forms of technology as communication becomes more advanced. Without compromising the written Word of God, the framework and foundation of a Believer's spiritual growth, regardless of geographical location, must be uniform and grounded in the teachings of Jesus Christ—not based on man-made cultural traditions, religions, or their organized beliefs, but on Jesus Christ and His body (of Born-again Believers/Christians) and the work of the Holy Spirit Who is in the earth and is responsible for the operation of the ministry of Jesus Christ church of Believers.

Basic biblical principles and some narratives which provide a greater understanding while maintaining godly doctrines are addressed in this book as Jesus Christ wants to reach every life with His Gospel. This is what lead to the expansion and title change of the 2007 publication, *Who Is Jesus Christ? And What Was His Purpose On Earth?* to *Who Is Jesus Christ? And What Is His Purpose in Our Lives?*

Man's Beginning

When God the Father, God the Word, and God the Holy Spirit (the three-in-one God) created man, He spoke the words, "Let Us create man in Our image, according to Our likeness; let them have dominion over the fish of the sea, over the birds of the air, and over the cattle, over all the earth and over every creeping thing that creeps on the earth" (Genesis 1:26 NKJV). "For by Him all things were created that are in heaven and that are in earth, visible and invisible" (Colossians 1:16 NKJV).

The Bible states, "By the Word of the Lord the heavens were made and all the host of them by the breath of His mouth. For He spoke and it was done; He commanded, and it stood fast" (Psalm 33:6, 9 NKJV).

God who is Spirit and the Giver of Life created man in the likeness of Himself. He created the spirits of the male and the female, and He called them both man. "So He created man in His own image; in the image of God He created him; male and female He created them" (Genesis 1:27 NKJV).

God placed a physical man on earth to be in control of it, to take care of it, to make decisions, to rule with authority, and be a master over all that He made on earth. God formed man's body from earth's material, the dust or ground of the earth, and breathed into his nostrils His God breath—the breath of everlasting life—and man came into physical existence on earth. So both the male-man and the female-man's spirit entered into a physical body from the breath of God. The Bible states, "And the Lord God formed man of the dust of the ground and breathed into his nostrils the breath of life: and man became a living being" (Genesis 2:7 NKJV). (The word being in the context of this verse does not mean "self-existent." It means man came into "being alive" or a *nephesh* in Hebrew which means self, person, soul. God is the only one who gives life.) He is the only self-existent life, and all life comes from Him.

Man is a spirit, he has a soul and he lives in a body. The spirit in man's body is a reflection or a mirror of God, who is Spirit. The Breath of Life or the Spirit of Life that came out of God and went into man's body was man's *ruwach* in Hebrew, which means "wind, breath, life, spirit." Man's spirit is the real life in his body. The body is simply the vehicle or transportation in which man's spirit travels. For example, when a man rides in the body of a car, that car does not make the man a car too. Similarly, the spirit of a man only "rides" in his body.

God's intent was for man, His likeness, to represent Him in the earth, to speak like Him, to decree, to declare His Word in the earth, and to act like Him: kind, loving, faithful, and holy. Man is the mirror image of God Himself, "a god-man" in the earth, with similar characteristics as He, God in Heaven. There are three parts to a man in the earth: the spirit, soul, and body. The soul of a man consists of the **will**—ability to choose, **mind**—thought, thinking, reasoning, memory, imagination, intellect, knowledge, understanding, perception, and emotional state: feeling and emotion. God, who is Spirit, lives forever; therefore, male, female—man's spirit and soul—also lives forever. God and man are spiritually immortal: endless, ceaseless, perpetual, eternal. God placed man in a garden to take care of it. This garden was called Eden. Like any parent, God told man what to do and what not to do. He told the first man not to eat of the fruit of one of the trees, which was the Tree of Knowledge of Good and Evil. He told him that he would die if he ate from that tree. He could, however, eat from any of the other trees in the garden. "And the Lord God commanded man, saying, 'Of every tree of the garden you may freely eat; but of the tree of the knowledge of good and evil you shall not eat, for in the day that you eat of it you shall surely die'" (Genesis 2:16-17 NKJV). This means man would be cut off from the image/ likeness of God in him.

The first man's occupation was to name every animal—beast and bird of the air in the earth, but none of God's creations looked like man. God wanted to give him a suitable helper. Therefore, God put him into a deep sleep and took a rib out of Adam, the name of the first man. It is important to note that the name Adam represents all mankind, which are both male- and female-man together, not him as an individual. God separated the female-man out of Adam and made a woman who became Adam's wife. His wife was the female gender of man, or the feminine man called a woman (*ishah* in Hebrew means the female-man who was taken out of the male-man). The word *ish* means "male-man" as an individual person/husband in Hebrew, the male gender of man or the masculine man. God instituted marriage for the male and female Adam to be joined together as one Adam, or Mankind, who would multiply and populate the earth that He gave to them to rule. "He created them male and female, and blessed them and called them Mankind in the day they were created" (Genesis 5:2 NKJV).

Genesis 2:20–23 (NKJV) states, "So Adam gave names to all cattle, to the birds of the air, and to every beast of the field. But for Adam there was not found a helper comparable to him. And God caused a deep sleep to fall on Adam, and he slept and He took one of his ribs and closed up the flesh in its place. Then the rib which the Lord God had taken from the man, He made into a woman and He brought her to the man. And Adam said, 'This is now, bone of my bones and flesh of my flesh; She shall be called Woman. Because she was taken out of Man.'"

When Adam looked at the woman, he saw that she looked like none of the species he named. She was of his same flesh and bone. They were both of the human race and made up of the same genetic DNA, which is the base material of chromosomes. Chromosomes transmit hereditary patterns called genes, which are microscopic bodies that pass on hereditary characteristics to future offspring such as personality, genetic traits, and habits. After the fall of Adam even certain sicknesses and diseases are passed down through generations to grandparents, to parents, and to the child. Sin is also passed down in the spirit/soul of man.

There was an evil serpent, which was the Devil or Satan within the serpent's body. He befriended Adam's wife and told her that she would not die if she ate the fruit from that particular tree of which God said not to eat. The evil spirit within the serpent told her that God was lying to her and her husband. He knew that if they ate the fruit from that tree, their eyes would be opened and they too would be like God, knowing good and evil.

Satan gave them this dishonest suggestion in order to deceive and betray God's Truth, His Word, and who they already were– god-like or God's image. Note the serpent's lying, deceitful words from Genesis 3:4–5 (NKJV), "Then the serpent said to the woman, 'You will not surely die. For God knows that in the day you eat of it your eyes will be opened and you will be like God, knowing good and evil.'" Like an unbelieving and disobedient child, Adam's wife listened to her lying, evil friend, the serpent Satan, and ate the fruit from the forbidden tree and gave it to her husband, who also ate it, choosing to believe the evil deception and lie instead of conforming to God's Will and command. God gave them a choice: do not eat of the tree and good will follow or eat of the tree and evil will follow.

They were both to dominate, rule, manage, and govern Earth with God-given words. This principle of operation within their lives in earth was for both the male and the female man, who were previously separated by God and brought back together as one Adam or mankind in the institution of marriage established by Him. God the Father, God the Word, and God the Holy Spirit are three-in-one, but they each function in different roles. Within a marriage covenant the husband and wife also function in different roles or assignments. The role of the husband is to be the initiator of enforcing the Words given to him by God. God's Word is His Will, His truth, authority, command, and law in the earth when spoken, confessed or acted upon by humankind. The wife is to be her husband's helpmate, companion and assistant in enforcing God's Will or Words. They were to dominate/rule in the earth with God's Words. The husband and wife were caretakers of the earth God created. They were authorized to proclaim God's Truth, which is His will, and the words they hear Him say, just like an ambassador speaks on behalf of the country he represents. Therefore, the question from God to Adam. His authorized voice in the earth was, "Who told you, you were naked?" (Genesis 3:11 NKJV) The rich relationship God had with man was disrupted by the words of a lying, evil spirit hiding in a serpent's body. The moment Adam's wife added the words, "touch the fruit", the enemy had an open door to deceive her because God's instruction was not to eat the fruit. He said nothing about touching. Therefore, adding a lie unto God's Word of Truth is sin. Lying was an open invitation for the serpent to deceive. Therefore, the serpent could then give her deceptive, erroneous instructions. Adam, the male-man, believed and obeyed his wife's instructions to eat what God told him not to eat. Satan willfully interfered in God's divine order of submission in this marriage covenant. Adam's wife submitted to the serpent's crafty instruction instead referring it to her husband. Her husband submitted to her and the serpent's words instead of God's. Paul, in the New Testament, regarding God's unchanged divine order in marriage and the Church of Christ states: "But I want you to realize that the head of every man is Christ, and the head of the woman is man, and the head of Christ is God" (1 Corinthians 11:3 NIV). According to this verse, Adam rebelled against the divine order and instruction given by God. The woman submitted and obeyed the serpent instead of her husband.

And they heard the sound of the Lord God walking in the garden in the cool of the day, and Adam and his wife hid themselves from the presence of the Lord among the trees of the garden.

Then the Lord God called Adam and said to him. "Where are you?" So he said. "I heard Your Voice in the garden and I was afraid because I was naked; and I hid myself." And He said, "Who told you that you were naked? Have you eaten of the tree of which I commanded you that you should not eat?" (Genesis 3:8–11 NKJV)

This great man who dominated the earth and named all the animals of the earth was reduced to someone who described himself as fearful, naked, and who had to hide himself from God. Receiving or accepting Satan's lies over God's truth will always reduce one to inviting the presence of fear, shame, and a hiding or cover-up spirit. The goodness, moral excellence, integrity, virtue, and righteousness, which was God's glory on them, departed. "I call heaven and earth as witnesses today against you, that I have set before you life and death, blessing and cursing; therefore 'you' choose life, that both you and your descendants may live" (Deuteronomy 30:19 NKJV).

The consequence of their decision was called sin, which is the word God uses whenever He is disobeyed. Remember that God told the first man, "The day you eat of that fruit you will surely die" (Genesis 2:17 NKJV). God's Words were commands that were not regarded or believed as truth. The truth of God's spoken Word was His Will and could not be changed. He had told Adam the consequences of disobeying Him. Adam and Eve had rejected Truth, so they disobeyed Him. Because of this, sin came into existence and sin causes death.

Remember, I told you that God is Spirit, and the spirit part of man looks and behaves like God. After Adam and His wife sinned, their spirit became separated from God. They could no longer call Him Father. His presence no longer came from Heaven to commune and have fellowship with them in the Garden of Eden. He still loved them, but He could not undo the fact that they were disobedient to Him. Therefore, they were driven out of the Garden of Eden. Before they were driven out of the Garden of Eden, Adam called his wife Eve because she was the mother of all living people (Genesis 3:20). Eve conceived a son and called him Cain in Genesis 4:1.

Satan's explanation and interpretation of what God already told Adam was not the truth. Words of complete truth have never been spoken by this "belly-crawling snake," as there is no truth in him.

Satan said to Adam's wife, "You will not surely die. For God knows that in the day you eat of it [the fruit] your eyes will be opened and you will be like God, knowing good and evil" (Genesis 3:4–5 NKJV). It was a fact that they were already like God because they were made in the nature and likeness of God, the same way you can be like your mother and father in physical structure, feature, or mannerism, but you are not your mother and father.

God has already placed within Adam and Eve a photograph of Himself, and because man is from God, this photograph of God's Spirit within them is similar in feature and mannerism to the Spirit of God. Not only was their spiritual feature a picture or copy of God, they were God's representative in the earth. God was not responsible for earthly transactions, they were. They were His children in the earth. Satan knows that a person can use his/her will to adhere or conform to good or evil, to believe or not to believe, to obey or disobey God.

Numbers 23:19 (NIV) states, "God is not human, that He should lie, not a human being, that He should change His mind. Does He speak and then not act? Does He promise and not fulfill?" God's Word must be used as a person's standard or way of knowing the truth or knowing what is good or evil, right or wrong. A person's will or choice can, therefore, be guided by God's Word, which is truth. In Psalm 91:4 (NKJV), David states, "His truth shall be your shield and buckler." Because man has a will that exists in the area of his soul, he is free to live by his own choices. God gave him the privilege of choosing, and therefore, God has to allow man to make his own choices, whether good or bad. But God's choice for man is always to embrace His will, which is good or truth. Now, where the truth of God's Word is knowingly rejected, one can knowingly perish. For example, Adam knew the truth about what God said to him and rejected it. Therefore, he knowingly perished. God has principles called rules or laws, and when His Truth or Word is unbelieved and not heeded (because it is impossible for Him to lie), man could be disciplined, judged, and sentenced. The penalties or the consequences for violating His Truth: rules laws, commands, or words have already been established by Him. Acting on God's truth, by believing will produce good results. Not believing Truth, unbelief will not produce God's desired results. Therefore, the consequences of sin are evil, wicked, and destructive. These are not from Him, but are from Satan as a result of transgressing God's Truth. God does not make up rules each time someone sins. Therefore, if one does not desire the consequences, one should abstain from committing the sinful act.

God is a Holy Judge of sin. He upholds His standard of Holiness to His Word. Unbelief is an act of dishonor, disrespect, and rebellion against His Word or Commands. This violation can have negative consequences.

Another example is of Adam and Eve's offspring, Cain, and his disobedience to God. "Now Abel was a keeper of sheep, but Cain was a tiller of the ground. And in the process of time it came to pass that Cain brought an offering of the fruit of the ground to the Lord. Abel also brought of the *firstborn* (emphasis added) of his flock and of their fat. And the Lord respected Abel and his offering, but He did not respect Cain and his offering. (Did he bring of his leftover crops and not the first allotted portion of his harvest to God?) And Cain was very angry and his countenance fell. So the Lord said to Cain, "Why are you so angry? And why has your countenance fallen?" If you do well, will you not be accepted? And if you do not do well, sin lies at the door. And its desire is for you, but you shall rule over it" (Genesis 4: 2b-7 NKJV).

The solar system, galaxies, planets, and seasons were put in place by God and function by His commands, principles, or laws. They do not have their own will or choice as to how they operate. They operate according to God's Will. However, man has free will and can choose to defy God's Will or Laws. Therefore, to cover man's sin temporarily, in the Old Testament as an act of forgiveness for sin, God allowed man to sacrifice animals and use their blood to cover/atone for his sins. In this era of judgment, man did not have a Savior or a mediator between him and God. He did not have a lawyer to represent him and to satisfy God's wrath toward sin until Jesus Christ came and shed His delivering blood. All this will be explained in upcoming chapters.

The Result of Sin

God separated His presence or Spirit from Adam and Eve; therefore, there was no further Father and Son/Daughter relationship with Him. Adam's and Eve's bodies, with their spirits disconnected from God, lived on until their bodies got old and died natural deaths. When this happened, their spirits and souls were released from their bodies. Again, remember that the spirits and souls of men are everlasting. The spirit and soul go to Heaven or Hell when the body dies. Man's spirit and soul separated from God is called spiritual death, meaning man's spirit or the *ruwach* (Hebrew for spirit) or life that God breathed into Adam, has no connection with God. Because of his sin, God's presence came out of his spirit and left it spiritually dead or empty. God was no longer Adam's Father but Satan's, and he is still the father of all whose spirits are without God's presence in it.

Separation of the spirit and soul from the body is called physical death, meaning the spirit and soul left the body and the body is dead. Instead of man ruling the earth and the world's operations that God gave him to manage, Satan now has rule over these operations or world systems—the government, health, education, politics, judiciary, agriculture, atmosphere, aviation, finance, entertainment, and all the other world systems. God is the owner and creator of the earth. However, Satan and his satanic kingdom of darkness, which rule over spirits of evil and wickedness, got the position of operations manager or landlord. This gave him the power to control, rule, make decisions, be in charge, and to become the master over the living in the earth. Adam gave the earth and himself over to Satan when he believed Satan's words/lies instead of God's Words. "The earth is the Lord's, and all its fullness, the world and those that dwell therein" (Psalm 24:1 NKJV). Satan represents spiritual and physical death, so when man disobeyed God, death and suffering came upon mankind and all living, which includes the animal kingdom and the earth. Mankind's behavior and nature became like Satan's—evil and wicked. Man without God became mainly dependent on his own efforts, labor, and work to earn his livelihood. When connected to God, man had an easier life where he did not have to struggle with the ground to get food. He had a personal and spiritual relationship where God spoke into his spirit and told him *all things* and *all* the information of the universe.

Man, without God, now must function mainly by his own knowledge, education, intellect, or learned experiences. Here is an example of rulership transfer:

A teenage boy was told by his parents that the consequence for disobeying his teacher was that the toughest teacher at school would go home with him to manage and run their house and he would be kept apart from his parents. Authority, rulership, and the freedom to dominate his house had been passed on to his teacher. This boy was now separated from his parents' hugs and kisses, and it was entirely his fault. Ownership of the house was still his parents', but his teacher was now in charge and was free to rule, take over their home operations, make decisions, and reign in his parents' house.

Likewise, because of man's disobedience, Satan ended up dominating, ruling, and reigning in our house—the earth that God gave us—creating evil, lies, injustice, chaos, and confusion that come out of the minds of men that Satan now rules over. But God loves us so much that He had a plan to annul the thievery of Satan.

Man had to get reconnected to God in order to get back into friendship and communication with Him. God knew that man's spiritual separation from Him would keep Him and mankind eternally apart because Adam's sin was transferred to all of humanity. Good and evil became a choice of man when Adam ate from the Tree of the Knowledge of Good and Evil.

The Plan of God

Here was God's plan. God is three in one: God the Father, God the Son or Jesus Christ or the Word before He put on flesh, and God the Holy Spirit. "For there are three that bear witness in heaven: the Father, the Word and the Holy Spirit; and these are three in one" (1 John 5:7 NKJV).

In the beginning was the Word, and the Word was with God and the Word was God. He was in the beginning with God. All things were made through Him and without Him nothing was made that was made (John 1:1–3 NKJV).

This is an example of a human functioning in three different roles. This example is for clarity only and not to be compared to the three-in-one God:

A housewife may function in three different roles but remains the same person. She is a professional nurse, a minister of the Gospel, and a homemaker. The housewife is one person operating in three different roles in an earthly body. However, she is limited to the earth's environment and one location at a time and one role at a time. In contrast, God is not limited to specific locations or the environment. He is everywhere. He is all-knowing and all-powerful. He is one God and functions as God the Father, as God the Word, and as God the Holy Spirit all at the same time.

God Sent Jesus

God sent His Word from Heaven to earth and named His Word Jesus, Savior, and Son of God. He placed His Word into the Virgin Mary's womb so He would be born into the earth as a man. John 1:14 (NKJV) says, "And the Word became flesh and dwelt among us." Mary was only a carrier of Jesus' body. Galatians 4:4 (NKJV) states, "But when the fullness of time came, God sent forth His Son, born of a woman." God placed the "Seed" or the Word of Himself into the womb of the Virgin Mary. "And the angel answered and said to her, 'The Holy Spirit will come upon you, and the power of the Highest will overshadow you; therefore, also that Holy One who will be born will be called the Son of God'" (Luke1:35 NKJV).

Jesus' body was from God and not from Mary. Her womb kept Jesus' body until it was time for Him to be born into the world. Anyone born after Adam and Eve had to come out of the womb. God spoke fruitfulness and multiplication into the lives of the first man and woman at creation. They were to multiply themselves on earth. God made the first body of Adam, and He also made the last body of Adam, who is Jesus. As it is written, "The first man Adam became a living being/person." But the last Adam [became] a life spirit (1 Corinthians 15:45 NKJV). Jesus entered the earth as a man and was therefore subjected to earthly elements. Hebrews 10:5 NKJV states, "A body You have prepared for Me." God sent His Word to the earth in the form of a man. This is the same God who created the earth with Words. Jesus Christ is the expressed image or Word of God. Everything that God is can be found in His Word who became flesh—Jesus Christ. Note the Holy Spirit, who is the mighty power of God, creates the Word of God whenever God speaks it.

This is how Jesus Christ was born. A young woman named Mary was engaged to Joseph from King David's family. Before they were married, she learned that she was going to have a baby by God's Holy Spirit. Joseph was a good man and did not want to embarrass Mary in front of everyone. So he decided to quietly call off the wedding. While Joseph was thinking about this, an angel from the Lord came to him in a dream. The angel said, "Joseph, the baby that Mary will have is from the Holy Spirit. Go ahead and marry her, then, after her baby is born, name Him Jesus, because He will save His people from their sins. So the Lord's promise came through just as the prophet had said, "A virgin will have a baby boy, and He be called Immanuel," which means "God with us." After Joseph woke up, he and Mary were married, just as the Lord's angel had told him to do. But they did not sleep together before her baby was born. Then Joseph named Him Jesus [Yeshua-Savior] (Matthew 1:18–24 CEV).

The Use of the Blood During the Old Covenant

In the Old Testament of the Holy Bible, God used the sacrificing and shedding of animal's blood—such as the blood of a goat, sheep, or bull—as a way to cover and forgive sins. God who is Holy can not have fellowship with unrighteous man. In those days, He received animal sacrifices that were offered up to Him as a substitute to cover man's sins. Without the sacrificial substitute and the shedding of the animal's blood, God would extend judgment to sinful man. However, because of the blood shed, He extends mercy to His chosen people who were descendants of Abraham and were also the nation of people that He used to bring Jesus the Messiah into the earth.

In the Old Testament, God also instituted the law that required the entire nation of Israel's sins, which were committed in ignorance, to be forgiven by the yearly sacrificing of animals. The animals' shed blood would purify, cleanse, and forgive its sins, until the next year, when they had to do the same thing all over again because the nation's sins were only forgiven once a year. "For the life of the flesh [or body] is in the blood and I have given it to you upon the altar to make atonement or cover for your souls, for it is the blood that makes atonement for your soul" (Leviticus 17:11 NKJV).

Therefore, God used blood to forgive sins. Why? This is God's law, order, or command. "And almost all things are by *His law* purified [cleansed, forgiven], with blood [God has to "see" the sacrificial blood covering sin] "And without shedding of blood; there is no remission" [of sin] (Hebrews 9:22 NKJV). In other words, the sacrificial shedding of these animals' blood enables God to extend forgiveness and mercy, not punishment.

God's goodness, holiness, and righteousness can not look at sin and not judge and punish it. Sin can not live in the presence of a Holy God. Keep in mind that the word *atonement,* meaning *to cover over,* can only be used regarding the Old Testament people. We do not speak about blood covering sins when referring to New Testament Believers. New Testament Believers are under the new agreement/covenant of Jesus Christ, whose blood took away man's sinful spirit, not covered it. This will be explained in upcoming chapters.

Before I go further, I will give you some of other biblical reasons for the significance of blood. The main reason though is God's command in Hebrews 9:22 (NIV), "...without the shedding of blood there is no forgiveness."

The shedding of blood represents the giving of life, confirmed a covenant or oath, brings into being an end/death to something or someone.

It brings authenticity to an oath, agreement, or law and declares the new law now effective and the old canceled.

For example, if a person has a *will* (a written legal document that tells what a person wishes or desires to be inherited by others after death), it does not go into effect until that person died.

When that happens, the inheritor of the *will* can get the benefits. Therefore, the shedding of blood signifies proof of death and the end of a life, law, or agreement. The result causes the *documented will* to go into effect.

When a person dies, their *will* is read to the family and it now goes into effect. This is the same with Jesus Christ. His crucifixion on the cross and the shedding of His blood was used to end Adam's sin and end man's sinful nature.

Hebrews 9:22 (NKJV) says, "Without the shedding of blood, there is no remission" (remitting of sin).

According to the legal law of God written in the scriptures, Jesus Christ the Messiah/Anointed Savior's blood was the only blood shed that canceled, eradicated, annihilated, destroyed, and did away with Adam/mankind's sin and sinful nature that had been inherited from Satan, the thief. Now, the Will and Testament of the New Covenant that Jesus Christ left His family, the Born from Above, are His divine promises written in the Bible. They are now in effect after His death, burial, resurrection, and ascension. Jesus Christ is now seated at the right hand of the Father God in Heavenly places. Therefore, if you want to know what you inherited and what was given to you after Jesus Christ's death and resurrection and ascension and seating, Ephesians 1:20. Read the *Will*, the Bible (the Believer's Old and New Covenant Manual).

In the case of a *Will*, it is necessary to prove the death of the one who made it because a *Will* is in force only when that person has died; it never takes effect while the one who made it is still living. In Hebrews 9:16-17, Jesus told us that the New Covenant was in His blood according to His Will, which He left to the New Testament Believers. They no longer have to sacrifice animals as an offering to God or use their blood to cover or forgive sins to avoid being punished by "the law of sin and death." Jesus' blood now washes away all sins, gives eternal life, and renders mercy and forgiveness to all sinners. There is now the law of Grace, Mercy, Love, Remittance, and Pardon for sins. Love is now law in the New Testament and Covenant or the Word of God. Sin remains sin, but now it had a Mediator or Lawyer called, Mercy and Love, Who is Jesus Christ. He said, "This cup is the New Covenant in My blood; do this whenever you drink it, [the wine, symbolic of My Blood], in remembrance of Me" (1 Corinthians 11:25 NIV).

There are covenant blood promises given to Believers for every day of the year written in the New Testament Will of Jesus Christ and are sealed in the power of His blood. There is power/authority, life, and truth in God's Word, the New Testament Will left to us by Christ our Savior;

it can never lose its power or authority and it can not be erased because it is life and life eternal. Satan has no legal will, agreement, contract, or covenant with Believers who are in Christ Jesus. He is an evil spirit. Evil spirits can not shed blood to eradicate sin, because sin is from Satan. His words are false and they are lies, which are sin, and sin brings death. Believing and declaring Satan's words can not bring or give life, only death, sickness, and poverty. Read Hebrews chapter 9 for further scriptures on the purpose of the blood. Let's continue to explain the use of blood during the Old Covenant. According to Leviticus 16:1–34, once a year, the high priest would bring two goats to the Tabernacle. One would be killed. The blood was used to atone or cover the sins of the people of the nation of Israel only for a year. In this once-a-year ceremony, the High Priest would enter the Holy Place, which is the first room of the Tabernacle, and then the second room, which is the Most Holy Place or the Holy of Holies. The people stayed outside in the courtyard during this ceremony.

The first and second rooms were separated by a veil. No one but the High Priest went behind the veil and into the Holy of Holies where the Ark of the Covenant and God's presence was. The Ark of the Covenant was a box-like structure that contained the tablets of stones with the Ten Commandments written on them, which were God's righteous demands to man that could not be changed by man. God's laws are now written not on stones in a box but in the minds or the conscience of men, where there is a sense of right and wrong. They can not be erased or changed by man. Consequently, if you lie, you know that you are lying. If you steal, you know that you are stealing.

The Ark of the Covenant contained Aaron's rod, which budded, speaking of the high priestly authority God gave to Aaron to serve and minister before Him in the wilderness tabernacle. God made His rod sprout buds, blossoms, and ripe almonds to show the people and other leaders that Aaron was especially chosen by Him (Numbers 17:1–13). Aaron was the brother of the famous leader and prophet of Israel, Moses. Believers in Christ, just like Moses and Aaron, are also chosen to serve God in the purpose He has given to him or her.

Now, every Believer is a priest to God in their body, which is now God's. "To Him who loved us and washed us from our sins in His own blood, and as made us kings and priests to His God and Father, to Him be glory and dominion forever and ever. Amen" (Revelation 1:5–6 NKJV). Let's continue to share what's in the Ark: a pot of manna is symbolic of the spiritual eternal life given by God, who is Jesus Christ, sent from Heaven.

Manna was the food that God sent from Heaven to feed the Israelites while they were in the wilderness. The nutrition from this food kept them alive. This manna or "bread' was food from Heaven, symbolic of the Words of God that we now "eat" daily from the Bible to give us our anointed, spiritual nourishment. The presence of God resided on the counter or on top of the Ark of the Covenant. Two goats were brought to the tabernacle. The High Priest would kill one of the goats as a sacrificial offering for the nation's sins and sprinkle its blood on top of the Ark of the Covenant between two angelic statues called cherubim. This place had a special name called the Mercy Seat. The cherubim watch over and guard the Mercy Seat. The nation's offering, which is the goat's blood to cover their sins for a year, was received from the Mercy Seat. As the blood was sprinkled, God's presence on the Mercy Seat took the sacrifice. The high priest would then confess and put the sins of the people on the head of the remaining goat and send it away in the wilderness, an innocent scapegoat that bore the sins of a nation of people. That scapegoat's body would disappear into the wilderness, and the body could never be found. Therefore, this nation of people could never go back and revisit their forgiven sins by trying to find the scapegoat. This is symbolic of the New Testament Believer's sins being washed away by the blood of Jesus Christ, and like the scapegoat in the Old Testament, these sins can never be found again.

Jesus Christ Became the Curse

God made a law in the Old Testament: "If a man has committed a sin deserving of death, and he is put to death, and you hang him on a tree, his body shall not remain overnight on a tree: but you shall surely bury him that day, so you do not defile the land; for he who is hanged on a tree is accursed of God" (Deuteronomy 21:22–23 NKJV).

Galatians 3:13 (NKJV) states, "Christ has redeemed us from the curse of the law, having become a curse for us for it is written, cursed is everyone who hangs on a tree." God said anyone who hangs on a tree was cursed. Jesus's death for mankind's sin was upon a cross made from a tree. Curses came upon Jesus when He took on mankind's sin by surrendering to God's will to go to the cross. In Luke 22:42 (NKJV), Jesus said, "Nevertheless not My will but Yours be done." Even though He was innocent of committing sin, that did not negate the fact that God's law also said, "Cursed is everyone who hangs on a tree." "Who Himself bore our sins in His own body on a tree" (1 Peter 2:24 NKJV).

Jesus was cursed with sickness, diseases, poverty, and physical and spiritual death. Jesus became Adam's and mankind's substitute and took his and all of our sins upon Himself. Isaiah 53:5 (NKJV) states, "He was wounded for our transgressions or disobedience, He was bruised for our iniquities, [*sins, wicked acts*]."

The Blood of Jesus Christ: The Blood of the New Covenant

Instead of using goat's blood to cover or atone for sins on the particular year Jesus Christ died, God required Him to bear mankind's sin in His body, and His blood was used to take away mankind's sin. The blood of animals could only cover sins for a year. However, God used Jesus Christ's blood not only to cleanse and to purify mankind's sin, but also to remove it. So, you see, there was no further need for the yearly sacrificing of animals and using their blood to forgive sins.

John, who was a messenger, was sent by God to prepare the way for Jesus. The next day, John saw Him coming toward him and said, "Behold the Lamb of God who takes away the sin of the world!" (John 1:29 NKJV). Jesus Christ's blood did not cover mankind's sin. His blood removed mankind's sin and sin nature. Jesus Christ had to be willing to die and shed His sinless blood to take away mankind's sin. He became our sacrificial lamb. His sinless life, His obedience to God, and His blood redeemed, purchased man back to God. "You were slain, and have redeemed us to God by your blood, out of every tribe; tongue and people and nation" (Revelation 5:9 NKJV).

Jesus Christ is the Savior because His blood was used to once and for all purify, cleanse, and remove Adam's sin from mankind. In order for Him to do this, His physical body died and His blood was shed. Remember, I told you God is a Holy God and His Holy nature has to judge and punish the sin of mankind. Jesus Christ became mankind's sacrificial substitute instead of the goat. In the Old Testament, the sins of the people were placed on an animal substitute. The punishment for a spiritually dead spirit is to be placed in Hell. Jesus Christ went to Hell because all of mankind's sin was placed upon Him. Jesus Christ was the physical body that mankind's sin was placed on. "Christ suffered for our sins once for all time. He never sinned, but he died for sinners to bring you safely home to God. He suffered physical death, but he was raised to life in the Spirit" (I Peter 3:18 NLT).

Jesus Christ's Sacrifice

Let me give you an example of the phenomenal sacrifice Jesus Christ made for us:

There was a gentleman named Mankind Murray who lived in a city called Bay Pen. He was in prison because he got into trouble with the law of his country. He was charged with a serious crime, found guilty, and was sentenced to death. The judge ordered him to be crucified on a cross. The end came for Mankind Murray. This was it! He had no connection or relationship with God. There was no hope of him going to Heaven after his death. He knew that his body would be buried, and his spirit and soul would go to Hell. However, Mankind Murray had a friend called Jesus who offered to take Mankind Murray's place on the cross. Jesus was innocent. He never committed any crime. He convinced the sentencing judge to let Him die instead of His friend. The executioner loosened the handcuffs and chains from Mankind Murray's hands and feet. He was now a free man. They placed his handcuffs and chains on Jesus, whipped Him mercilessly, pulled out His beard, spat in His face, blindfolded Him, slapped His cheek with the palms of their hands, and asked Him, mockingly, "Prophesy! Who slapped You?" and threw Him in prison.

On the day of the crucifixion, Jesus was seen dragging Mankind Murray's cross on the dirt road to the place of His death. He was carrying the cross of His friend. Because Jesus was weak, the men who carried Him away laid hold of a man named Simon, a Cyrenian, to help Him carry the cross part of the way. However, for the rest of the journey, Jesus stumbled with the cross to the place of His crucifixion. The executioners continued to whip Him, beat Him, and even plucked out His beard. They showed him no mercy. They said He was foolish and mocked Him for calling Himself the Savior of Mankind Murray. They put a crown of thorns on His head to represent the king that He called Himself. "King of who? Mankind! Haha! Haha!" They laughed. They nailed His feet, stretched out His hands and body, and hanged Him on Mankind Murray's cross. He was beaten beyond recognition. They gambled for His garment, gave Him bitter vinegar to drink, and pierced His side with a sharp spear. Out spewed blood and water. He bled profusely, suffering for a crime He never committed to save the life of His friend Mankind Murray. He died in extreme agony.

What Happened to Jesus Christ's Sacrifice?

Jesus's spirit and soul, the eternal part of Him, went to Hell. It is also the place where the spirits and souls of those spiritually disconnected from God go after death. Jesus's spirit spent three days and three nights in Hell where He released from Himself the sin of mankind that He had carried there.

Jesus, before He took His last breath and gave up His Spirit/ or *ruwach* in Hebrew, made His Father God the caretaker and overseer of His spirit saying, "Into Your hands, I commit My Spirit" (Psalm 31:5 NKJV).

"For as Jonah was three days and three nights in the belly of the great fish, so will the Son of Man be three days and three nights in the heart of the earth [which is Hell's location]" (Matthew 1 2 :40 NKJV).

In Hell, Jesus gave back Adam's sin—every sickness, every disease, every lack, every curse, and every form of evil placed on mankind. Jesus returned them all to Satan where they came from. God used the shedding of Jesus Christ's pure, sinless blood to remove the authority or power of sin over mankind, whom Satan legally held in his possession.

Jesus's death and shedding of His blood stripped Satan of his rights and of the contract or agreement that he made with the first man, Adam, which said, "Do not believe the Truth and die spiritually. Give up everything that you, man, have dominion and rule over. Believe my deceptive, dead words and allow me, Satan, to keep you, man, in bondage to sin and darkness and be separated from God."

"Having disarmed principalities and powers, He [Jesus] made a public spectacle of them, triumphing over them [Satan and his demons]" (Colossians 2:15 NKJV).

Jesus took back mankind's rulership, dominion, and the authority of this earth that was given to him by God from the beginning before Satan stole it. God raised Jesus and mankind out of Hell and eternal death. "For You will not leave My soul in Sheol, nor will You allow Your Holy One to see corruption" (Psalm 16:10 NKJV). Jesus presented His sinless blood to God, on behalf of mankind, for the forgiveness of sins. God received Jesus and His sinless, blood sacrifice, which He used to legally remove the sentence of everlasting death on mankind. "In whom [Jesus] we have redemption through His blood, the forgiveness of sins" (Colossians 1:14 NKJV).

When Jesus went into Hell, He had another mission to accomplish. Ephesians 4:8 (NKJV) states, "He led captivity captive." He went into the area called Paradise where the spirits of the righteous, those who believed God, stayed when their bodies died. We know this because Jesus spent three days and three nights in the heart of the earth. He told the thief that was crucified with him that he would be with Him in Paradise (Luke 23:43). Jesus had to redeem mankind or, in other words, pay back the price for Adam's sin. This had to be done before God would receive the spirits of the Old Testament/Covenant men and women into Heaven because their spirits were not Born Again from Above. God gave the promise of righteousness to them. Basically, these saints, before Jesus came, got a "promissory note" for their belief in God. This gave them righteousness, but the full purchase for their righteousness was paid when Jesus Christ came to earth and shed His blood for the remission of mankind's sin, which included them.

The Paradise location in this chapter that Jesus Christ spoke about was in the "Underworld" or heart of the earth. After Jesus died, He was resurrected from Hell and ascended to Heaven. Paradise's location moved to Heaven because those who believed God were now redeemed and Born Again because of the saving, delivering, redemptive Blood of Jesus Christ.

Paradise, Heaven, Abraham's Bosom—these places are synonymous in that they state the abode of a righteous man and woman's spirit after physical death. Luke 16:20–31 gives us the name of *Abraham's Bosom*, the abode of the beggar Lazarus's spirit after he died. The Apostle Paul also states in 2 Corinthians 12:2-4 that he was caught up into the third Heaven, which is also called Paradise. All references to Heaven's location are the third Heaven where God is.

The Old Covenant godly saints that died such as Abraham, Moses, Samuel, David, Esther, Ruth, Jeremiah, and Isaiah must have roared and cheered with exceeding gladness when they saw their deliverer—Yeshua, Jesus Christ of Nazareth, the Messiah and the Son of the Living God coming to get them from their present location in the "underworld" Paradise and into the Heavenly Paradise.

We can be assured that our righteous Born-Again-in-Christ loved ones, who have gone to Heaven before us, are in a glorious place.

"He also first descended into the lower part of the earth? [Hell.] He who descended is also the One who ascended far above all the heavens" (Ephesians 4:9–10 NKJV).

The high priest in the Old Testament came before God on behalf of the people with goat's blood in an earthly tabernacle for God to cover their sins for a year. Jesus came before God in a Heavenly Temple with His own blood to remove sin indefinitely. However, you must receive what Jesus Christ did in Heaven. God does not have to validate His Truth or Word by you physically seeing it displayed. He can not lie.

You must believe His Word, His Truth. You must believe in mankind's representative, Jesus Christ, without seeing a thing. John 3:36 (NKJV) states, "He who believes in the Son has everlasting life, and he who does not believe the Son shall not see life, but the wrath [judgment] of God abides on him." Remember, the people who were gathered once a year in the courtyard of the Tabernacle could not go into the Most Holy Place with the earthly high priest. They had to believe in him going behind the veil. In other words, they had to trust their representative to stand in the presence of God on their behalf and offer goat's blood to cover their sins for a year.

Picture Jesus as your Heavenly High Priest entering the Holy of Holies with His own sinless blood, and on mankind's behalf, offering it up to God by sprinkling it on the Heavenly Seat of Mercy where God's throne is, the Seat of Authority, being watched over by real angels or cherubim. Jesus sprinkled His Holy blood on the Mercy Seat of God, and it was received by God. So powerful was Jesus' blood that God remitted and forgave man's sins all the way back to Adam. Jesus Christ's blood removed Adam's sin and its eternal death sentence from mankind. Jesus said, "I am He who lives, and was dead, and behold, I am alive forevermore. Amen. I have the keys of Hades and Death" (Revelation 1:18 NKJV).

The physical tabernacle with the earthly high priest was only a replica, a type, shadow symbol, or picture of God's Heavenly Temple. Jesus was both the scapegoat that took mankind's sin in His body and the sacrificial innocent lamb that was killed, and the blood offered up to God. You see, even though mankind was wrong to sin, God gave mankind mercy and made eternal life available to mankind again, through the last Adam, Jesus, who did not sin against Him. Jesus Christ is the only one who made it possible to reunite man's separated spirit to God. That is why He is called Savior/Yeshua, the Messiah, The Anointed Deliver, sent to earth from Almighty God (Genesis 17:1), and the Most High God (Psalm 7:17). No one else can qualify for this title. No one else saved mankind from Hell and everlasting death. Jesus Christ paid the price to keep mankind out of Hell by shedding His sinless blood.

"Without the shedding of blood there is no remission of sin" (Hebrews 9:22 NKJV). Jesus Christ only can say, "I am the way, the truth and the life. No man comes to the Father except through Me'" (John

14:6 NKJV). You must believe in Jesus Christ. He is the representative, or High Priest "behind the veil," in the Heavenly Temple where God is.

Instead of offering God the blood of animals to cover sin, like the High Priest did on behalf of the people in the Old Covenant, you only have to come to God through faith in the blood of Jesus, who removes your sin. Receive what He has done for you and confess Him to be the Lord or Owner of your life. God will now accept you as being in right standing with Him. He can now give your spirit and soul eternal life with Him. God forgave and removed the sin of Adam from mankind and He can personally remove it from you, but there is one condition. You must choose to accept, receive, and confess Jesus Christ as your Lord and Savior, it must be a choice of your own free will. No one can make you receive what Jesus Christ has done for you, but you. "Their sins and lawless acts I will remember no more. And where these have been forgiven, sacrifice for sin is no longer necessary" (Hebrews 10:17-18 NIV). Jesus was the final sin sacrifice.

Scriptures That Support Jesus Christ's Death, Burial, Resurrection, Ascension, and Seating in Heavenly Places

"Christ died for our sins according to the Scriptures, and that He was buried, and that He rose again the Third day according to the Scriptures" (I Corinthians 15:3-4 NKJV).

Thus it is written, and thus it was necessary for the Christ to suffer and to rise from the dead the third day (Luke 24:46 NKJV).

Him God raised up on the third day, and showed Him openly, not to all the people, but to witnesses chosen before by God, even to us who ate and drank with Him after He rose from the dead (Acts 10:40 NKJV).

"Yet it pleased the Lord to bruise Him; He has put Him to grief. When you make His soul an offering for sin" (Isaiah 53:10 NKJV).

He also first descended into the lower parts of the earth? [Hell.] He who descended is also the One who ascended far above all the heavens (Ephesians 4:9–10 NKJV).

And what is the exceeding greatness of His power toward us who believe, according to the working of His mighty power which He worked in Christ when He raised Him the dead and seated Him at His right hand in the Heavenly places (Ephesians 1:19-20 NKJV).

Those Who Hesitate to Receive Jesus Christ

Jesus Christ is now seated in Heaven at the right hand of God. "But this Man, after He had offered one sacrifice for sins forever, sat down at the right hand of God" (Hebrews 10:12 NKJV). Those who receive what Jesus Christ has done for them have the opportunity to be seated with Him in heavenly places. The spiritual part of you, not the physical part, is now transferred from the Kingdom of Darkness and Death (Satan's kingdom) into the Kingdom of Light and Life.

"He has delivered us from the power of darkness and conveyed us into the kingdom of the Son of His love" (Colossians 1:13 NKJV). God is King of Kings over His Kingdom and you can be kings and priests in the Kingdom of God (Revelation 1:6).

When you receive Jesus Christ as Savior and Lord, God will receive you into His dominion of healing, prosperity, soundness of mind, wholeness, and eternal life. He has rules that you now must live by, which are in His Holy Word. Sickness, poverty, lack, and bondage are from Satan and not from His kingdom. Receiving Jesus as your Lord and Savior shows Satan that he is not your owner anymore. You have regained your rightful position with God.

Remember, God is Spirit. He is unseen by your physical eyes, but He exists. Your spirit, which is the real you, is a photograph or image of God. It is unseen, but it exists. This position of authority will also give you the right and power to conquer Satan's weapons—such as perversion, affliction, sickness, disease, poverty, curses, spells, and death—when they present themselves to you. "Behold I [Jesus Christ] give you the authority to trample on serpents and scorpions [or evil spirits and demons] and over all the power of the enemy, and nothing shall by any means hurt you" (Luke 10:19 NKJV). Will you receive the truth of what Jesus Christ has done for you? Would you like to be free from Satan's evil authority and receive eternal life with Jesus Christ?

Can God Receive a Horrible Sinner Like Me?

A question not meant for the Believers reading this book.

Adam ate the fruit from the Tree of the Knowledge of Good and Evil and disobeyed God, and that was a sin. Think of all the other heinous sins of mankind since Adam. Jesus Christ's blood, ever since it was shed two thousand years ago, is still forgiving all kinds of sins. Jesus Christ dying for mankind and using His blood to take away sin from mankind was not a contract made with you based on your good works. Remember, you have Adam's defiled blood, so there is no way you will ever qualify to stand before God as a high priest and present your blood to remit your sinful nature received from Adam. In the Old Testament, the earthly high priest, Aaron, had to offer up blood to atone or cover his sins and his household by killing a bull. Whenever he went into the Holy of Holies, he had to go into the presence of God according to God's specification once a year on the day he offered up goat's blood to atone for the sins of the people. "Thus Aaron shall come into the Holy Place: with the blood of a young bull as a sin offering" (Leviticus 16:3 NKJV).

"Aaron shall offer the bull as a sin offering, which is for himself, and make atonement for himself and for his house" (Leviticus 16:6 NKJV). "And Aaron shall bring the bull of the sin offering, which is for himself and for his house, and shall kill the bull as a sin offering which is for himself" (Leviticus 16:11 NKJV). If not, he would have fallen dead.

During the once-a-year Atonement Service (description also given on previous pages), Two goats were brought and presented before the Lord at the door of the tabernacle of meeting. "Then Aaron shall cast lots for the two goats: one lot for the Lord and the other lot for the scapegoat. And Aaron shall bring the goat on which the Lord's lot fell, and offer it as a sin offering. But the goat on which the lot fell to be the scapegoat shall be presented alive before the Lord, to make atonement upon it and to let it go as the scapegoat into the wilderness" (Leviticus 16:7–8 NKJV).

The people who waited in the court would listen to the ringing of the bells strapped to the high priest's garment. Then they would know that the high priest was still alive as they would ring as he moved about. Let's imagine that the high priest did not enter the Most Holy Place according to God's specification. He would die before the presence of God. God's instructions had to be followed as specified. Leviticus 10:1–2 states that Aaron's sons Nadab and Abihu burnt incense in the tabernacle on the altar of incense, which contained unholy ingredients not specified by God. They died before the Lord. However, this Heavenly High Priest called Jesus Christ went into the presence of God with no sin in Him. Remember that Mankind Murray was guilty of committing a crime and breaking the law of the land, but Jesus Christ took his death sentence and went to Hell in his stead. Now, imagine Jesus Christ doing this by putting Mankind Murray's death sentence along with everything else that comes with sin—such as sickness, diseases, poverty, stealing, fear, and lying and putting it all in a backpack, strapping it on, and going to Hell with it. When He reached Hell, He took the bag of sin off His back and left it there. He then entered the Holy of Holies with His pure, spotless blood and offered it up to God in exchange for Him to do away, remit, or cancel all of mankind's sin.

No one except for Jesus Christ could come to God to remit their sins by their good behavior, acts of kindness, praying, fasting, or ceremonial washings. Adam disobeyed God; therefore, every human disobeyed God. Without Jesus Christ, nothing man was capable of doing on his own will ever be received by God for payment of sins. The binding covenant transaction to remit and pardon mankind's sin was between Jesus Christ (His Son who was a sinless man) and God. The deal was closed, padlocked, and sealed with the blood of Jesus Christ. No other man or woman, born from Adam, can have access to God without being invited and received by God. This can not be accomplished any other way except through Jesus Christ's sinless blood. Earthly kings and queens' individual guests are required to follow certain specifications. You cannot even access certain items, for example, a computer, without predetermined rules and specifications; how much more, the God of Creation. Again, as John 14:6 (NKJV) states, "Jesus Christ said 'I am the way, the truth, and the life. No one comes to the Father except through me.'" Sorry! Period! Case closed!

God's presence in the wilderness tabernacle could not be accessed by anyone but the high priest and only at a specific time of the year. There was only one gate or entrance to the tabernacle, which was through the eastern gate. Today, the only entrance to God is through Jesus Christ, who calls Himself "the door." Jesus said, "I am the door, if anyone enters by Me, he will be saved" (John 10:9 NKJV). As I have said before, Jesus Christ is our sacrifice. You do not have to bring another sacrifice into the courtyard of the tabernacle for the priest to offer. No lamb, sheep, or goat's blood sprinkled on the Mercy Seat for God to extend mercy to you today. Jesus Christ already took your sinful nature when He became your sacrifice. God extended mercy, love, and forgiveness because of Jesus Christ's blood sacrifice on a lifted up altar called a cross.

When Jesus Christ returns to earth, He will not be coming back as a sinless, sacrificial lamb. God will judge those who refuse to receive what He has done through Jesus Christ. Remember, I said God can not look at or see sin without judging it. Therefore, without Jesus Christ's blood on you, you will be judged a sinner. In Revelation 22:20 (NKJV), Jesus Christ said, "Surely I am coming quickly."

What Is Confessing the Word of God & Receiving Jesus Christ (Yeshua) as Your Savior and Owner (Lord)?

Confessing the Word of God is to say the same words that the Word of God says about you. You then repeat or read back aloud so that your ears can hear what you are saying. You should believe what you say when you repeat or confess what God says about Jesus Christ. You do not have to make up or invent your own words. God's desire is for you to agree with His plan to save you spiritually and believe that Jesus Christ is both Savior and Lord. When you believe His Words and declare it from your mouth, it will never return void (empty or dead to Him). "So then faith comes by hearing, and hearing by the word of God" (Romans 10:17 NKJV). You stop speaking your words and begin speaking God's Words. He can trust His Words coming from your mouth, not your unspiritual, untrustworthy, flaky, made-up ones that will twist, turn, and change with circumstances. The supernatural power of faith comes to you when you declare God's Word.

To confess Jesus Christ as your Savior, read the following:

"If you confess with your mouth the Lord Jesus and believe in your heart that God has raised Him from the dead, you will be saved. For with the heart [spirit/soul] one believes unto righteousness, and with the mouth confession is made unto salvation" (Romans 10:9-10 NKJV).

"Whoever confesses that Jesus [Christ] is the Son of God, God abides in him, and he in God" (I John 4:15 NKJV).

"Whoever believes that Jesus is the Christ is born of God" (1 John 5:1 NKJV).

"But as many as received Him [Jesus Christ], to them He gave the right to become children of God" (John 1:12 NKJV).

"That which is born of the flesh is flesh, and that which is born of the Spirit [Spirit of God or the Holy Spirit] is spirit. Do not marvel that I said to you, 'You must be born again'" (John 3:6-7 NKJV).

"He who has the Son has life; he who does not have the Son of God does not have life" (1 John 5:12 NKJV).

Please say the following:

God in Heaven, I confess and believe that Jesus Christ is the Son of the Living God. I believe that God has raised Him from the dead because of His obedience and the shedding of His sinless blood to take away sin from mankind, which includes me. I receive Jesus Christ as my Savior and Lord. I now declare that I am righteous, that I am saved from eternal death and Hell, and I now have eternal life forevermore with God. Thank you, Father. (Now you can call God your Father) In Jesus Christ's name. Amen!

If you have said the above, you now have legal authority or delegated authority over Satan. Next time you see a police officer, look at what he is wearing. He wears a uniform of authority, which states who he is. He wears the badge of the country or city he represents, and he carries his armor with him at all times–armor that the country he represents has given him permission to use. This authority means the police officer has been given delegated authority by his country to enforce the law. Therefore, in a busy street, the police officer stands and stretches out his hand. He may be small and petite, but because of the authority he has been given, he stretches out one gloved hand and a huge truck comes to a complete stop before him. He uses legal governmental authority to command it to stop and to go. You now wear the uniform of your legal authority given to you by Jesus Christ. Jesus [Christ] said, "All authority has been given to Me in heaven and on earth" (Matthew 28:18 NKJV). The badge on your uniform shows you represent the government of the Kingdom of God. The weapons you have on and carry at all times are speaking the Words of God, the name of Jesus Christ (Yeshua), verbally or symbolically applying the blood of Jesus Christ with anointed oil and prayer. After you are Born Again, Jesus Christ commands you to get power from the Holy Spirit (Acts 1:4). Baptism or infilling of the Holy Spirit power is not only to speak in Holy Spirit tongues and to be used with the nine gifts in 1 Corinthians 8-10, but also to be a bold witness for Jesus Christ. These will be discussed in upcoming chapters.

There are various prayers such as the following: prayer of request or petition prayer, agreement prayer, and intercessory prayer, and prayer which also involves praying in the Holy Spirit. You can receive the infilling of the Holy Spirit with the evidence of speaking in other tongues. To pray in the Holy Spirit or in a heavenly language, you must have confessed and received Jesus Christ as Lord and Savior. Other weapons are praise and worship, taking communion, decreeing and declaring the blood of Jesus Christ, anointing oil, fasting, and spending time in prayer and the Word of God. (Please refer to other biblical sources and a physician before attempting to fast.)

You have been given the authority to use your weapons! The devil does not see you as a new Believer. He sees you as having the authority to stretch out your hands and stop him in his tracks when you use the authority that Jesus Christ has given you. If you do not use your spiritual authority and weapons to stop him, he will run you over like a huge truck. You are not powerless over evil, but now you are powerful with the life of Jesus Christ in you.

"You are of God, little children [that's us, the born again], a nd have overcome them [Satan and his demons], because He who is in you is greater than he who is in the world [the devil]" (1 John 4:4 NKJV).

You need your weapons because you won't be wrestling against flesh and blood or people, but the spirits that may be operating and controlling people like spirits of anger, lust, and hate. Ephesians 6:12 (NKJV) states, "For we do not wrestle against flesh and blood, but against principalities [high-ranking demons over territories, countries, and regions], against powers, against the rulers of the darkness of this age." Demons rule or legislate using people to carry out their ungodly operations. They may operate in lies and deception or darkness. The same way Satan operates in the world is the same way he wants to operate in your life, even as a Son or Daughter of God, so do not be naive. He may use slick-talking wolves in sheep's clothing to approach you. They may even be sitting right in the church saying "Amen." Be on your guard.

Here is an example of Jesus Christ teaching in the synagogue or church. He was spoken to by a demon-possessed man who came to church dressed up like everybody else. Jesus Christ did not turn on the man but on the spirit that was using the man:

"Now in the synagogue [or church] there was a man who had a spirit of an unclean demon. And he cried out with a loud voice, saying, "Let us alone! What have we to do with You, Jesus [Yeshua] of Nazareth? Did You come to destroy us? I know who You are—the Holy One of God!" But Jesus rebuked him, saying [that's what we need to do], "Be quiet, and come out of him!" And when the demon had thrown him in their midst, it came out of him and did not hurt him. Then they were all amazed and spoke among themselves, saying, "What a word this is! For with authority and power He commands the unclean spirits, and they come out" (Luke 4:33-36).

You use your authority in the name of Jesus to throw them out of whatever situations or circumstances they are in. Notice that Jesus Christ did not use His authority to cast them from the earth. They are still around even today, in the second heaven, on earth, and in dry places and the depths of the sea. The third Heaven is where God is, and the first heaven is the one you can see above, so be vigilant or watchful.

Whenever you have evil thoughts against someone, mean, harmful, malicious speech, or thoughts to do an evil act, pull it out from your mind, throw it down, and step on it. Your mind is responding to evil because it is aware of both good and evil. You first have to think it, then act on what you thought. "Casting down arguments and every high thing that exalts itself against the knowledge of God, bringing every thought into captivity to the obedience of Christ" (2 Corinthians 10:5 NKJV). Satan is a spirit and you have a mind or a soul. Satan as a spirit can influence or speak through your mind. Ephesians 6:13 (NKJV) states, "Therefore take up the whole armor of God, that you may be able to withstand in the evil day, and having done all, to stand." You will be attacked; however, the sooner you find out about Satan's devices in your godly, Christ-like walk, the more prepared you will be in using the weapons we discussed earlier. Remember, you are not helpless or hopeless as a Born-Again Believer. Your spiritual fight is not with physical people. Ephesians 6:13-17 tells you the specific spiritual armor to keep on because as a child of God, the Kingdom of Darkness hates you and is at war continually against you. Keep truth on your waist: Believe God only, never the devil. Keep on the breastplate of righteousness: Know that you are righteous, just like Jesus Christ. Have your feet fitted with gospel of peace: That is the message of peace to proclaim. Carry the shield of faith: Trust God always. He protects and is your defense. Put on the helmet of salvation: State you are a Born-Again Believer in Christ and the Sword of the Spirit, which the word of God: Respond with the Word of God always, never to the circumstances from the devil. It's a fight when your mind wants to believe the devil and not God's Word. "For the weapons of our warfare are not carnal [physical or fleshly, but spiritual] but mighty in God for pulling down strongholds [or demonic fortresses]" (II Corinthians 10:4 NKJV).

The armor from Ephesians chapter 6 is to be kept on always and never taken off. However, there are weapons that are meant to be taken up such as prayer, the Word, and communion.

Never underestimate your authority or your weapons of power that Jesus Christ has given you. You could be crossing the road when you notice an eighteen-wheeler truck barreling toward you. With prayer, the Word of God, the blood and name of Jesus, you can stop the devil in his tracks while laughing from ear to ear! Just like the police officer with the white glove, there is no ability in his hand to stop a truck. The power, authority, and strength are in the government he represents. That's what the truck driver sees. He sees the representative or the ambassador of authority requesting him to stop his humongous truck and he obeys. You are an ambassador and a representative of Jesus Christ. You have been given the authority and power by the Holy Spirit to heal the sick, raise the dead, cast out devils, and speak with new tongues (Mark 16:17). So, do not be fearful of using your spiritual authority. "The truck driver," Satan, will stop because he sees the blood of Jesus Christ on you.

"Therefore if anyone is in Christ, he is a new creation; old things have passed away; behold, all things have become new" (2 Corinthians 5:17 NKJV). Your spirit, not your physical body, is now new. Your spirit is that part of you that is like God and has eternal life. Your mind must be renewed in the Word of God to change your old way of thinking and speaking. Find a Bible-believing, Word-teaching church that will teach you about God the Father, God the Son, and God the Holy Spirit.

Who is Jesus Christ? He is now your Savior, Deliverer, Healer, Provider, Protector, and more! He has given you His life again. The life that was dead because of mankind's sin is now alive to God. You can never die spiritually again! You have life forever! You are now in the body of Jesus Christ! "He who has the Son has life; he who does not have the Son of God does not have life" (1 John 5:12 NKJV).

The spiritual part of you is transformed immediately and now has eternal life, instead of eternal death, and is alive to God and His Word. We all have to go through a longer process of getting our soul renewed, healed, delivered, and set free from the nature of Adam's sin. We were all physically born into and have inherited that sin which infected our souls before we knew Christ. All that trash must be hauled out of our souls that a life of sin has placed there. With the Holy Spirit's help, he will show you how to do this. The first thing one should do is forgive others and repent. Forgiveness and repentance are for soul restoration. The soul is restored, with God's Truth or Word and Jesus Christ's blood, to the original mindset of God's Word. The soul is continually being cleansed, but the spirit is cleansed by the blood of Jesus once and for eternity. In addition, you must begin thinking good thoughts as opposed to evil thoughts. Ask God to heal your soul, to wash away the dirt, brokenness, hurt, and tragedy with the blood of Jesus Christ. No one is excluded, not even a newborn Christian. Start renewing the mind/ soul with God's Word. That will keep it out of darkness.

What Does it Mean to Be Righteous?

This chapter is for the persons who are Born-Again Believers [Born of God, Born from Above, Christ Jesus is now your Savior and Owner] and are serious about maturing spiritually and following Christ.

The Holy Spirit is the one who convicts sin and brings sinners to Christ. You should have an inner witness or absolute knowing from your alive spirit in Christ that you are saved. You may have said the above salvation prayer and not believed it; therefore, there will be no changes in you. He who has the Son has life; he who does not have the Son of God does not have life. Be very serious in this decision because it is not a religion, but a relationship. Jesus Christ has to know you and you know Him. You do not want to hear these words from Christ: "I never knew you; depart from Me, you who practice lawlessness" (Matthew 7:23)! Jesus Christ paid too great a price for your eternal destiny. So be sure you know Jesus Christ as your Savior and Lord. God needs to see the blood of Jesus on you, which enabled Adam's sin to be cancelled and remitted. Because with this, you will be judged a sinner. (Matthew 7:21 NKJV).

After you say the prayer to receive, confess, and believe that Jesus Christ is the Son of God, you now have a relationship with God. Jesus Christ transformed the spirit part of you from sin and unrighteousness and gave you righteousness. You have a right to stand or go before God, just like Jesus Christ. You are now holy before God, just like Jesus Christ. You are sanctified or set apart as one of His saints. You are justified. God sees you—specifically your spirit, not your soul or body, as He sees Jesus Christ. "You," meaning spirit, is righteous, not your body. "But you are washed, but you were sanctified, but you were justified in the name of the Lord Jesus Christ and by the Spirit of our God" (1 Corinthians 6:11 NKJV).

God sees you with the blood of Jesus Christ in your spirit. God did not change your position of righteousness because you wore makeup, earrings, or pants (for a woman). These are external and flimsy sayings by the enemy who can not give eternal life. Remember, the transaction to remove your sins had nothing to do with the sinful you. God will never see Jesus Christ's blood as impure; He was a sinless man. So when He looks at you, "you" meaning your spirit, God sees Jesus Christ's blood on you, which is pure and sinless. Your spirit was delivered from Hell, which is, therefore, an everlasting deliverance. It was not for a certain number of years or a temporary position. This transaction cannot be voted in or out after a number of years like a politician's office.

When you said that prayer, it was a covenant, which is a strong, binding oath, sealed by the sinless blood of Jesus Christ. No person can erase it. Your words of confession can be spoken without sincerity, but only you and God have that knowledge. Romans 10:10 (NKJV) states, "For with the heart one believes unto righteousness, and with the mouth confession is made unto salvation." His Word is forever settled in Heaven (Psalm 119:89) and the Word of the Lord endures forever (1 Peter 1:23).

Remember, without God seeing the blood of Jesus Christ on you, which declares mercy and not judgment, God will judge sin and the sinner. Sinful man cannot declare you righteous. When God declares you righteous, you are righteous. So by the blood of Jesus Christ, your righteousness is not portable or mobile. One of the names of God is *Jehovah Tsidkeenu*, "the Lord our Righteousness." His righteousness was given to us. With salvation, God gave us His very nature of righteousness. "For He made Him who knew no sin to be sin for us, that we might become the righteousness of God in Him" (2 Corinthians 5:21 NKJV). Hallelujah! He who has the Son has life everlasting! Therefore, because God is always right, you are in the right. God is Truth; therefore, you are in the truth. Goodness comes from being in the right. Thus, you are righteous, which is a legal position, state, or stand, and it is fixed. The Law-Giver God gave you this authority, power, and truth in Him.

The opposite of truth/good is lie/evil. You have been taken out of the lie/evil legally with the sinless blood of Jesus Christ. So, legally, you cannot be put back into your former evil and lying nature, without removing the blood of Christ which took away Adam's sin. Because He took away Adam's sin, all of mankind's sin was taken away—yours, mine, and whosoever truly confesses, professes or declares, and receives Jesus Christ as Savior. In order to continue in the lying, evil, sinful nature, Jesus would have had to undo His death and His shed blood, which removes/remits sin from you. Therefore, mankind's sin would have remained, and that's a lie of the devil. God did not make an agreement with people or sinful man, to put you in the right with Him. He made it with His Sinless Son, Jesus Christ. This free pardon or acquittal you received is called Grace, which is also called free love, free mercy, free favor, freely given; so always be appreciative and thankful to God.

That "evil snake" Satan would not want you back anyway. You know too much about his lies. If you are told that you will lose your free gift of salvation, you have to work for this free gift, and this free gift can be returned because you have been naughty and not nice—that's a lie too and guess who made it up!

If I were a child, I would probably imagine my mother putting eight grown kids back in her womb because we were naughty. You are righteous because God gave you righteousness (right standing with Him, He puts you on the right side of Him, and it is a permanent stand) when you received His Son, Jesus Christ. You signed for the free gift (Jesus Christ). Why would the devil want anything to do with your righteousness? If you have never received Jesus Christ, how can you return a gift you have never received? The Holy Spirit is the Person that convicts sin. Did you respond to His conviction when you heard the good news of Jesus Christ? The Holy Spirit is the one that must prove to you that you are a prisoner of sin because of your sinful nature from Adam that has you blinded from seeing Christ. Jesus Christ said, "And when He [the Holy

Spirit] has come, He will convict the world of sin, and of righteousness, and of judgment: of sin, because they do not believe in Me" (John 16:8-9 NKJV). "For the gifts and calling of God are irrevocable" (Romans 11:29 NKJV). The gifts are salvation, righteousness, the infilling of the Holy Spirit with the evidence of speaking in tongues, and all the other gifts God gives freely. (Holy Spirit infilling will be explained in upcoming chapters.)

"God is not a man, that He should lie, Nor a son of man, that He should repent. Has He said, and will He not do? Or has He spoken, and will He not make it good? Behold, I have received a command to bless; He has blessed, and I cannot reverse it" (Numbers 23:19-20 NKJV).

"For as by one man's disobedience many were made sinners, so also by one Man's obedience many will be made righteous...so that as sin reigned in death, even so grace might reign through righteousness to eternal life through Jesus Christ our Lord" (Romans 5:19, 21 NKJV).

How Do I Live a Righteous Life?

After declaring/professing Jesus Christ as your Lord and Savior, you must follow that up with action. Now remember that Jesus Christ gave you a new spirit, which means the legal power of the old, sin-filled spirit no longer exists. You said you believed that He is the Son of the Living God who died and used His blood to eradicate your sinful nature, the one you received from Adam. You could not do that for yourself. The Holy Spirit gave you that faith, trust, and evidence to believe in Jesus Christ and what He did to save you. That belief in Jesus Christ confession made you Born Again. However, your soul, which is also eternal, consists of the mind, will, personality, and attitude, was not made new. The legal authority of sin to reign in your soul and body no longer exists. However, you can still allow sins such as anger, malice, and hate to enter your soul. Sin cannot enter your Born-Again spirit. Jesus dealt with that Sin- the sin of Mankind/Adam. Therefore you are no longer called a sinner or a son of Satan and death, but a Son of God because of Jesus's redemptive blood. Satan is still in the atmosphere. You can therefore indulge yourself in his bondages: which kills, steals, and destroys. Still he does these by using: fear, stealing, murder, fornication, mental and physical, evil works of darkness.

Similar to an infant at the very beginning stages of its life learning to crawl, you are a spiritual infant at the beginning stages of your Walk with God. You will now have to start learning the ABCs of the Word of God. Just as a baby moves from milk to regular food and from diapers to being potty trained, you must move from ungodly talk and actions such as lying, gossiping, stealing, and perversion to following God's Will and direction for your life. Find consistent time to read the Word of God. Your mind gets transformed by renewing it or changing its thinking process with the Word of God.

"And do not be conformed to this world [which means Satan's ways of operating, which is disobeying God's words], but be transformed by the renewing of your mind, that you may prove what is that good and acceptable and perfect will of God" (Romans 12:2 NKJV).

The acceptable, good, and perfect will of God is the Word of God. You no longer live by the world system or Satan's rule book. Remember, your body is still open to sinning or engaging in sin. It will do what the unrenewed mind tells it to do. "That you put off, concerning your former conduct, the old man which grows corrupt according to the deceitful lusts, and be renewed in the spirit [means soul] of your mind, and that you put on the new man which was created according to God, in true righteousness and holiness" (Ephesians 4:22–24 NKJV). You must do it, and not live spiritually according to your soul, flesh or body, but by the Word of God. The redeemed or saved spirit in you, led by the Holy Spirit, will convict your soul when you disobey God. He will correct you. He will tell you not to sin. He will say, "Do not steal that," "Do not tell that lie," or "Do not go there," but it is up to your soul to obey. He will not force obedience on you. God gave you a free will and He will not violate it. Therefore, to keep from being tempted, you will have to guard your mind and body at all times until Jesus Christ returns, like a soldier guards himself from his enemies.

"Let no one say when he is tempted, "I am tempted by God"; for God cannot be tempted by evil, nor does He Himself tempt anyone. But each one is tempted when he is drawn away by his own desires and enticed" (James 1:13-14 NKJV).

This particular story tells of a soldier who was so overworked that he needed to sleep. So, he went to sleep with one eye open and one hand on his weapon, ready to attack. Likewise, Born-Again Believers in Christ need to keep their minds and bodies from being deceived by Satan's deceptions and lies. Remove yourself from any compromising situation, ungodly, bodily desires, and any evil imagination. It is better to be called a fool than to get involved with conscious, willful, purposeful, and repetitive sin. God's grace and kindness do not give us license to disobey Him and wallow in the pigsty of a sinful lifestyle. In the Old Testament, there was a basin of water in the courtyard of the tabernacle built by Moses as instructed by God. This basin, called the *laver*, was where the priest washed his hands and feet before going into the tabernacle to minister to God or do his duties in the tabernacle. Whenever he would look into the water, he could see his reflection that showed him who he was to God, a chosen priest who ministered unto God (Exodus 30:17–21).

The laver of water is symbolic of the Word of God. Whenever it is read, you should see your reflection in the Word of God. We all must strive to be a mirror image of the Word of God whenever we read it. Reading the Bible daily cleanses our minds of ungodly thoughts. In other words, it bathes us from the impurities and thoughts of the "old man or woman" who did not receive Jesus Christ as Savior. The image you should see as you "wash" in the Word are His healing, provision, protection, deliverance, and salvation—His promises reflecting or looking back at you. You are legally entitled to access not only salvation, but all of the above promises of God due to the shed blood of Jesus at the cross. "I am the resurrection and the life. He who believes in Me, though he may die [physically], he shall live. And whoever lives and believes in Me shall never die [spiritually]. Do you believe this?" (John 11:25–26 NKJV).

There are certain biblical and nonbiblical phrases that Believers think qualify them to lose or keep their salvation and righteousness.

"Backslide"—Used in the Old Testament by God in His relationship with the children of Israel (not a New Covenant word). *Backslide* from *Webster's* means "to become less virtuous: less morally excellent in the soul: mind, will, personality and attitude; to turn back into the direction of immorality of an unrepentant, unforgiving soul." This is a person who does not repent of sin. Repenting allows one to use the blood of Jesus Christ to wash away sin. If one does not believe the Word of God, then one cannot use it to renew the soul. This person may not have received a relationship with Christ Jesus if they remain in a continual, unrepentant state of sin. If you are unsure of salvation, rededicate your life to Jesus Christ.

"Miss the mark"—A Believer thinking his own self-righteousness should measure up to God's standard of being righteous. Only Jesus Christ was the perfect man. He was the only one who was right with God. He never sinned, nor was His blood defiled with sin. Therefore, God was able to use His blood to forgive and wash away sin, which enabled mankind to become righteous. The perfect, sinless blood of Jesus Christ forgave mankind's sin and made His spirit perfect in Christ. Roman 3:23 NKJV says, "For all have sinned and fall short of the glory of God." However, when the righteous man does evil, he can repent and use the same forgiving blood of Jesus Christ that made him righteous before God to cleanse and wash away that unrighteous act. 1 John 1:9 says, "If we confess our sins, He is faithful and just to forgive us our sins and to cleanse us (with His blood) from all unrighteousness (sins)." The Bible also says, "Therefore you **shall be** perfect, just as your Father in heaven is perfect" (Matthews 5:48 NKJV). Our soul/bodies one day will be made perfect. A Born-Again Christian's spirit is made perfect in Christ Jesus.

"Not worthy"—We Believers are not righteous and do not become "worthy" by ourselves. We are righteous because we are in Christ Jesus. Long ago even before He made the world, God loves us and chose us in Christ to be holy and without blame in His eyes (Ephesians 1:4). *Note the words "in Christ."*

"An old sinner"—Continual confession of these words as present state of righteousness with God. "If you openly declare that Jesus is Lord and believe in your heart that God raised him from the dead, you will be saved. For it is by believing in your heart that you are made right with God, and it is by openly declaring your faith that you are saved" (Romans 10:9-10 NLT). When you do this, God uses the forgiving blood of Jesus Christ to wash away the sin of Adam that separated your spirit from the Spirit of God. We are now made-over in the image of God. Psalm 103:12 (NKJV) says, "As far as the east is from the west, So far has He removed our transgressions [sins] from us." These are crimes, errors, evildoings, faults, iniquity, misconduct, and misdeeds. Your personal sins have names. It is important when repenting to name the type of sin: murder, abortion, wrongdoing, slander, gossip, etc.

"Wondering if I will make it in"—Referring to heaven; not sure of salvation due to guilt, present or past sins; condemnation from Satan, feeling unrighteous and guilty even after receiving Jesus Christ as Savior in their life. "And this is what God has testified: He has given us eternal life, and this life is in his Son. Whoever has the Son has life; whoever does not have God's Son does not have life. I have written this to you who believe in the name of the Son of God, so that you may know you have eternal life" (I John 5:11-13 NLT). Condemnation and false accusation come from Satan (Romans 8:2). God cannot keep an account of Adam's sin in your spirit because there is none. Righteousness is a statue or fixed position in God because of Christ's blood that washed away the sin of Adam in your spirit. "Therefore, if anyone is in Christ, he is a new creation; old things have passed away; behold, all things have become new [in the spirit-man]" (2 Corinthians 5:17 NKJV). However, *you* need to keep your soul and body cleaned out with the forgiving blood of Christ Jesus whenever you sin.

Even though the soul and body are not renewed instantly after receiving Jesus Christ like your spirit, God sees them renewed through the blood of Christ. However, you have to enforce that victory with the Word of God, the cleansing blood of Christ, forgiving others, and repentance.

"Walk the straight and narrow path"—Trying to earn righteousness by being good, following the rules, staying out of trouble, and staying off the broad way that leads to destruction (Matthew 7:13–14 NKJV). This should all be done, however, this is not how righteousness and salvation are received. Perhaps you are a Believer in Jesus Christ and you are doing works to please God, keeping the Law of Works instead of the Law of Love/Grace. "God saved you by his grace when you believed. And you can't take credit for this; it is a gift from God. Salvation is not a reward for the good things we have done, so none of us can boast about it. For we are God's masterpiece. He has created us anew in Christ Jesus, so we can do the good things he planned for us long ago" (Ephesians 2:8-10 NLT).

You should never use the phrase "walk the straight and narrow path" if you have a true Born-Again experience. Whenever you do wrong/evil and distance yourself from God, Jesus, and the Holy Spirit, just like a child goes to his/her parents to ask their forgiveness when he/she has done wrong, you can go to God and confess His Word because God responds to His Word. If the sin is envy, James 3:16 (NKJV) states, "For where envy and self-seeking exist, confusion and every evil thing are there."

Pray: Help me, Father, through the Holy Spirit, not to envy, in Jesus Christ's name, Amen!

Now, I realize that there are some theories that suggest you no longer have to confess sin once you give your life to Christ. You simply have to repent and change your behavior. You are already righteous. Jesus has already forgiven your past, present, and future sins. However, I personally revere God too much not to confess God's Word that declares how Christ Jesus, the Word, wants me to act. For example, if I commit the sin of worry, I pray: Father, I will not worry because you said in your Word I should not fret (Psalm 37:8). If you are remorseful over your sin, that is the work of the Holy Spirit in you. Therefore, confess His Word that declares your behavior unholy from scripture. If you tell a lie, pray:

Father, Your Word says You hate lying (Proverbs 6:17). Therefore, help me, Holy Spirit, not to speak that lie again, in Jesus' name. I repent! Amen!

He never distances Himself from you or stops loving you. He hates that you have chosen unbelief or disobedience, but like a prodigal son or daughter, you will remain a son or daughter. No human gets transformed into a four-footed animal when they do evil. A son remains a son. However, you may have consequences to deal with.

Your spirit was reborn, which is an everlasting transaction. Jesus Christ is not going to go back on the cross again every time a person sins. "Not with the blood of goats and calves, but with His own blood He entered the Most Holy Place once and for all, having obtained eternal redemption" (Hebrews 9:12 NKJV). If you are not sure about your salvation for whatever reason, you can say the salvation prayer over again to be assured of your salvation.

"For you died, and your life is hidden with Christ in God. When Christ who is our life appears, then you also will appear with Him in glory. Therefore put to death your members which are on the earth: fornication, uncleanness, passion, evil desire, and covetousness, which is idolatry" (Colossians 3:3-5 NKJV).

The Righteous and Sin's Price Tag

Yielding your soul/mind and body to sin will make you an open target for the Devil. Sin will kill, steal, and destroy your soul and ultimately, your body. It may come in the form of offense, guilt, worry, fear, doubt, gossip, malice, hate, shame, unforgiveness, sickness, disease, poverty, unbelief, and lying. Yes, worry is a sin! "The wages [consequences] of sin is death" (Romans 6:23a NKJV). For a Believer, this is physical death, not spiritual death, which is separation from God. Daily, unrepented sins can affect your spirit-man negatively. It can open the door for Satan to attack, torment, and wound your soul [mind, will, and personality]. This can cause sickness and disease to manifest in the body. Repent and correct the wrong direction of your mind/thoughts and confess God's Word about the aforementioned sins quickly. If you don't, the Holy Spirit will be grieved and you can become cold and distant to the things of God. The complete scripture in Romans 6:23 says that the gift of God, meaning the gift of salvation, is eternal life, which you received in your spirit, the eternal part of you.

Your soul is also eternal; however, you may go to heaven with an unrenewed mind/soul in the Word of God. When God looks at you, He cannot see you or your spirit as a sinner anymore. He sees you with Jesus Christ, His Son—righteous, pure, and with His undefiled blood on you. He sees you as righteous. Can you imagine this blow to Satan? He thought he had God all figured out when he told the first man to disobey God's command of not eating from the Tree of Knowledge of Good and Evil and, as a result, Man would be eternally dead. He had no idea that God would use His own blood to erase sin from mankind and remove the eternal death sentence from his spirit. This is why Satan hates Man so much. God had the audacity to forgive and redeem man's sin eternally and give him, Satan, eternal punishment. Satan is still around, so today's Believers should remain alert because he continues to influence and deceive us into not believing, obeying, or confessing God's Word.

"I have been crucified with Christ; it is no longer I who live, but Christ lives in me; and the life which I now live in the flesh I live by faith in the Son of God, who loved me and gave himself for me" (Galatians 2:20 NKJV).

Remember, a Born-Again Believer's spirit belongs to God and not Satan. Jesus Christ made that possible. A Believer, therefore, cannot be called a sinner. However, the body and soul/mind/will can choose to do acts that are sinful. A Believer is a three-part being. Only the spirit birth determines his eternal destination, not his soul or body. Sin is a curse, and if you involve yourself in this curse, the results will infect the soul and body with a curse. For example, if you bring roaches into your home, you will have a roach-infested house. Your house did not become a roach. However, it can be called a "roach house" and receive the effect of roaches living there, but the house will always be a house. In the same way, sickness is a curse that Satan can bring into your house (body).

I did not say your spirit is cursed. Galatians 3:13a states that "Christ has redeemed us from the curse of the law" (that *us* are Born-Again believers' eternal spirit-man that is created in God's image). For example, if you open the door of your house, flies could come inside and infest your food. This is the same with your soul and body. Whatever you allow in that is sinful can affect you negatively. Here is another example: the doctor prescribed blood pressure medication to control Tom Day's high blood pressure, but he refused to take them or do anything his doctor suggested to lower his blood pressure. Therefore, he ended up having the effects of uncontrolled, high blood pressure. The effects of natural laws and spiritual laws still exist on earth. While serving God, as a Believer, you should be mindful of taking care of the natural body with its physical needs, coupled with the spiritual laws or the Word of God.

Believers' spirits has been redeemed from the curse of sin and they can never be separated from God. However, that does not mean sin, which brought about sickness and disease and came into the earth because of Satan's takeover, does not still exist on earth. We all share this earth with sinners, [the unsaved], Sons of God, Satan, and all his demonic forces. Do not get infected with his sin.

You Are Righteous, Not Unrighteous

You can allow yourself to engage in unrighteous acts. The soul/mind and body of a righteous person can still be bound by your individual sins when you continually yield to them and ignore God's Word. "Stand fast [do not move] therefore in the liberty by which Christ has made us free, and do not be entangled again with a yoke of bondage [or sins]" (Galatians 5:1 NKJV).There is a knowing and a witness in your inner man or spirit when you receive Jesus Christ as your savior. Practicing sin will become repulsive. In 1 Corinthians 5:5 (NKJV), Paul talked about a man who was a member of the church, but was practicing an unholy, evil lifestyle: "deliver such a one to Satan for the destruction of the flesh [or body], that his spirit may be saved in the day of the Lord Jesus" (NKJV).

Remember, Mankind Murray, on previous pages was a criminal. He was saved from eternal spiritual death because of Jesus Christ. Therefore, you are saved because of Jesus Christ, not because of how good you are or how rich or educated you are, or how self-righteous you are, but because of how good Jesus Christ is. "In Him we have redemption through His blood, the forgiveness of sins" (Ephesians 1:7 NKJV).

"There is none righteous, no, not one" (Romans 3:10 NKJV). When you feel like patting y ourself o n t he b ack, remember this, "For by grace you have been saved through faith, and not of yourselves; it is the gift of God, not of works, lest anyone should boast" (Ephesians 2:8 NKJV).

When you are tempted to ask these questions: How could God love that person? How could God forgive me? How could that person be righteous?—Remember, it is because of Jesus Christ.

You also can not call yourself righteous without the witness of the Holy Spirit within you. "Therefore I make known to you that no one speaking by the Spirit of God calls Jesus accursed, and no one can say that Jesus is Lord except by the Holy Spirit" (1 Corinthians 12:3 NKJV). Jesus Christ asked His disciples, "Who do you say that I am?" (and He also asks that of every one of us). Simon Peter answered and said, "You are the Christ, the Son of the Living God." Jesus answered and said to Him, "Blessed are you, Simon Bar-Jonah, for flesh and blood has not revealed this to you, but My Father who is in heaven" (Matthew 16:15–17 NKJV).

Knowing Jesus Christ as Lord must be an inner witness in a person's spirit. People will not be able to verify this for you. Only you know that you can call Jesus Christ Lord after you have believed/declared and received Him as your Savior.

"Most assuredly, I say to you, he who hears My Word and believes in Him who sent Me has everlasting life, and shall not come into judgment, but passed from death to life" (John 5:24 NKJV).

Jesus answered and said to him, "Most assuredly, I say to you, unless one is born again (born from above), he cannot see the kingdom of God" (John 3:3 NKJV).

If you declare with your mouth, "Jesus is Lord," and believe in your heart that God raised Him from the dead, you will be saved. For it is with your heart [soul/ spirit] that you believe and are justified, and it is with your mouth that you profess your faith (confess God's Words about Jesus Christ) and are saved (Romans 10:9-10 NIV).

Soul Restoration

I never fully understood why David said, "He restores my soul" (Psalm 23:3 NKJV). You may have understood everything I said previously about being righteous and your position in Christ because of your Born-Again spirit being born alive to God. However, you also need to understand that with salvation, you now need God to restore your soul to the original man before Adam soiled it with sin, just like your spirit was Born Anew.

You must renew and change the evil instructions that were given to your soul by Satan. God could use your soul as it is with the old programs of Satan, but He will be using a soul injured and wounded by sins such as worry, anxiety, fear, bitterness, envy, jealousy, rebellion, rejection, and more. According to the *Webster's Dictionary*, the word *restore* means "to give back, return to a former position or condition." God declared separation of His image from man's spirit when Adam sinned. This is eternal death—no eternal life, no eternal likeness, and no eternal image of God in his spirit. However, you became reunited with God as your Father when you received Jesus Christ as your Savior. On the other hand, your personal sins can continue to hide their evil presence in your soul, which will keep it from being healed, delivered, and set free from evil habits and every kind of wickedness that it is afflicted with.

You may be thinking, *I thought God already took away all my sin when I received Jesus Christ?* Yes, He did, but He did it spiritually. He took all your sins: Adam/Mankind's sin and your personal sin of the soul and body. Jesus Christ became owner of your spirit, soul and body the instant you received Him as your Lord and Owner, but you are still the caretaker and keeper of your soul, [mind, thoughts, will, emotions] and your body. Christ shed His blood on the cross. He died and was buried. He was then resurrected, ascended, and is now seated in Heaven. This not only freed your spirit from eternal death, this now gives you the opportunity to keep out the unwanted spirits of darkness that once operated freely in your soul and body. "Do you not know that your bodies are temples of the Holy Spirit, who is in you, whom you have received from God? You are not your own" (1 Corinthians 6:19 NIV).

The presence of the Holy Spirit now abides in your recreated spirit with these good characters: goodness, peace, joy, meekness, faith, love, and self-control. John 14:17 (NKJV) states, "The Spirit of truth, whom the world cannot receive, because it neither sees Him nor knows Him; but you know Him, for He dwells with you and will be in you" (your spirit). Your spirit is now a new creation: Born Anew, Born from Above or Born Again *IN* Christ Jesus; the old spirit passed away. Old sins of the soul and body no longer exist. The old sins in them were spiritually deleted. That means God does not have an old sinner account of you anymore because the old "sinner man" record no longer exists. God forgave you when you confessed His Son to be your Lord and Savior. He then used the sinless blood of His Son, Jesus Christ, *Yeshua Hamashyach*, the Savior and the Messiah, to remit, wash away the sin of Adam, or Mankind, and created a new spirit within you, made in His image.

Because your soul and body were not recreated or Born Anew as your spirit was, you can invite hatred, ungodly anger, and unfaithfulness back into your soul and body. Your soul and body are still the same. If your mind and body were sick the day before you got saved, they may still be sick after, but you now can be healed and delivered as these are part of your privileged rights as a Believer. Now you must keep from sinning, as all evil and wicked acts are from Satan. Jesus Christ, when He heals, will say, "Go and sin no more." Remember, God does not see you/your spirit as a sinner.

Your spirit is now recreated in God's image. You are Born Again and you look like Him. Remember, you are a three-part being. However, your soul and body were never reborn and they can revert to sinning, but your spirit cannot sin again. The Holy Spirit's presence is in it. Jesus Christ's blood made that possible. God is willing to cleanse you when you sin in your soul and body. Repent and confess that sin (1 John 1:9). For example, if you told a lie, pray: Father God, Your Word says I must not lie (Proverbs 6:19), I repent/change. Ask others to forgive you if you have wronged them. You do not necessarily have to ask God to forgive, because He already forgave you of all sins when you received Jesus Christ. The Bible says, "And if he (meaning a person) sins against you, rebuke him, and if he repents forgive him" (Luke 17:3b).

The effects of your personal sin make wounds in the soul, as there are consequences to every sin you engage in. Sin affects your soul [mind, will, and emotions] (the law of cause and effect). Only the blood of Jesus Christ can take away the Satanic sins you get involved in. Use the blood of Jesus Christ to cleanse your sin so that your soul can receive healing and deliverance (set free). Use the Word of God to declare your healing and deliverance. Decree it out of your mouth. The Holy Spirit's anointing power on the Word of God will raise your soul out of that bondage and set you free. Find one or two scriptures that you can meditate on and declare it/them. The scripture must be placed down in your spirit man and meditated on for the Holy Spirit to breathe life on it, heal, and raise you out of darkness.

Therefore, name the kinds of personal, Satanic sins you need to be free from. God was specific when He declared that Jesus Christ would be raised out of Hell after three days. The Holy Spirit's power was there to perform God's Word and resurrect Jesus Christ. You can use the scriptures that are already in your spirit. If they are healing scriptures, say it over your body and soul. These words are alive with the Holy Spirit power to heal and resurrect you.

For example, if you were a diabetic or had high blood pressure before you became Born-Again, you may still have these conditions after salvation. Remember, healing is now yours. If you are addicted to cigarettes, you can be delivered from nicotine addiction. You must remind these sicknesses that Jesus Christ already redeemed you. You are simply waiting on the physical manifestation of your healing, which also means that you are doing things in the natural to assist with your healing. Salvation, through Jesus Christ, made these benefits available—healing, deliverance, provision, and protection to provide restoration to your soul and body.

This enemy called Sin may have already caused significant damage to your soul and body throughout your life. Satan did that to a man called Job in the Bible. Satan killed all his children, destroyed all his earthly possessions, and plagued his body with sickness. Job's wife told him to curse God and die. His friends gave him no encouraging or comforting words. This man had a tremendous amount of trauma done to his soul and body. He could have died with the sin of bitterness in his soul, but instead, he trusted God, repented, and was forgiven. Job said, "I have heard of You [God] by the hearing of the ear, But now my eye sees You. Therefore I abhor myself, And repent in dust and ashes" (Job 42:5–6 NKJV). He repented of his soul sins, forgave, and prayed for his friends. God restored his losses and healed him of his trauma and wounds of his mind and body. This proves that there is no devastation that God cannot heal or restore.

Do not allow the spirits of darkness such as bitterness and all forms of fear to enter your soul; it wounds the mind, will, and emotions. Sins committed either by you or your parents that resulted in hurt, abuse, pain, and trauma need to be repented of. All wrongdoing done by you against others or others against you as a result of this sick, fallen world needs to be forgiven. Restoration and healing of your soul with the Word of God brings peace and love when you allow Jesus Christ's blood to cleanse and heal it of the sins that wounded it.

Genesis chapter 4 gives us the account of Cain and Abel. Cain became angry with his brother Abel because his offering to God was accepted, approved, and honored by God, while his was not. Instead of Cain repenting, asking God's forgiveness, changing his ways, and bringing to God the required offering, he allowed the sins of jealousy, rage, and hate to overtake him. This created a wound in his soul [mind/thought, will, and emotion/feelings]. Even his countenance reflected the depression, madness, and rage that were in his soul. Where did these sins and rebellious spirits come from? They were passed on to him from his father, Adam. From where did Adam get those demonic spirits? Satan! This was the nature Adam received when he sinned by disobeying God. These sins are from Satan's rank of evil workers in his kingdom of darkness, "the rulers of the darkness of this age" (Ephesians 6:12 NKJV) that defiled Cain's soul, which filled it with darkness and caused him to ultimately murder his brother.

Judges chapters 13–16 tells of Samson born to Mano-ah and his wife, who was previously barren. Samson was a Nazirite, a person chosen by God to live a separated life unto Him. He was not to drink wine or cut his hair. He was a very strong man because of this. However, he loved the Philistine women, who were pagan and idol worshipers. The Israelites, which included Samson, were people of God, but they were in Philistine captivity. His parents did not approve of his relationships, but he rebelled, dishonored them, and took these Philistine women as wives. He even went to a prostitute. Samson was lured into confessing to Delilah, his wife, what caused his strength–his hair had never been shaved. He was eventually captured by the Philistines who shaved his hair and gouged out his eyes. He became their slave and showpiece. He died with them as he took vengeance. Indulging in sin can also wound the souls of others. Samson wanted what Samson wanted, regardless of it being wrong.

Soul sin brings sorrow and wounds souls, but God is the restorer of wounded souls. You say you are not a gambler or a thief, but you may have an arrogant, critical, and judgmental spirit and a sharp tongue, even though you have trained that sharp tongue to say, "Praise the Lord, sisters and brothers," on Sunday mornings. Some saints wound their souls while going into church services. They do this by being disobedient and rebellious to the parking lot attendant or to the usher's direction. Some saints even gossip about other members. Each member in the Body of Christ is an anointed priest unto God. Revelations 1:5–6 (NKJV) states, "To Him who loved us and washed us in His own blood, and has made us kings and priests to His God and Father." The Word says, "Do not touch My anointed ones, And do My prophet no harm" (1 Chronicles 16:22 NKJV).

Every Born-From Above, Born-Again Believer is an anointed member of Jesus Christ's Body. We inherited not only Jesus/Yeshua's name, but also Christ, Messiah, *Ha-Mashiyach* (Hebrew): the Anointed One and His anointing in our spirits. Members of the Body of Christ are also anointed for leadership services and the same Holy Spirit power that's in Jesus Christ is in every Believer's spirit who receives His presence and anointing.

We should repent of our rebellion toward each other, to our leadership, and to our authorities. As the Bible says, "For rebellion is as the sin of witchcraft" (1 Samuel 15:23 NKJV). You are wounding your soul with these sins. These sins, such as rebellion, will keep you a servant bound to Satan, even if you are Born-Again and redeemed with the cross, blood, death, burial, resurrection, and ascension, and also seated with Jesus Christ. You will be free in your spirit, but still will be under the attack of Satan as he will be able to operate in your soul [mind, thought, will, choice, imagination, and emotion] with his darkness of anxiety, fear, depression, etc. Ask God to restore/heal your soul by washing those sins away with His blood. Then have the Holy Spirit's power of praying in the Spirit and the Word of God to resurrect your soul out of these bondages. You may need to use the weapons of forgiveness, repentance, and communion in the name of Jesus Christ.

As the Bible says, "The blood of Jesus Christ His Son cleanses us from all sin. If we say that we have no sin, we deceive ourselves, and the truth is not in us" (1 John 1:7–8 NKJV).

Dear Father God, I have invited the spirit of fear, ungodly anger, hate, worry, pride, rebellion, disobedience, stubbornness, and jealousy to operate in my soul. I repent because I have rebelled against your Word that says, I should not indulge in these wrongdoings. I bring them to the cross for you to remove them. Heal me of these wounds in my soul. Remove them with the blood of Jesus Christ and wash them away. I close all doors to where they may have entered. Therefore, I go all the way back with the blood of Jesus Christ to my childhood, birth, and past generations where there were traumas and wounds of the soul that may have allowed these openings (some individuals may not need to do this, but some of us do, who have had long-standing unhealed soul traumas). I uproot them from my family line and from myself. I declare that Jesus Christ has taken me and the past generations out of this evil, demonic darkness by the resurrection power of the Holy Spirit. The Bible says, "But if the Spirit of Him who raised Jesus from the dead dwells in you [your spirit], He who raised Christ from the dead will also give life to your mortal bodies [souls] through His Spirit who dwells in you [your spirit]" (Romans 8:11 NKJV). In the name of Jesus Christ, I bind these Satanic bondages and command every root to dry up, wither, and die. I wash them out of my soul with the shed blood of Jesus Christ. I cast them out from the roots and send them into the depths of the sea and bind them there never to return to me in the name of Jesus Christ, Amen.

You may say when you became Born Again, "I repented," which means you took a different course of action, to think differently, to change your mind or purpose. This change is done in the soul, which is the mind, will, and emotions, not in the spirit. God in His mercy will accept this prayer because of a lack of knowledge about the free gift of salvation. When your spirit became Born Again, it was not because of a mind change or repentance. When you received Christ Jesus into your spirit-man, that was the work of Christ's shed blood. He did the forgiving and remitting of the sin of Adam from your spirit-man with His blood: "Not with the blood of goats and calves, but with His own blood He entered the Most Holy Place once and for all, having obtained eternal redemption" (Hebrew 9:12 NKJV).

No amount of repenting, which means taking a different course or action, from your personal sins can save you from the sin of Adam that came up on mankind. You were physically born into his sinful nature. You asked Jesus Christ to be your Savior and Lord because you acknowledged that He is the Son of the Living God who was sent by God to use His sacrificial blood to not only forgive and cleanse your sins, but to wash away the sin of mankind. That is why your spirit became born of the spirit of God. Romans 10:9 (NKJV) says, "If you confess with your mouth the Lord Jesus [not sins] and believe in your heart that God has raised Him [Jesus] from the dead, you will be saved." Saved from what? The penalty of YOUR sinful nature which is death. (You received death from Adam and Adam received death from the "Snake" Satan.) "For with the heart one believes unto righteousness, and with the mouth confession is made unto salvation" (Romans 10:10 NKJV).

This work of the Holy Spirit, who drew you by conviction to God, now makes you right with God, your Heavenly Father. This is true because you received His Son, Jesus Christ who paid the penalty for Adam's sin that came upon all Mankind when he disobeyed God. God now sets you apart or sanctifies you as holy, truthful, and good to Himself. Remaining set apart (sanctified) in your soul and body is an ongoing process that you have to work at daily. Now you need to repent/change, get healed, and be delivered from sins of the soul. Why? Because your soul was not Born Again. You were given a brand-new spirit when you received Jesus Christ as your Savior and Lord. There are no sins in your spirit. The Spirit of God cannot live in a spirit with sin or Satan. Satan is death, and his dead spirit was washed away. God has replaced it with a living one, which His presence is alive in. However, Satanic sins committed in your body and in your soul, for example: abomination, immorality, and misdeeds, which are all under the heading *iniquity*, need to be repented of and turned from. Use the blood of Jesus Christ, that cleanses and heals the soul and body, to continuously wash away that mindset of sin.

Born-Again Believers think that it is the soul that gets born again. No, you have the same old soul and body as you had before. You must continuously cleanse yourself from sin, like you would your body, or

Satan, with his evil stench of sin, will keep creeping back in. Even though you have the same old soul and body, they are alive or more sensitive to sin—in other words, sinning won't be fun anymore.

You need to wash away the sins from your soul with the same cleansing blood of Jesus Christ because you may still possess the same complaining, argumentative, angry, selfish, quarrelsome, and strife-filled attitude. These are sins that you never received from God with your new spiritual birth. These sins in your soul will keep the blessings of God from you. Sin in your soul gives Satan a foothold in your life to not only steal your finances, but to ultimately kill and destroy you. He does that in Born-Again Believers through their souls. Philippians 2:12b (NKJV) states, "Work out your own salvation." This is what sanctifying your soul is about. It is a working process to bring about, to remove all hindrances, to straighten out, and in this case, to deliver your soul from its previous lifestyle. One of the meanings of *salvation* in the Greek means "*soteria*" or "deliverance of spirit, soul, and body."

Jesus did the work of saving and delivering man from sin. Sin separated the spirit of man, that is made in the image of God, from his God. Getting our spirit back from Satan with Jesus Christ's blood was God's job because our spirits belong to Him. However, your mind, will, and emotions God gave to you to be the caretaker of. It is your responsibility to train your soul to live within God's realm, where sin does not work, but God does. God tells you to maintain your body and soul by cleansing it and washing away the sins from it with the blood of Jesus Christ: "And the blood of Jesus Christ His Son cleanses all sin" (1 John 1:7 NKJV).

Sins in your soul may need to be healed or delivered, just as your body needs to be healed or delivered when you have the flu. You need to get rid of that flu/sin that has your soul sick. For example, you could have negative reactions after a traumatic event that may have happened years ago. You may have been involved in a traffic accident on the freeway with your parents at two years old and family members died as a result.

Now, at fifty years old, you refuse to drive on the freeway. That trauma caused fear, and that fear is sin. Some of these sins are hidden in the subconscious: "How much more shall the blood of Christ, who through the eternal Spirit offered Himself without spot to God, cleanse your conscience from dead works (and your mind) to serve the living God?" (Hebrews 9:14 NKJV)

That wound in your soul that has caused that spirit of fear needs to be healed/delivered and cast out of the body and the soul with the name and blood of Jesus Christ. Then have the Holy Spirit's anointing power raise you up out of that pit. The same power that raised Christ from the dead lives in your spirit.

A healed soul can more easily bind spirits of depression/fear and cast them out in the Name of Jesus Christ. A wounded soul is like having your foot on the brake of a car and expecting it to be able to drive. After twenty years, you will still be in park. This is equal to having sins in your soul—it causes no forward movement. You must move your foot off the brake and put it on the gas. This is equivalent to healing/delivering your soul, restoring it to the place of peace, love, and joy where Adam was before he sinned.

Remember that Jesus Christ already healed you.

You can not heal your own soul. Jesus Christ already did the healing for you, but you may not have come into the full physical manifestation of it. However, spiritually you were healed two thousand years ago at Calvary's cross. Therefore, declare that you believe your soul is healed and delivered, even from the sin of worry, the moment you prayed and repented. There is no *going to be, shall be,* or *will be healed* with God. Understand that God's benefits are accessed in the now; when you pray, you receive (Mark 11:23–24). He is in the now. 1 Peter 2:24 (NKJV) states, "Who Himself bore our sins in His own body on the tree, that we, having died to sins, might live for righteousness—by whose stripes you WERE healed." This means Jesus Christ bore all sicknesses of the soul and body; you were healed spiritually at the cross of Calvary. He paid the price for sickness and disease because they were caused by sin. Sickness, disease, and infirmities, whether we cause them or the effects of being in an imperfect body and a fallen, disease-plagued world causes them, are not from God. They do not exist in Heaven. We receive healing and deliverance from Satan's grip as we forgive, repent, bind and cast Satan out. Once we repent, we must forgive, apply, and wash away soul or body sins that cause sickness with the blood of Jesus Christ. You will need to enforce and maintain the victory of what Jesus already did on the cross by praying, taking communion, decreeing and declaring God's Word. Do not assume that Satan and his demons are going to adhere to any legalities and that Jesus Christ gave you the victory over them at the cross. They are bandits, liars, and thieves who are plotting your death and downfall every second of the day. You have to conform to God's rules, laws, government, protocol, and policies within His Kingdom, where you now live. Satan and his dark kingdom of bandits are opportunists that will take advantage of your ignorance, unbelief, disobedience, and every open "crack" in the door of your life.

You can raise yourself out of sicknesses with the same Holy Spirit power and anointing that resurrected Jesus from the dead when you believe Him. Bind and cast that sickness out of your soul/ body in Jesus Christ's name. A healed soul will enable your spirit man to rule and dominate in you because there will be no soul sins to hinder the Word of God from operating in your life. Philippians 4:8 (NKJV) states, "Whatever things are true, whatever things are just, whatever things are pure, whatever things are of good report, if there is any virtue and if there is anything praiseworthy–meditate on these things."

The book of Judges chapter 6 tells the story of the Israelites, God's chosen people. They were constantly being attacked by the Midianites, who were destroying and stealing their crops and cattle. The Israelites had to hide themselves in the caves and dens in the mountains. This left them greatly impoverished and with nothing to eat. God had told them not to worship the gods of the lands around them, including the Midianites, but they disobeyed. Therefore, God left them in the hands of the Midianites for seven years. They were very cruel and came upon the Israelites like locusts, destroying everything in their path. They cried out to God, so He sent an angel to a man named Gideon to rescue them. The angel of the Lord found Gideon threshing wheat in the wine-press and hiding from the Midianites. He instructed him to first tear down his father's altar built to Baal and cut down the Asher-ah (Canaanite goddess) pole beside it. These gods represented demonic spirits that the Israelites were bowing down and making sacrifices to. God had freed them from Egyptian captivity, but they returned to another captivity by being bound to demonic strongholds whenever they worshiped these foreign gods. As soon as Gideon tore down Baal's altar (*false god*) and the Asher-ah pole, he used its wood to burn the offering sacrifice of bulls to God for the Israelites' sins. Those demonic powers behind the gods of Baal and the Asher-ah pole "sent" the Midianites, Amalikites, and the people of the east to come against the Israelites like locusts to make war against them. This is the reason God constantly warns us not to go back into sin, because we invite the evil spirits behind those sins into our souls and bodies.

The mind of a Born-Again Christian must be renewed with God's Word. Without the Word of God, the mind and soul will automatically go back to its "old house of sins," that it once moved out of. You must take possession of your soul by tearing down the gods, idols, and images of the old "house" of your soul and body that sin once ruled in. When your memory wants to return to the "garbage" thoughts you came out of, cast down those Baal/gods (demonic thoughts) that want to return. Have you ever moved out of a house to a new one, and while driving from work you found yourself automatically driving back to the old house? You have to tell your mind, "You are no longer the owner of that house." Do the same and tell Satan he is no longer the owner of your house/spirit, soul, and body anymore. The new owner and occupant of your spirit is Jesus Christ. His blood legally paid for you. The old house no longer exists. You were redeemed/purchased at full price. Those Baal gods/ demons that used to tell you to sin in choices, thoughts, and feelings are now illegal. These bad choices, thoughts, and feelings will attempt to reenter your soul and body by manifesting themselves as a bad temper, a bad attitude, false religious beliefs, and false doctrines such as "speaking in tongues is not for today." They also manifest themselves as keeping old friends who love to sin and are a bad influence on you. Satan uses such friends to persuade you to go back to a perverted lifestyle because it is acceptable in this satanic world. You are then deceived into believing that "just a little taste, a little talk, or a little look won't hurt." Other manifestations include hating another ethnicity, declaring negativity or "bad-mouthing" yourself or others, while denying the truth of what the Word of God says, hating another ethnicity, and deceptions that say. Remember, Ephesians 4:27 (NKJV) states, "Nor give place [opportunity] to the devil."

God told Gideon to pull down the Baal altar and goddess pole, as those things represented demonic spirits. God also told him that He would be with him and that he would not be defeated when the Midianites and their allies tried to attack them. God used three hundred men in Gideon's army to defeat the hosts of their enemies. Again, spiritually, a Born-Again Believer already won every victory over Satan, who is sin. As I stated before, neither sin nor Satan has any legal right to operate in your soul or body. However, you, the Born-Again Believer, now has to take possession of them. You should not give Satan an open invitation because he will be carrying sin with him because he is SIN. Like Gideon, tear down and cast out the gods of the Midianites. These are the ones that are already in your land, the ones that want to come into your land, and the ones you should keep away from your land, which are your soul and body. You won't be using physical weapons and fighting flesh and blood like Gideon and his army. You will be pulling down and casting down spiritual enemies to keep Satan the "Midianite" from stealing, destroying, and killing your crops/ finances, jobs, children, and earthly possessions. Use the cleansing, healing, and delivering blood of Jesus Christ which destroys and washes away sin along with forgiveness, repentance, and the resurrection power of the Holy Spirit in the Word of God. You have authority in the name of Jesus Christ. Communion, anointing oil, prayer, and fasting are all weapons that we have been given to restore our souls.

"For the weapons of our warfare are not carnal but mighty in God for pulling down strongholds" (2 Corinthians 10:4 NKJV).

The Ten Commandments
The Old Covenant Era of God's Judgment

In the Old Testament of the Bible, God's requirement was for mankind to keep the law, which were written on tablets of stone and given to Moses. Know that Jesus Christ is the only one that kept all the laws, meaning the Ten Commandments and every law of the scriptures. If a person broke one of the laws, this person broke all the laws. We have all broken at least one of those laws. See Exodus 20:1–17 for the Ten Commandments.

For whoever shall keep the whole law, and stumble in one point, is guilty of all (James 2:10 NKJV).

Now behold, one came and said to Him. "Good Teacher, what good thing shall I do that I may have eternal life?" So He said to him, "Why do you call Me good? No one is good but One, that is, God. But if you want to enter into life, keep the commandments." He said to Him, "Which ones?" Jesus [Christ] said. "'You shall not murder,' 'You shall not commit adultery,' 'You shall not steal,' 'You shall not bear false witness,' 'Honor your father and your mother,' and, 'You shall love your neighbor as yourself.'" The young man said to Him. "All these things I have kept from my youth. What do I still lack?" Jesus [Christ] said to him, "If you want to be perfect, go sell what you have and give to the poor, and you will have treasure in heaven; and come, follow Me." But when the young man heard that saying, he went away sorrowful, for he had great possessions (Matthew 19:16–22 NKJV).

This young man was selfish. He loved his riches more than his neighbor. He stumbled in one point. He could not keep all the laws in order to receive eternal life, as the Old Testament/ Covenant Law required. Love–that's who Jesus Christ is! He was not selfish. He did not sell what He had. He gave up everything that belonged to Him because He loves Mankind and wanted Mankind back desperately. He was the perfect Son of God who fulfilled the law. "But all the law is fulfilled in one word [love, which represents Jesus Christ], even in this: 'You shall love your neighbor as yourself'" (Galatians 5:14 NKJV).

The first five books of the Bible are called the Torah or the book of the law, but in this writing, I have specifically selected the Ten Commandments. "For the law was given through Moses, but grace and truth came through Jesus Christ" (John 1:17 NKJV).

When Jesus Christ died for us, God did away with the Ten Commandments, which were contained in a box-like structure called the Ark of the Covenant. It was made of acacia wood and laden with gold. There were two cherubim or statured angels on each side. The Ark of the Covenant was located behind a veil or curtain that separated the Holy Place from the Most Holy Place. The veil in the temple was torn in two from top to bottom by God (Matthew 27:51). This means that the presence of God was no longer on top of the Ark of the Covenant behind the veil, but is now transported into the spirit of a Born-Again Believer, whose spirit is no longer separated from God. As Luke 17:21b (NKJV) states, "the kingdom of God is within you." He now lives in you and me, the saved. His laws are now written in our hearts and minds (or spirit). He is now our God and we are His people. No longer do we have to go through an earthly high priest to communicate with God. The veil that separated the people of God in the temple in the Old Testament has been torn down in the New Testament/Covenant. Born-Again Believers can now go directly to God in the authority of Jesus Christ. He is the only High Priest or Mediator between God and Man. That is God's choice. "I will put My laws in their mind and write them on their hearts; and I will be their God, and they shall be My people…for all shall know Me… For I will be merciful to their unrighteousness, and their sins and their lawless deeds I will remember no more… "A new covenant," He has made the first obsolete" (Hebrews 8:10–13 NKJV). "Or do you not know that your body is the temple of the Holy Spirit who is in you" (1 Corinthians 6:19a NKJV). Do not let anyone call you unrighteous. Jesus Christ's blood, sacrificed on the altar called the cross, declared you righteous before God. It extended mercy to you and not judgment. Jesus Christ is your only personal legal attorney, ambassador, and representative.

It is the Spirit who gives life; the flesh profits nothing. The words that I speak to you are spirit and they are life (John 6:63 NKJV).

The New Covenant Era of Grace: Mercy, Forgiveness, Love, and Favor

God gives man an allotted time or era of grace, mercy, forgiveness, love, and favor. It could be years, decades, centuries, or generations. Love is a New Covenant commandment given by Jesus Christ. Mankind is now living in this era of love. "A new commandment I give to you, that you love one another; as I have loved you, that you also love one another. By this all will know that you are My disciples, if you have love for one another" (John 13:34–35 NKJV).

When Jesus Christ died and we received Him as our Savior and Lord, we received the love of God, which gave our spirits eternal life. His love gave us mercy and forgiveness. God extended to us the favor we did not deserve or work for. "For God so loved the world that He gave His only begotten Son, that whoever believes in Him should not perish but have everlasting life" (John 3:16 NKJV).

The Old Covenant gave us the law of judgment. It pronounced us guilty and gave us no mercy whenever we broke it. We were already guilty of inheriting Adam's sin, so we had no way of coming out from under the curse of sin. However, it was replaced by the New Covenant that Jesus Christ gave us, the law or commandment of love, which forgives sins.

"But now we have been delivered from the law, having died to what we were held by, so that we should serve in the newness of the Spirit [new covenant or contract of love] and not in the oldness of the letter [Speaking of the law]" (Romans 7:6 NKJV).

Love won't gossip cheat, hate, covet, envy, find fault, be selfish, rude, judgmental, slander, backbite, devour, kill, lie, and avenge its neighbor. Satan will influence you to do the above, but you must continually say with your mouth what Galatians 5:22–23 says. What should come out of a Born-Again person's mouth is love, joy, peace, long-suffering, kindness, goodness, faithfulness, gentleness, and self-control. Therefore, when you are tempted to be mean, say to yourself, "Love is not unkind, but kind." Study 1 Corinthians 13 and Philippians 4:8. To love is a law or commandment. "For all the law is fulfilled in ONE word, even in this: You shall love your neighbor as yourself" (Galatians 5:14 NKJV).

When Jesus Christ hung on the cross between two criminals, (Luke 23:39–43) He could have lashed out at Mankind in His agony and demanded His right to die without being further tormented by the soldiers. He could have cursed and blamed God and man, but because of love, His words were "Father, forgive them, for they do not know what they do" (Luke 23:34 NKJV). Love did not demand its rights! One of the criminals, who was hanging on the cross next to Jesus Christ, said to Him, "Save Yourself!" However, the other criminal responded differently. He spoke of Jesus Christ's innocence and their guilt. He saw the love of Jesus on display without Him preaching a word. Jesus Christ did not state that He was the Son of God nor did He demand respect. He endured being wronged without ever lashing back. Therefore, one criminal observed and saw the Savior in Jesus Christ and asked Him to remember him when He came into His Kingdom.

Who is that one unsaved person that is watching us when we are being persecuted or lied on? Can we swallow our pride, lay aside our ego, and respond in love to save that person who is in the corner of the room observing? Jesus Christ helps us to love! Even the soldiers exclaimed, "Surely this man is the Son of God (Matthew 27:54)!"

Jesus said to the criminal, "Today, you will be with me in Paradise" (Luke 23:43 NKJV). Jesus kept someone who was bound for eternal hellfire from going there, even though He was suffering.

Are we as Christians capable of doing the same thing? Can people see the same character of love in us that Jesus displayed? Through this love, can we convince a sinner to receive Jesus Christ so that they too can go to Heaven? If not, say with me,

"Father, I declare Your command to love. Forgive me for not loving others. I repent of this sin. Heal my soul from the spirit of hatred and erase it with the blood of Jesus Christ. Raise me also out of every sin in my soul because they too cannot hold me. I renounce and curse the spirit of hate, self-hatred, and all other evil spirits that hang onto it—bitterness, anger, and all forms of fear. I choose to love myself first. Only then can I let others see the love of Jesus Christ in me. In the name of Jesus Christ I take authority over evil operating in my soul [mind, will, emotions]. I cast them out and command them to wither, die, and go into the depths of the sea. I bind them there, never to return to me. I choose to love others. Amen!"

Most assuredly, I say to you, he who believes in Me [Jesus Christ, the one who loves you] has everlasting life (John 6:47 NKJV).

Condemnation and Accusations

Do not allow the devil to accuse or condemn you by making you feel guilty of past sins. Tell him that he is out of touch with the times, as Jesus Christ has already erased your sins. The blood of Jesus has never lost its power to destroy sin. Remind Satan you are no longer in the Garden of Eden where Mankind/Adam died spiritually. He is such a liar! He knows his job description. How can a liar condemn you of your past? When did the condemning liar become a goody two-shoes? He is an opportunist and can not play fair. "There is therefore now no condemnation [not guilty] to those who are in Christ Jesus, who do not walk according to the flesh [sin], but according to the Spirit" (Romans 8:1 NKJV). God's grace and His forgiveness through Jesus Christ's shed blood removed all guilt and the sin of Adam from your spirit once and for all. It also removed the sins of your soul. However, you must repent of the sins of your soul whenever you put them there. You should be progressing in your walk with Christ, not regressing due to indulgence in Satan's sins such as angry outbursts, cheating, gossip, etc.

Satan will harass you if you do not handle him with the Word of God. Follow your spirit, not your flesh.

As far as the east is from the west, so far has He removed our transgressions from us (Psalm 103:12 NKJV).

Massa Lad Accuser

There was a slave living in a remote country. His master or owner was called Massa Lad Accuser. Every night, the slave would bring out the master's favorite rocking chair, fix the pillow just right, prop his feet up, put on his warm slippers, give him a hot cup of chocolate and his favorite cigars, and lastly, turn the radio to the news station. When the news was finished, he would call the slave into the room where he was and say to him, "My favorite slave, you call yourself a Christian, but mark my words, you will never amount to anything. You will always work for me. You are supposed to be broke and suffer when you are sick. You can never be healed. Healing does not belong to you. Don't bother to pray, read the Bible, or speak in tongues around here! Just speak my words, you will get better results." This continued day after day. One day, while the slave was cutting some wood, he slipped and fell. Ever since that day, he began having severe back pain. He convinced Massa Lad Accuser to let him use the horse to go into town to see the doctor.

On his way back from the doctor, with his medication, he noticed there was a tent crusade across the street. The banner said *Healing Service*. He had learned to read when he was a child, so he was very proud of himself. The service was in the middle of the day, so he had plenty of time to get back home before dark. Therefore, he decided to go to the crusade and stay for a while. Although he was in pain, he did not want to take his pain medication before he reached home. He had gotten saved a long time ago, and even got filled with the Holy Spirit with the evidence of speaking in tongues [or in a heavenly language] while listening to a broadcast on the radio. Massa Lad had fallen asleep, and so the slave listened to the whole service, but he didn't have a Bible.

The preacher at the tent service told him about all the benefits that were now his when he received Jesus Christ, and that included healing. He laid his hands on him, and immediately, he felt different. There was no more pain. They gave him a Bible and told him where he could start going to church. He went home rejoicing. He did the routine things for Massa Lad Accuser that evening. Then, after the radio news broadcast, Massa Lad Accuser told him to have a seat and he began to speak. "You know, you are my favorite slave," he said. "You are deathly sick, aren't you? You know you'll never get better, as a matter of fact, you will die… you and your whole family will eventually be with me in Hell!" The slave shot up like lightning and said, "I am not your slave! You are not my Lord! You are not my owner! You are the devil! You and your lying words are beneath me! How dare you come into my house! Get out of my house, you lying demon! You aren't stealing my healing…or my life! Today a preacher read to me Psalm 91:16 which says if I chose not to, I can't die until I am satisfied with long life! When I am finished with you, all my household will be saved, says Acts 16:31. The preacher read that scripture also.

Therefore, Mr. Accuser, you are the only one that's going to the pit of Hell, devil! As a matter of fact, let me throw you out right now!" With all his might, he picked up the rocking chair and threw it through the window, into the woods. "Come around here again and I'll put my size sixteen foot on your neck! (Joshua 10:24). The preacher read that scripture too, rat!"

Even though this story is fiction, please remember that Satan is a very dangerous, destructive, and wicked spirit. He is not a rat. He may look like one, though! When Satan harasses or torments you, always remember to give him God's Word. This person thought he was a slave and a servant to Satan's tormenting, lying, deceiving, paralyzing, death-filled words, even after he became a Christian. However, he took control of his thought life when he began declaring the Word of God to the devil, his mind, and his household.

Remember the thief comes to kill, steal, and destroy and torment your minds with his evil reports and lies (John 10:10). Renounce and cast his words down (2 Corinthians 10:5).

Curse Satan's words from the roots and command them to wither and die, go into the depths of the sea, and never return to you.

Remind the devil who you are in Jesus Christ: the righteous, delivered, healed, etc. Even though this gentleman was filled with the Holy Spirit, he did not have a Bible and knew no scriptures about his legal authority as a Believer. He did not know that he was already victorious. He was, therefore, not able to renew his mind until he went to the tent crusade and, in a short time, he got ahold of a few scriptures and meditated on them [muttered them over and over]. They renewed his mind, and he used them as a hand grenade to throw at the devil. God's Word is spirit and life. Oxygen helps us to breathe, but the Word of God breathes life into our spirit, soul, and body. Christ said, "I have come that they may have life, and that they may have it more abundantly" (John 10:10b NKJV).

The Word of God is one of the main spiritual weapons we can use to cut off the serpent's head. Hebrews 4:12a states, "The Word of God is, living and powerful, and sharper than any two-edged sword." Isaiah 49:2a says, "And He has made My mouth like a sharp sword" (NKJV). Jesus Christ is the Word, and He did just that when He descended into Hell and cut that "belly-crawling snake's head off," which was his authority. Satan is now "headless." Jesus Christ will never leave us or forsake us, and His Word "sword" is in our mouths and in our hearts [spirit/soul]. Satan knows He has no unsettled, legal right or claim to keep Believers in slavery with his words. Jesus Christ has already stripped him of all legal authority to be our slave owner. The blood of Jesus Christ defeated the judgment of death against us. Therefore, no evil, Hell, death, sickness, or poverty can hold us in bondage as we are now Jesus Christ's legal representatives in this earth. Because Satan has no authority "head" or legal power over a Born-Again Believer, he will try to use his "tail" to intimidate you. There is no legal power in his "tail." Use your sword (the Word of God) to get rid of that too when he tries to invite himself into your life through circumstances. Genesis 3:15c "He (Jesus Christ) shall bruise your head." Cut off Satan's head or his legal power/authority over Mankind. This prophecy by God has been fulfilled:

"There is therefore now no condemnation to those who are in Christ Jesus, who do not walk according to the flesh, but according to the Spirit" (Romans 8:1 NKJV).

Then I saw an angel coming down from heaven, having the key to the bottomless pit and a great chain in his hand. He laid hold of the dragon, that serpent of old, who is the Devil and Satan, and bound him for a thousand years; and he cast him into the bottomless pit, and shut him up, and set a seal on him, so that he should deceive the nations no more till the thousand years were finished (Revelation 20:1–3 NKJV).

Then He arose and rebuked the winds and the sea, and there was a great calm (Matthew 8:26b NKJV).

"Or how can one enter a strong man's house and plunder his goods, unless he first binds the strong man? And then he will plunder his house" (Matthew 12:29 NKJV).

"Assuredly, I say to you, whatever you bind [clip off, break off, plunder, stop, cut off, wall up, restrain, fortify, make inaccessible] on earth will be bound in heaven, and whatever you loose [allow] on earth will be loosed in heaven" (Matthew 18:18 NKJV).

"When the unclean spirit goes out of a man, he goes *through dry places* seeking rest, and finds none" (Matthew 12:43 NKJV).

"He [Jesus] rebuked the unclean spirit, saying to it: "Deaf and dumb spirit, I command you, come out of him and *enter him no more*" (Mark 9:25b NKJV).

"So the demons begged Him, saying, "If You cast us out, permit us to go away into the herd of swine" (Matthew 8:31 NKJV).

"And Peter, remembering, said to Him, "Rabbi, look! The fig tree which You cursed has withered away" (Mark 11:21 NKJV).

Jesus Christ showed us Born-Again Believers how to bind, loose, rebuke, cast out, curse, command, and renounce Satan [the devil] and his unclean, demonic spirits.

Why Do You Take on the Name of Jesus Christ (Yeshua)?

When you were Born Again or Born from Above by the Spirit of God, God required you to use the name of Jesus Christ in the relationship. When a woman gets married, the law requires her to take on her husband's name. She is immediately engrafted into or adopted into a family that's not her birth family. She is legally one of the owners of her husband's assets and the in-law to her husband's relatives. That's the marriage law. God also used this law. He instituted that without the shedding of blood, there is no remission of sin. Therefore, He used His Son Jesus Christ's perfect blood to erase Mankind's sin and to engraft him/her to become His legal son and daughter, who legally have the same rights and privileges as Jesus Christ. In other words, Jesus Christ became "married" to you by using His blood. On earth it is called a marriage covenant. God the Father did the marriage ceremony once and for all when He gave you righteousness and right standing with Him. Of course this symbolic marriage depiction of Jesus Christ with His Body of Believers called the Church is spiritual. This marriage is not a physical depiction.

You now have the right or privilege to go boldly to His throne. You are now an heir of God and His blessing and a joint heir with Jesus Christ (Romans 8:17). You are seated with Christ in heavenly places (Ephesians 2:6). You are given the right to be children of God (John 1:12). Therefore, we are all gods because our spirits are made in the image and likeness of God and GOD IS SPIRIT. He created man's spirit like HIMSELF FIRST before He breath man's spirit and soul into a formed body made from the dust of the ground Genesis 1:26 states: "Let US: (God the Father, God the Son or the Word and God the Holy Spirit) make man in Our image according to Our likeness." Therefore, Jesus is exactly right when He quoted Psalm 82:6a in John 10:34, "Is it not written in the law, I said (I, meaning, Jesus-The Word) you are gods?" You, of course, are not God the Father, angels, or idols, but because you are made like God, you are little gods, meaning you are god-like in the earth. Anyone who is like God and has His nature is very precious.

He made us kings and priests to our God (Revelation 5:10 NKJV). He calls us sons and daughters and heirs of God through Christ (Galatians 4:7). The high court of Heaven does not divorce, so you are stuck with God the Father, the Son, and Holy Spirit for ever and ever. Amen!

"I will greatly rejoice in the Lord, my soul shall be joyful in my God; For He has clothed me with the garments of salvation, He has covered me with the robe of righteousness, as a bridegroom decks himself with ornaments, And as a bride adorns herself with her jewels" (Isaiah 61:10 NKJV).

You are now wealthy and prosperous. You were "married" into royalty. Why deny your marriage (covenant) rights and live as if you were single (without covenant)? Blessed are those who are called to the marriage supper of the Lamb! (Revelations 19:9 NKJV)

Marriage is a picture of God's love for Mankind, and we can call it nothing else. It is love, mercy, favor, goodness, and kindness, which is unmerited and unselfish grace. Marriage is without fault finding or condemnation, which Christ the Redeemer and Savior has given to humanity. By asking sinful man to get into a marriage covenant with Him, He exchanged man's filthy sin nature for His righteousness. This grace was shown in God's redemptive plan in the Old Testament book of Ruth, where Boaz redeemed Ruth in marriage. They became King David's ancestors or his great-grandparents. Ruth, Naomi's widowed daughter-in-law, was a Moabitess. She was a foreign woman from a pagan, idol-worshiping land and not from the tribe of Israel or Jewish. She was engrafted by marriage into Abraham's lineage and the seed of righteousness. She was given Boaz's name and His Jehovah God to call upon. Not only was she in the lineage of King David, but also Jesus Christ the Savior. This is the redemptive work of Christ: Boaz and Ruth's marriage was a foretaste of God redeeming sinful man back to Himself through His Son, Jesus Christ. Please read the full account in the Old Testament book of Ruth.

"Therefore, my brethren, you also have become dead to the law through the body of Christ, that you may be married to another—to Him who was raised from the dead, that we should bear fruit to God" (Romans 7:4 NKJV).

Faith in God

Faith is acting on Truth. Another name for Truth is the Word of God. Faith is not natural like the shoes you wear. It is spirit. "The words that I speak to you are spirit, and they are life" (John 6:63 NKJV). Faith will only operate within God's promises, Will, Word, or commands, and also within your belief to His written or personally spoken Words to you. In order for faith's manifestations to be birthed in the natural or for you to see the results of your faith, your soul, mind, will, and emotions must choose to trust, believe, and receive God and His Word. Your spirit received a measure of faith when you were Born Again. You received your Born-Again FAITH when you heard the gospel. This was given to you by Jesus with the help of the Holy Spirit. You believed on the name of the Lord Jesus Christ (Savior) to be saved and declared with your mouth that Jesus is Lord or owner of your life, not Satan. You believe in the Savior Jesus Christ, whom God had raised from the dead (Romans 10:9-13). If He says you are healed, act on that intangible word. You may not physically see or feel faith, which makes it harder to understand, because faith is not seen it is believed. Because you are spirit, you now operate in the spiritual realm by believing God's Word. As you move in this operation, it is called faith. Satan's strategy is to get Believers in Jesus Christ to choose to believe his words, which is death. There is no life in his words. Satan's words are opposite of God's Word. This is the faith that operates from your spirit: trusting, believing, and doing God's Word independent of your will or mind. In other words, it does not matter what your mind or will decides or says to you. You will only respond to and believe the Word of God. "For we walk by faith, [which is the Word of God/spirit] and not by sight [the realm of the senses]" (2 Corinthians 5:7 NKJV).

To perform any type of transaction now in God's Spirit realm or in the Kingdom of God and His principles, you must use faith or believe. Believe Who? God Who is TRUTH or FAITH. Therefore, doubt is unbelief in truth or trying to prove the integrity of God's Truth/Word.

Your spirit walks by truth or trusting God's Word, which is called faith. It does not walk according to your will, mind, or emotions from your soul. Your spirit will hear and receive God's Words, but you must also train your soul to hear and receive God's Words from your recreated spirit. Your spirit should be leading your soul (mind) as you follow God's Word/Spirit.

Faith in God's Word will grow in your spirit and soul as you abide in, spend time in, or hear His Word. Faith is speaking, decreeing, declaring, and acting on the supernatural Word of God to change the natural. Using God's Word to speak to and move mountains does not appear in you overnight. God is Spirit, His Word is Spirit, and you and I are spirits. The Word of God speaks to your spirit. Your mind and your will are only channels for God's Word to pass through. However, if untrained in His Word, they can block the Word of God and your carnal, fleshly nature will still dominate you. For example, a baby will hear his/her parents' call to jump into their arms without thinking about the danger of possibly falling because the baby trusts and believes in his/her parents. The baby is innocent. There is nothing negative to block or mistrust the parents' words. The Holy Spirit will teach you. (Receiving the Holy Spirit's infilling will be discussed in upcoming chapters). He will reveal the Spirit of God to you as you study in your unique way, as everyone is unique to Him. "But seek first the kingdom of God and His righteousness, and all these things shall be added to you" (Matthew 6:33 NKJV).

In the Old Testament, David did not suddenly develop faith in God to slay Goliath on the same day He killed him. He spent time in God's presence, hearing His Word. He trusted God first to help him kill a bear and a lion. When it came time for him to kill Goliath, he knew he had to move in that same supernatural Holy Spirit power, which is faith in God's Words, or he would be a dead man. Therefore, spend time in the Word of God, which is very important to develop trust in Him. Then, you can move from trust to the supernatural, which is your faith acting on His Word. Therefore, when Jesus says "Come," you can walk on water to get to Him and not sink (Matthew 14:25-31). "Trust in the Lord with all your heart and lean not to your own understanding [intellect, mind, reasoning]; in all your ways acknowledge Him [Holy Spirit presence], and He shall direct your paths" (Proverbs 3:5–6 NKJV).

In addition, be careful not to put your trust in the circumstances or situations that come against you because fear can cause you to sink. You should not only confess God's Word, but also build a relationship with Him, which involves spending time in His Word, praying, praising, and worshiping. God, in His mercy toward man, may operate in the working of supernatural, miraculous signs and wonders, which are divine, spiritual gifts of the Holy Spirit found in 1 Corinthians 12. The gift of miracles may not be a daily happening in a congregation of Believers. For example, Believers may not experience the miracle of a limb growing out every Sunday or the dead being raised. However, Believers may use their faith/belief/trust in God and His Promises daily to heal, provide, and deliver. Personally, I believe God will once again manifest His great miracles, such as parting the Red Sea, for His Church.

Faith is what pleases God. You cannot believe and act on God's Word, and at the same time, act on and believe the Devil's words. Light always eliminates darkness. Therefore, darkness cannot survive in light. Speak and act on God's Word, which is light, and He can drive out your darkness. It is not up to God to use your faith for you. For example, you may say, "It's up to the Lord to heal me." He provided healing the same way He provided your body. However, it is up to you to exercise your body, which is working your physical muscles. In the same manner, it is up to you to exercise your spiritual faith muscles. "If you abide in Me, and My words abide in you, you will ask what you desire, and it shall be done for you" (John 15:7 NKJV).

The branch of a tree cannot live without the trunk of the tree. In other words, you get your nourishment from the words you abide in. Spend time in the "gym" of the Word of God, not just quoting scriptures, but also hearing the written or spoken Word because that's how faith comes. Be diligent. "So then Faith comes by hearing, and hearing by the word of God" (Romans 10:17 NKJV). The more time you spend with God and His Word, the more you will trust Him. The Devil will have a harder time derailing your faith. "This Book of the Law shall not depart from your mouth, but you shall meditate in it day and night, that you may observe to do according to all that is written in it. For then you will make your way prosperous, and then you will have good success" (Joshua 1:8 NKJV). God told Joshua this, and he only had five books of the law to meditate on! However, you may be speaking God's Word, never confessing unbelief, acting on His Words, living right and holy, and forgiving others, but you are not seeing the manifestation of what you are believing Him for. Then, ask God to show you what's hindering the manifestation.

The Word evidence in Hebrews 11:2 is the Word of God that you bring to Him. Just like a judge in a court of law, evidence must be presented to the judge to decide the claim. The sign or evidence you bring to the court of God is your belief and action, which is your faith in God's Word. His Word cannot be seen. It is presented to Him with your voice.

The same way when you first heard the gospel, your belief justified you to God. It made you righteous when you believed in the words that said Jesus Christ is the Son of God, He is the only way to God, and He is the only way to receive eternal life. Because you believed, you acted on your belief by speaking. You confessed Jesus Christ to be the Son of the Living God and your Savior, Owner/Lord.

"The Words that I speak to you are spirit, and they are life" (John 6:63b NKJV).

Nothing is impossible to you if you believe in the God of impossibilities. Matthew 17:20 (NKJV) says, "Nothing will be impossible for you." It takes endurance to reach this point in your faith. Having the God kind of faith will be tried and tested. The book of James 1:3 (NKJV) states, "Knowing that the testing of your faith produces patience [endurance]." Much like training your muscles to lift 5 to 100 lbs of weights, training your faith will take patience, endurance, and standing, even under great pressure. This endurance will not come from your physical strength or your human mind. It will be a divine capability and ability that God will place in your spirit-man to endure the trials and tests that oppose your faith.

While you are standing on God's Word to bring into physical manifestation what you asked Him for, Satan will use anyone, anything, and every circumstance to derail your faith in God's Word. God, His Word, and Faith are alive—breathing, moving "muscles." John 6:63 (NKJV) states, "It is the Spirit that gives life; the flesh profits nothing. The words that I speak to you are spirit, and they are life." Faith is one of the fruits/ingredients of your Born-Again spirit. Faith is **now** because God *is* in you continually, not was, past tense. Hebrews 11:1 (NKJV) states, "**Now** faith *is* the substance [*material, ingredient*] of things hoped for, the evidence of things not seen." Faith has and is evidence, the Word of God, is not seen but heard, declared or voiced. You cannot have faith in God without hearing the Word of God. Because God's Word is Truth, it is proof. Faith is the ingredient that comes out of believing and acting on God's Word. Faith void of the Word of God is not faith, which is unproven trust in God. You only develop faith through God's Word [hearing it, saying it, meditating on it, abiding in it, etc.], the God kind of faith, that is. This is God's "DNA," and this faith must become your and my lifestyle. Faith not only prospers you; it saves, delivers, heals, forgives, and loves the unloving. Faith in God and His Word, when acted on, causes you to endure, move mountains, and believe the impossible.

Hope is dreaming or having a vision, feeling or desire in the soul, but it may lack the material or ingredient of faith or a desire held on to truth, which is God's Word planted deep in your spirit. Consequently, there may be no belief that results in action. Hope may be the feeling or emotion in the mind/soul void of faith, which is the material of the healing Holy Spirit's power in God's Word to bring about visible manifestations. Hope may stay in the soul as a feeling or emotion of uncertainty that states, "I hope I get well," but faith is believing and acting on every promise in the Word of God. Faith moves God's Holy Spirit's power into action, not hope. However, hope can be expressed negatively or positively, with positive hope, you can possess your dreams or aspirations with determination, skills, achievements and hard work.

My mother was an excellent seamstress/ dressmaker. She would imagine a dress design, then create a pattern to make the dress. She, then, would buy her choice material and make the dress from the pattern. If she did not do that, the dress she hoped for and dreamed about would have stayed in her mind as an image. However, she put action to the image in her mind and brought the dress out of the invisible into the visible. The manifestation, which was wearing the dress, came into being when she put action to the image in her soul, which came into creation because of faith or belief in a gift, naturally acquired skill or knowledge in a craft. Hope, as a dream/vision, is good and can be used as a goal setter. However, she did not keep hope for the creation of the dress lingering in her imagination, but put faith in her skills into action.

Sometimes hope in the natural is also used as a stepping stone to get to spiritual healing. For example, you will need faith in God's Word to be healed of arthritis. You received divine faith when you received your salvation (Romans 12:3). Now you are going to use that faith in a healing scripture that has been dormant, as far as renouncing bodily disease is concerned. However, you needed and received prescribed medication as a remedy which you hope to use as the stepping stone or goal until faith in God's Healing Word takes root in your spirit. Remember you have faith which is a belief in God's healing SCRIPTURES, but you may need to confess and decree it over your arthritic joints until the bones and joints begin to hear and obey those healing scriptures coming from your spirit. Remember, Jesus spoke words to a barren fig tree (Mark 11:14) and a stormy sea and they obeyed His words (Matthew 8:25). Hope is taking the bus until your faith confession over your tithes and offerings scriptures manifests a car. Therefore, hope sets the marker or goal until faith declarations in God's Word is believed spiritually. Do not use the word hope when you are believing for healing or standing on the Word of God because God's promises are already accomplished, but your faith in it may be 0%. So then faith will have to come to you by hearing and hearing by the Word of God on a healing, provision, or protection scripture, verse; promise. "So then faith comes by hearing, and hearing by the Word of God" (Romans 10:17 NKJV).

Hearing God's Word on healing creates a spiritual image in your spirit called belief, which when acted on or declared is faith. Faith believed and declared creates and brings the Word of God into manifestation. When you believe and act on God's Word the invisible becomes visible. The Word of God is the "material" (evidence, sign, or proof). Whenever you believe, it is a sign/evidence of your faith, coupled with your speaking, declaring, confessing, or any other action. A healing manifestation would be in the physical.

A police officer brought into a court of law a weapon that was used in a crime. This weapon was used as evidence or proof of a crime committed.

How do you handle evidence that you cannot see in the natural? God requires us to do this with His Word. His Word cannot lie. It is already the evidence that you will have to bring to Him, the Judge, and the Devil, your false accuser. As your defense, you must trust God's Word by faith [the ingredient] to show the evidence/sign/proof of your belief in the face of your false accuser, the Devil. You will win the charges against you every time. It does not matter if the charge is sickness, poverty, or bondages; the faith verdict is not guilty. James 1:22, 25 (NKJV) states, "But be doers of the word, and not hearers only… but a doer of the work, this one will be blessed in what he does." There are many people in the Bible whose faith is recorded. Their faith in God involved action. They not only believed God, but also their faith acted on the Word of God. Therefore, living by faith is moving on God's Word.

I am thinking about the woman who touched the hem of Jesus's garment in Mark chapter 5. Jesus Christ felt her faith touching His garment. That was a spiritual touch, not a natural one. That was the trust, the belief in her Anointed Messiah put into action. Faith in God will make you stand out to Him in a crowd when no one else sees your actions/belief in God. This too was the action of the poor widow in Luke chapter 21, who put two mites into the treasury. Christ saw her giving and called it faith. By giving her all, she made a statement to poverty that God was her provider, not the two mites she gave. She believed in putting G od first, even though she needed that money.

The faith of these women was recorded in the Bible just like Moses, Noah, and Abraham's faith were. How about the Canaanite woman who had a demon-possessed daughter and came to Christ pleading with Him for help in Matthew 15:21–28. Jesus Christ answered her not a word, even though she cried after Him and His disciples. When He answered, He told her He was not sent to her "class of people" and what belonged to the house of Israel was not for "little dogs." Her people were not Israelites. Was she offended? Did she allow hurt feelings to get in the way of receiving her child's deliverance? No! Was her faith tried and tested? Yes! Did it take patience and endurance to withstand the odds that had come against her? Yes! Was she holding on to her faith, believing in the Messiah, even though she was not Jewish? Yes! Did she have all the right college degrees, seminary, religious, and theological qualifications to receive God's healing promises that were given to His people? No! Faith/belief in Jesus Christ the Healer was the evidence that qualified her for a healing. Did she believe this? Yes!

Was she disappointed when the disciples told Jesus Christ to send her away? Did she run away, feel hurt, offended, or rejected? Did she curse, walk away, and talk about Jesus Christ and His disciples behind their backs? No! Her faith was not moved by her emotions, her feelings, or her ethnicity. It was moved by believing and acting on who Jesus Christ was to her, the Messiah, Deliver, and Healer sent by God. Did she dig her heels in the sand and declare what the Word of God said about the Messiah, Jesus Christ? Did she believe that there was healing in the crumbs that the "little dogs" received that fell from God's healing table? Yes! Did this *work* on her part indicate to Jesus Christ and all the devils and opposition in her way that she was not moving without her daughter's healing? Yes! Because God, through the prophets, promised a Messiah, and He had all the evidence/signs of that Deliverer.

Did she *see* her child's healing first, without faith in Christ the Healer? No! Could Jesus Christ by the words that came out of her mouth spiritually hear her faith in Him? Yes! Did she know that she was speaking to the Savior, Deliverer, and Healer that God promised? Yes, she said, "Have mercy on me, Lord, Son of David! My daughter is severely demon possessed" (Matthew 15:22 NKJV). She acted on her belief that Jesus Christ was truly the Messiah sent from God, and that the demon possessing her child was a tormenting liar. Did Jesus Christ finally tell this socially-outcasted woman that she had great faith and then recorded it in the Bible? Yes!

Why did Jesus Christ test and measure her faith? Because, He knew she would receive according to the measure she had believed and acted on. What was her score from small to great, weak to strong? Was she a very bold woman to stand firm, believing what was in God's Word, not being a *daughter of Abraham and a Canaanite (Old Covenant)*? What happened to her severely demon-possessed child? Her extraordinary faith in Jesus Christ kicked that spirit into the depths of the sea, and it has never been back to that region. Jesus said to her, "O woman, great is your faith! Let it be to you, as you desire." And her daughter was healed from that very hour (Matthew 15:28 NKJV).

You start out with a measure of faith. When you become a Christian, it is now up to you to increase it. This has already been mentioned in this book, but every measure you have is going to be better than the last measure you had. For example, a little is better than the same measure you received at salvation. God will surely ask you, what did you do to increase the measure you received? Did you read your Bible? Did you hear the Word of God? Faith comes by hearing. You should test your faith in God's Word by asking for something small. Ask Him to provide you with bus fare before you ask Him to allow you to walk on water.

Functions of Faith:

1. Faith as fruit of your Born-Again spirit (Galatians 5:22). This is the fruit of faith that grows. Your faith in the Truth/ God can be measured and can increase. This faith has no growth limitation because faith has no limits. All it does is increase according to your faith released or exercised, even at 101 years old.

2. The Holy Spirit gift of faith is also manifested in and through a Believer (1 Corinthians 12:9). This kind of Faith is one of the nine supernatural miraculous gifts of the Holy Spirit.

3. Faith as a work of God. Only God is the Creator of this faith. Faith is who God is, and faith is believing in Him, who is Truth (John 3:36, John 3:16, John 6:29). Faith is also given to you by the Holy Spirit to save you from the wrath of sin, to believe God, the work of Christ, and what He did to redeem you from eternal death.

4. Faith is the ingredient you need for God's Word to speak to you personally. This is called *the Word of God to you*. *The Word of God to you* are scriptures that you asked God to give you, have meditated on, or Words God has spoken to you directly. Romans 10:17 (NKJV) states, "So then Faith comes by hearing and hearing by the word of God."

You will know that you have faith because you have the evidence, proof, material, substance, or ingredient which is the Word of God. You believe and act on it. That is faith. For example, if you are unable to walk and Jesus commanded you to "stand up and walk," your belief will be in Jesus's Word, "stand up and walk." The healing ingredient of faith comes into action when you stood up and walked. You are no longer crippled. That is faith manifested. You cannot have faith without the Word. When you eat an apple, the ingredient or substance in the apple is the vitamin and the fiber. An apple does not exist without these. The evidence or sign in the ingredient is vitamin C and the fiber within the apple. The outcome, sign, or evidence that you are not lacking in vitamin C is that you have energy and your bowels function normally because of the fiber in the apple. The ingredient or substance of faith in the Word of God is unseen, just like the ingredients in the apple, but they are there. II Corinthians 5:7 (NKJV) states, "For we walk by faith not by sight." (Faith is the unseen ingredient in the Word of God). Just like you put your natural fruits in a blender and drink the fruit juice, which gives you antioxidants and energy, put the Word of God in your spiritual blender, your mouth. It will give your spirit, soul, and body all the nutrients and energy it needs. Healing and prosperity ingredients are in the Word of God. Put them into your mouth, ingest them, and declare their healing, delivering power in your body and soul.

Your spirit already knows and believes God. It has the Holy Spirit's presence within it. Feed your spirit and soul the Word. Your spirit will bring it to your soul when you need it. You must meditate on the Word until your spirit grasps it. However, any unbelief in God's Word is a sin. Satan will use this against you and your stand of faith. Your faith in God's Word is spiritual, however, it can be influenced by the belief or unbelief in your soul [mind, will, and emotion]. Whatever is confessed out of your mouth or your actions is evidence of belief or unbelief.

God is your, "I AM WHO I AM" God. (Exodus 3:14). Notice that *I am* is in the present tense. Even though the natural man has past, present, and future tenses regarding time, God's answer to your prayer is in the now or present tense. Use "I am," the present tense, just like God. If you have a million dollars or more in the bank, your confession would be "I am rich." Well, healing is more than a million dollars in your spiritual bank, so keep your confession in the now or present. Healing, prosperity, and salvation are ever present with you continually, even at 124 years old. Hebrews 11:1 states that faith is, *not was*. NOW FAITH IS, *Now God is*. Declare, "I am righteous! I am saved! I am holy!" However, His answer can manifest instantly or over a process of time, e.g., healing. Your confession during the period of waiting for your manifested healing should be "I am healed" or "I was healed when I prayed" (1 Peter 2:24). When you received salvation, you also received righteousness, healing, deliverance, protection, and soundness of mind. These are all a part of your spiritual salvation package. You have these benefits because of your salvation in Jesus Christ. All the benefits are spiritually automatic, such as being righteous and holy. These are within your Born-Again rights. You must activate or gain access to your benefits through prayer and prayer requests for a specific need to be met. For example: asking for healing or finances because you have healing and prosperity benefits. If you work for a company that gives health insurance benefits, you activate that health benefit every time you make a doctor's appointment. For financial benefits, you may get membership with financial or investment institutions; these may assist you financially as part of your company's benefits. You are activating your salvation benefits every time you ask God to heal or provide for your soul or body.

The soul and body must remain under submission to the Word of God when you use your faith. Sins in the soul allows Satan to give negative input to it. He will be able to infiltrate your mind, reasoning, and thoughts. Your mind will become confused. When this happens, focus on the Word, which will give you the sound, healthy mind of Christ.

There is a problem with unconfessed, unrepented soul sins such as gossip, jealousy, hate, and anger. Born-Again Sons and Daughters of God must live a delivered life in the soul and body, free of sins, because Satan roams about and looks for cracked-open doors of sins in your soul and body. Be sober and vigilant (1 Peter 5:8). A lie, big or small, is sin and so is bitterness.

Whatever is in your soul that is unhealed, ask the Holy Spirit to show you how to remove it. In the meantime, repent and ask forgiveness for the sins you have committed. In addition, use the blood and resurrection power of Jesus Christ and the Word of God to cleanse and heal your soul.

Soul wounds, trauma, and sin can cause sickness, financial problems, marriage problems, and mental issues, which can affect your anointing. It is better to have a healed soul, free of sins, when walking by faith.

Remember the Israelites in the wilderness, how they grumbled, complained, and rebelled against God? Remember how they stayed in the wilderness longer than they needed to and ultimately died in the wilderness? God is still the same God. He never changes. A life of murmuring is sin. Sin delivers you into the hands of Satan. Remember the prophet Moses of the Israelites and how his sister and brother criticized and gossiped about his wife's ethnicity, being an Ethiopian (Cushite)? Moses's sister, Miriam, got leprosy as a consequence for sinning (Numbers 12:1–10). Aaron did not enter the Promised Land that God had given to the children of Israel (Numbers 20:24–29). In the Wilderness of Zin, the Israelites needed water. God asked Moses and Aaron to speak to the rock and it would yield water, but instead, Moses struck the rock with his rod. This was called the water of Mer-i-bah, the water of contention *[struggle, argument]*, which the children of Israel did with the Lord to receive water (Numbers 20:1–13).

Moses sinned by disobeying God's command, and that sin had its consequence. He never entered the Promised Land (Deuteronomy 34:4–5). Remember, God is Now. He is everywhere. Therefore, when you criticize, judge, disrespect, and rebel against the anointed office of a leader and his/her family, this is sin. You are in great danger of Satan's attacks. You just gave him the legal right. He is the same crafty serpent today as he was in the garden of Eden that caused the first sin. Thank God the New Covenant believers have the sacrificial blood of Jesus Christ that forgives when one repents and confesses the Word of God, which heals and declares their deliverance from that sin. You do not have to bring an animal to the temple to be sacrificed to cover your sin, like the Old Covenant saints. We, the New Covenant believers, get rid of our sins with repentance: change of mind or turning in a different direction, and forgiveness. Unforgiveness in your soul toward others will allow the enemy, Satan, and his demons to torture you (Matthew 18:34). What soul sins are keeping us from going into our Promised Land?

I know you are saying, "Why talk about sin, sin, sin! You are too sin conscious!" I am not talking fiction, but theoretically, this knowledge has revolutionized my life. Remember, God gave dominion to man on earth. He also gave him dominion over his mind. Therefore, it is man's responsibility to train and monitor what goes in and out of the mind. God did not monitor what was going in and out of the Garden of Eden. He gave that assignment to man, Adam, and He was not going to disrespect and dishonor His own Word. He gave you a soul [with a will, mind, and emotion] to possess and to dominate, and He gave you His Word to do it with. He also gave you ways to keep yourself free from the spirits of fear, frustration, discouragement, anger, hate, racism, offense, slander, criticism, persecution, judgmentalism, false accusation, malice, bitterness, shame, and prejudice by being repentant and forgiving others. Applying Jesus Christ's blood cleanses all sin. His birth, death, burial, resurrection, and ascension made this possible.

When you go fishing, you cannot just eat the fish without first gutting it and then preparing it to be eaten. Unprepared fish will poison you. The Christian life is the same. It has a cleansing process. The position of Sanctification is when Jesus Christ takes your spirit that's made in the image of God out of Satan's darkness. He then remakes and transforms your spirit back into God's image. That is a fixed position where you are now called justified and righteous when you receive Him into your life as your Savior and Lord.

Because you are a three-part being [you are a spirit, you have a soul and you live in a body], it will take a great deal of work, over a period of time, to reprocess—clean out the gut—the belly of your soul, to make it spiritually productive. It too must be cleansed with the blood of Jesus Christ, which heals all bitterness, insanity, anger, and all Satanic darkness. III John 1:2 (NKJV) states, "Beloved, I pray that you may prosper in all things and be in health, just as your soul [mind, will, emotion, personality; attitude] prospers." These parts of your soul must also be separated out of darkness to become prosperous and productive. Then, your Father God's spiritual blessings can flow through, unhindered by Satan. No Born-Again Believer can be used mightily of God and be slanderous of his fellow brother and sister.

As a Born-Again Believer, speak evil of no one. You must not slander or be in strife. God's desire is for you to be peaceful, gentle, and to show humility toward all men. To grow up spiritually, Satan's tactics must be kept out of your soul by forgiving others and repenting. Use the blood of Jesus Christ to cleanse and heal the wounds in your soul. Use your authority to cast out demons and the resurrection power of God to raise you up out of every trap, strategy, and darkness of Satan.

The process of cleansing your soul is directly related to sanctification [being set apart as holy unto God]. Sanctification is divided into two parts. The first position of sanctification was done by Jesus Christ. He did the immediate work to make you justified with God (as if you never sinned), righteous unto God, and holy unto God. However, sanctification is a step by step, detailed and drawn out process, in which the soul must learn to become oriented to the things of God. Teaching the soul to be set apart unto God must be done at the pace of the Believer. It is not merely quoting and confessing scriptures. It is letting go of wrong thinking, wrong believing, and wrong habits. In other words, you must daily let go of the old sin nature (Satan's nature) and replace it with the nature of Christ. Even though God told Moses and Joshua He had given the Israelites a land flowing with milk and honey, Joshua had to possess what God had given to them. He had to go in and enforce the victory by annihilating the people who were already living in the land. In the same manner, you must possess your soul by defeating, not physical enemies like Joshua, but evil, spiritual enemies. In any battle you face, you can have the same victory as Joshua did through Jesus Christ. Please read the book of Joshua for the description of his battles and victories.

Attitudes That May Hinder Your Faith

One area that may hinder the manifestation of what you are believing God for is not walking in love [not loving people]. Love is a law and a commandment. You want to use your faith to acquire material possessions, receive healing, etc. However, you should, more importantly, use your faith to love yourself and others. If loving yourself and others is a problem for you, take comfort in knowing that it takes practice to develop this God kind of love. Remember the rich young ruler? He was selfish and could not love others enough to sell his riches, give it to the poor, follow Christ, and receive eternal life. God's commands are to love your neighbor as yourself, and all the other commands are fulfilled in this command. Remember, love is kind, not mean. It does not gossip, slander, or bear false witness against its neighbor. Ask God to give you the ability to love yourself and your neighbor (Mark 12:31). You cannot say you love God whom you cannot see and hate your neighbor whom you can see (1 John 4:20).

Having faith and love are both commands from God. You cannot have one without the other if God is to operate in greatness through you.

The following are examples of not operating in love:

You are on a job for forty years as a sales representative and you need a change. You want to change to a managerial position, but you are mean and unkind. You love to talk and look down on people. If you got that promotion, you would upset employees under you with your mean attitude.

You are a parent and you discipline your children, but you are mean and unkind. You show no love with your discipline. You call them unkind, derogatory names. "And you, fathers [and mothers too], do not provoke your children to wrath, but bring them up in the training and admonition of the Lord" (Ephesians 6:4 NKJV).

Because the children are not receiving love in their homes, they will eagerly wait for the day when they are old enough to leave home. In the meantime, they will be looking for love in all the wrong places. Everyone is born with an inherent need to be loved.

Parents, when you call your child a satanic name, you hurt the soul [mind, will, emotions], of that child. The damage can be so great that only Jesus Christ's death, burial, resurrection, and ascension can repair it. Repent of this sin. Ask the child to forgive you and ask God to heal the hurts. Child, you can still forgive your parents even if one or both are deceased.

Repent. Forgive this sin in the Name and blood of Jesus Christ. Psalm 147:3 (NKJV) says, "He heals the brokenhearted. And binds up their wounds [sorrow]." Remember, any form of unrepentant sins gives demons and Satan a voice to give suggestions into your soul. Your spirit is redeemed from darkness, but you must guard your soul. Calling a child derogatory names or being abusive can allow the enemy to form the wrong images or mental pictures in their souls [mind, thought, will, and emotions]. The wrong image or reflection of themselves once meditated on, idolized, looked up to, worshiped, or adored sets up false statues or monuments as truth and can become a stronghold.

As children grow up, they will believe the lie and formulate in their minds the concept of those words spoken to them, for example, "You are no good." A wrong or abusive action done to children can allow Satan to create a lack of confidence, fear of man, disrespect for authority, and low self-esteem. The children will believe that they are unimportant to God or to anyone else because they are unimportant to the people that mean the most in their lives. They may be hindered from esteeming themselves highly because no one else meaningful in their lives ever did. Therefore, they create their own idol—a false, satanic image of who they are outside of who God says they are, which is a sin.

Only God is to be adored, worshiped, and bowed down to. His Word can rebuild the confidence of a wounded soul. Receiving the Holy Spirit with the evidence of speaking in tongues will give you boldness and the courage to know that He is always with you. There are programs designed to overcome soul trauma and assist with the healing process, but sins, wounds, and hurts in the soul are caused by Satan. They must be eradicated with the repenting, forgiving, blood-cleansing cross of Jesus Christ and the saving, healing, and delivering, resurrection power of the Holy Spirit. As long as you have the idol, image, or the sin of being self-righteous and you think there is no need to get rid of these sins, Satan can keep you in bondage to sickness, disease, poverty, etc.

Walking in love is vital to the life of a Born-again Believer. Failing to do so can not only wound the souls of others, but it can also hinder the manifestation of what you are believing God for. For example, you asked God for a new truck. You have been waiting patiently for the manifestation, but in your heart/soul you said that you will use it to run over your neighbor's dog that has been messing up the grass on your lawn. Right now, you are using the worn-down truck you currently have to cut people off on the freeway. You show them the victory sign with your fingers as you drive by. Then you wonder why you haven't seen the new truck manifest! It is not because you have not been trusting God and declaring God's Word of provision.

Here is another example: You are driving an old broken-down car and you ask God for a brand-new, expensive one. Your neighbor walks to the same church, but you never offer a ride, although you have no passenger. One day, you even sped past the neighbor coming from church on a rainy day. The puddle of water you ran over drenched your neighbor as you sped past. In both examples, not operating in the law of love causes your manifestation to be hindered.

In your marriage relationship, as another example, you, the wife, constantly criticize your husband. You even call him a knucklehead and gossip about him to relatives on the phone. He tries to ignore your nagging and complaining, but often, in an outburst of anger, he raises his voice. He has, several times, slammed the door in your face, especially when you are too confrontational about issues that he believes are petty. You have both been making confessions for that nice house, the one down the street, on the corner with the big backyard where your kids could play. You did not get the house because someone else bought it.

The Word of God, that we continually decree and declare over our lives, sanctifies us or sets us apart—that is, our minds and bodies unto God, which is a form of cleansing. "Death and life are in the power of the tongue" (Proverbs 18:21a NKJV). The words that you repeatedly speak will give life or death to your marriage, finances, and health. "It is the Spirit that gives life; the flesh profits nothing. The words that I speak to you are spirit, and they are life" (John 6:63 NKJV).

You were given everlasting life and not only that, but life abundantly. That includes a supernatural life to create with words. If you speak the devil's words, you will create death in the natural and in the supernatural. "The thief does not come except to steal, and to kill, and to destroy" (John 10:10 NKJV). The devil may also plant negative thoughts into your mind. You must immediately cast these thoughts down or you will not only follow or believe them, but you will eventually act on them. You will act out what you believe or what you have been meditating on. Therefore, speak God's words to create life in your life and marriage. First Peter 3:7 (NKJV) states, "Husbands, likewise, dwell with them with understanding," which means every person is unique to God. Every person's fingerprint is different, even though the fingerprints are on the same hand. Honor your wife's uniqueness. "Giving honor to the wife, as to the weaker vessel [does not mean inferior vessel] and as being heirs together with the grace of God, that your prayers may not be hindered" (1 Peter 3:7 NKJV).

God told Jeremiah He ordained him to be a prophet to the nations. Marriage is also ordained by God. A husband and wife's roles within marriage (a God ordained marriage institution) is not the reason why a husband or wife exists. Their appointed ministry purpose is different. Their role in a God ordained marriage should not supersede God's assigned call to purpose. Example a wife's submission to her husband as the head chosen to lead in carrying out the will or Word of God is similar to Christ being the Head of His Church. God ordaining the husband or wife to Jesus Christ's Ministry is not by gender, but by His purpose for their lives or the reason for their living in the earth. Ephesians 4:11-12 (NKJV) states: "And He Himself gave **some** [not male or female] prophets, some evangelists, and some pastors and teachers, for the equipping of the saints for the work of the ministry, for the edifying of the body of Christ."

Father, I pray You open the spiritual eyes of husbands and wives to see Your truth about their marriages in Your Word, for there is abundance of life in Your Word for their marriages! According to Proverbs 3:6 (NKJV), "In all your ways acknowledge Him, And He shall direct your paths." In Jesus Christ's name, Amen!

Remember, Satan, the thief who comes to kill, does not need to have a gun to do it. He is a spirit. He uses words of death to do it. Another hindrance to faith's manifestation is being disobedient to God's commands or instructions He spoke to you personally or from the instruction manual, the Bible. We all have a purpose and an assignment in the Body of Christ, which is the reason for our coming to earth and having a body. Remember, we are spirits made in the image of God. Whether we are called to the five-fold ministry gifts: apostle, prophet, evangelist, pastor, and teacher (Ephesians 4:11); or the ministry of helps: church administration (government) (1 Corinthians 12:28); or other assignments, we each receive our own individual instruction or purpose from God. However, choosing to disobey God's instruction or deny your purpose can hinder spiritual, material, physical, and financial progress, blessings, and/or the manifestation of what you are believing God for. Choosing not to fulfill your purpose is to remain in bondage, but doing God's will is freedom.

"But seek first the kingdom of God and His righteousness, and all these things shall be added to you" (Matthew 6:33 NKJV).

To fulfill God's purpose is the primary reason we were sent to earth. Jesus Christ, when He was hungry, went up to a fig tree to see if it had any figs/fruit, but found only leaves (Matthew 21:18–20). In Genesis 3:17–18, it states that because of Adam's sin, the ground was cursed and brought forth thorns and thistles. Should Born-Again Christians bear fruit in the Kingdom of God or just have leaves, thorns, and thistles? We, as Christians, are supposed to bear fruit. Furthermore, we are able to bear fruit because Christ has redeemed us from the curse of the law with His blood by taking our curse (Galatians 3:13).

When Believers are obedient to walk in and fulfill their God-given purpose, the Holy Spirit then helps them to accomplish it. The work we do for God lives on forever, and it comes with rewards. "I can do all things through Christ who strengthens me" (Philippians 4:13 NKJV). Say this prayer:

Father God, You said I can do all things through Christ; therefore, with the help of the Holy Spirit, help me to do this assignment. In Jesus Christ's name, Amen!

Jesus Christ said, "You did not choose Me, but I chose you and appointed you that you should go and bear fruit, and that your fruit should remain, that whatever you ask the Father in My name He may give you" (John 15:16 NKJV).

All of the above may hinder your faith's manifestations, but unbelief will stop it. Receiving Jesus Christ as your Lord and Savior enables you to renew your mind from old/previous satanic thinking. "So then faith comes by hearing, and hearing (believing) by the word of God" (Romans 10:17 NKJV). We glorify and exalt God's presence in our lives as King of Kings when we, as a little child, simply chose to believe His Living Word. God's Word is always right. That is why He is called Righteousness. Unbelief is to doubt His Word being right or true.

Let me define doubt. Doubt is unbelief and unbelief is doubt. When someone says, "God cannot deliver me, God will not provide, God cannot use me, God cannot restore me, God cannot save me, or I do not believe, then this is doubt. For example, if God tells you to raise the dead and you say you will do it, then you will. However, if you say you cannot raise the dead, then you will not. If you say you will not live, you just said it—you will not live. If you say you are poor, you just said it—you are poor. If you say you are always sick, you just said it—you are sick. If you say you will never get a job, you just said it—you will never get a job. Put God's Word in your spirit and in your soul so that what you want God to hear, comes out of your mouth. You must repeatedly say what He says about you. This is what changes you. Believe in His Word no matter what the report is—good or bad. Unbelief or doubting God and His Word are sins of the soul that will block/hinder faith or the truth of God's Word from being received. Use the Word of God to renew your mind:

And do not be conformed to this world, but be transformed by the renewing of your mind, that you may prove what is that good and acceptable and perfect will of God (Romans 12:2 NKJV).

Do not be afraid; only believe (Mark 5:36b NKJV).

And the world is passing away, and the lust of it; but he who does the will of God abides forever (1 John 2:17 NKJV).

See Yourself as Christ Sees You

You must know that you are righteous in order to live strong day to day and year after year. You are believing and acting out what God says about you when you received Christ with authority, boldness, and confidence. You stand before Almighty God as righteous—without blame or guilt. Only then can you walk in bold faith and trust in God. You must not go back to declaring your unworthiness. He saved you even when you were a sinner. Therefore, you were never unworthy. You believed the lie. You cannot believe the lies of Satan and walk in bold faith. God did not create anything worthless. Therefore, you are not worthless. He said you were fearfully and wonderfully made. "For You formed my inward parts; You covered me in my mother's womb. I will praise You, for I am fearfully and wonderfully made" (Psalm 139:13– 14 NKJV).

Look at your big toe. Can the devil make a big toe? He cannot even make a frog's toe!

Doctors spend years practicing medicine to become qualified and proficient in working on the human body. Yet they still have not completely mastered the knowledge of it. Patients going on dialysis for the first time are often amazed at the size of a dialysis machine that is used to do the function of their small kidneys, as their own natural kidneys have stopped functioning. Amazing!

Celebrate the fact that you are worthy before the King of Kings. The four living creatures and the twenty-four elders that John prophesied about in Revelation worshiped God around His throne. The living creatures worshiped Him day and night (Revelation 5:14).

"You are righteous before me," says God! "Though your sins are like scarlet, They shall be white as snow!" (Isaiah 1:18b NKJV) "The blood of My Son has taken every trace of sin off you! No more shame! No more guilt! No more accusation! Come before me," says the Lord God of hosts. "I am not angry with you! Give me your burdens! Give me your trials! Give me your cares! Cast it off on me. Cast off bitterness, cast off hurt, cast off your unforgiveness, cast off being angry with Me and others! Cast off the fear of man, because I am God and there is nothing impossible with Me! There is healing in Me, there is provision in Me, there is restoration in Me! I am your Father," says God, "and I love you deeply."

Pray this prayer in response to the Encouraging Word spoken:

Father! Take my worries, take my cares, take my concerns. I yield them all to you, Lord. What am I doing with them anyway? You, Jesus Christ, took them from me two thousand years ago! Therefore God also has highly exalted Him and given Him the name which is above every name, that at the name of Jesus [Christ, Yeshua] every knee should bow, of those in heaven, and of those on earth, and of those under the earth, and that every tongue should confess that Jesus [Christ, Yeshua] is Lord, to the glory of God the Father (Philippians 2:9–11 NKJV).

You must saturate your mind with the Word of God. Without speaking and acting on God's Word [faith] or trusting God's Word, it is impossible to please God (Hebrews 11:6). Your Born-Again spirit-man is wired up to respond to the Word of God. Therefore, do not pollute your mind with ungodly thoughts because your spirit can not declare what is contrary to the Holy Spirit of God. Remember, your spirit is the eternal and supernatural you. It can create the Word of God that you consistently decree, declare, and confess. Because your spirit is made in the image of God and He is a creator, so are you. Therefore, guard your soul from all ungodliness, no matter how trivial it may seem, and follow

God's Word. Doing this will please Him. "Blessed is the man who walks not in the council of the ungodly, nor stands in the way path of sinners, nor sits in the seat of scornful; but his delight is in the law of the Lord, and in His law he meditates day and night" (Psalm 1:1–2 NKJV).

In the Old Testament, in the tabernacle or temple, the Holy Place had the table with what was called the showbread (Exodus 25:30), which is symbolic of Christ's Words, the living bread. Just as food sustains our lives, Christ, the Living Bread, who is also the Word of God, sustains our lives by giving us everlasting life. The lampstand, with the seven-branched candlesticks that gave the priest light, was symbolic of Jesus Christ, the light of the world. The oil in the candlesticks is symbolic of the Holy Spirit (Exodus 25:31–40). In the New Testament, this shows that Believers cannot live apart from Jesus Christ, His Word, and the Holy Spirit. We must be Believers who are lighted candlesticks, representing Jesus Christ with the anointing power of the Holy Spirit in us.

If your spirit is separated from fellowshipping, which is praying and worshiping in the Word of God, your spirit-man will become weak and anemic. You will revert to the old, carnal (not spiritual), sensual way, relying only on the five senses to live by. These are merely worldly, human senses, and not God-lead consciousness. Human senses speak and respond only to situations or circumstances in and of the world, and not God's Word. As a result, your soul and body will begin to control you instead of the Spirit of God within you.

Holiness. You became holy when you received Jesus Christ as your Savior. Holiness is not the name written over a church door. Holy is your spirit-man, just like the Spirit of Christ Jesus. It is not your white, long dress or the stiff, white collar around your neck. Our thoughts and actions may not be holy. However, our spirit is holy and set apart to God. "And by that will, we have been made holy through the sacrifice of the body of Jesus Christ once for all" (Hebrews 10:10 NIV). Unholiness cannot live there [in our spirits]. It is where the presence of the Holy Spirit dwells and He does not dwell in unholiness. However, in our souls [mind, will, emotions] and bodies, we can choose to allow unholiness in because we have a free will. We live our lives in holiness unto God in obedience to Him. "And that you put on the new man which was created according to God, in true righteousness and holiness" (Ephesians 4:24 NKJV).

Sanctification. You are set apart unto God. He sanctified, cleansed, and purified your spirit with His pure sinless blood. You became a saint the very second you were Born Again. However, the process of walking out your sanctified life in your soul and body is not immediate, as it was in your spirit. God rebirthed the old, dead spirit part of you. You now have a brand-new spirit that God's presence now occupies. You cleanse your soul [flesh] with the help of the Holy Spirit as you pray, listen to, and study the Word of God. This takes time. Do what God's Word has instructed you to do. Put on holiness in every aspect of your life.

The Word of God will work in your life to make you act and behave like Jesus Christ until He returns. "But of Him you are in Christ Jesus, who became for us wisdom from God—and righteousness and sanctification and redemption" (1 Corinthians 1:30 NKJV).

As your soul and body have less dominance over your spirit, people will begin to say that you are Christlike because they see Jesus Christ in you. Therefore, as long as you are on this earth with a soul and a body, you must continually pray in the Spirit, speak/pray God's Word, fast/consecrate, and separate yourself from what hinders you from living a holy/consecrated life to God.

Remember, confessing, repenting, and forgiving others heals your soul when you sin. An unrepentant and unforgiving soul will become corrupted with sin. These sins give Satan the legal right to keep you as his slave to all kinds of bondages, phobias, cravings, anxieties, nervousness, and even mental illness. If you are bound by any form of oppressive spirits and you do not know why, ask the Holy Spirit to reveal the source. Generational and familiar character traits are transferable in the DNA. DNA is the basic material of your mother and father's chromosomes, which are hereditary patterns that make up your soul and body composition.

Unfortunately, the sinful nature from Adam and your family's line also come through to your soul. Remember, your spirit received Christ as your Savior and Lord, but now you must cleanse your soul with the blood of Jesus Christ, that forgives sins of the soul and washes them away. Then, ask the Holy Spirit to raise you up out of that soul sin, just like He raised Jesus Christ out of the grave. I have been crucified with Christ. I was raised up with Him, and I am seated together with Him in heavenly places with Him right now! (Galatians 2:20, Ephesians 2:6) Bind and cast out those soul sins in the name of Jesus Christ.

If you have allowed the demonic roots of the tree of traumatic experiences, which causes wounds, injuries, damage, torture, and affliction to go down deep into your soul [mind, will, and emotions], then by now, they have become large roots that have been there possibly for decades—ten, twenty, forty, sixty, or even eighty years. Satan constantly tells you that they can never be uprooted and healed. He has now possessed, oppressed, and consumed your soul, not spirit, with so many sins that they have become a part of your life, personality, and character. Tell Satan it's time for him and those roots to get out of your soul. Command those roots to come out right now. The blood of Jesus Christ has dug them up. The blood of Jesus Christ has all power over those roots of darkness, (his spirits of) death, Hell, and the grave and it will never lose its power. The blood of Jesus Christ goes into every cell, every strand of DNA, every gene, and every chromosome, all of which have been passed down through familiar, ancestral, generational, demonic spirits that run in families.

Break the power of Satan over your soul! With the blood of Jesus Christ take authority over every perverted devil of molestation, incest, pornography, adultery, fornication, addictions, drug, alcohol, evil curses, fear, poverty, murder, stealing, diseases, sickness, strongholds, and every sin in the soul. The blood of Jesus Christ cleanses every sin and heals all injuries, burdens, wounds, and broken places in our souls. As the Word says, "For the Word of God is living and powerful, and sharper than any two-edged sword, piercing even to the division of soul and spirit, and of joints and marrow, and is a discerner of the thoughts and intents of the heart" (Hebrews 4:12 NKJV).

If we confess our sins *and repent* (e.g., being constantly critical of others), He is faithful and just to forgive our sins and to cleanse/sanctify us of all unrighteousness (behavior or sins that are not right with God) (1 John 1:9 NKJV).

And the blood of Jesus Christ, His Son cleanses us from all sin , (1 John 1:7b NKJV).

Very Important: Remember! Remember! Remember!

As a Christian, you are not living under the era of judgment under the law, but under the era or dispensation of grace, in which the coming of Jesus Christ implemented. At the last supper, Jesus Christ told His disciples, "This cup is the new covenant in My blood, which is shed for you" (Luke 22:20 NKJV). Please read the Gospels of Matthew, Mark, Luke, and John very carefully and note how Jesus Christ showed us examples of how to live under the New Covenant era of grace. We all deserved judgment because of sin, which brings death in our spirits, souls, and bodies, but Jesus Christ said, "For the Son of Man did not come to destroy men's lives but to save them" (Luke 9:56 NKJV). The scribes and pharisees wanted Jesus Christ to stone people who sinned. They did not want Jesus Christ to heal the sick or do any other miraculous works, such as opening blinded eyes on the Sabbath. They wanted to continue living under the law of Moses, that they had received from God hundreds of years before, which emphasized works to please God. They wanted to continue in the Old Covenant era of judgment. They were blinded to this era of grace, mercy, and favor that Jesus Christ came down from Heaven with, in order to save mankind from being punished with eternal death. Even with the coming of the Savior Jesus Christ, the Pharisees thought they should still live under the era of the law or judgment that God established through Moses. Moses came down from the mountain with the Law, written on stones (the Ten Commandments, Deuteronomy 5) to punish and sentence with eternal death if broken. Under grace, there is now forgiveness, mercy, love, and favor that is extended to man. You should even correct and rebuke in love.

There are people in the body of Christ who still favor judgment and works to please God. They believe they can help God eradicate evil from this world by calling down fire on individuals. They stop loving and start condemning, judging, and being unforgiving, even to themselves. "The scribes and Pharisees brought to Jesus Christ a woman caught in the act of adultery…Saying, Moses in the law commanded us that such should be stoned, but what do you say?" (What does grace and mercy say?) Jesus (Christ) said, "He who is without sin among you, let him throw a stone at her first" (John 8:3-9 NKJV). Then those who heard it, being convicted by their conscience, went out one by one. (The Holy Spirit will expose sin and "clean house" every time.)

They, the religious ones, who upheld the law brought this messy situation into the temple where Jesus Christ was teaching and threw the woman in the middle of the ground like a rag doll, as if to say their sins, or lack of it, were better than hers. Jesus Christ, after stooping down, wrote on the ground, then rose Himself up and said, "Woman, where are those accusers of yours? Has no one condemned you?" She said, "No one, Lord," and He said, "Neither do I condemn you: Go and sin no more" (John 8:10-11 NKJV).

Jesus Christ did not come from heaven to throw stones at sin, as the era of judgment did. He came and implemented the New Covenant era of forgiveness, mercy, grace, or undeserved favor. He gave this to man as a free gift. Sin pays its own wages and the paycheck is death. Sin is in sinful man who is not born from above. The solution is to remove sin from man's nature, not throw stones at it. Jesus Christ is the only one who can remove sin from man's nature.

With the forgiveness this woman received, she would never return to that lifestyle. She might have even joined Christ's discipleship that day because she found the love and mercy she was searching for, and it was not in those self-righteous, condemning, accusing men she was with.

This woman knew she had a problem, but accusations and condemnation could not change her. She needed a Savior, and she found Him—right in the middle of being condemned and accused of sin (John 8:3–5, 7–11).

Jesus Christ loves to take care of messy situations because He is the only one who can eradicate sin from our lives. You must continue to pray and intercede for those living in sin and declare their righteousness. Being in right-standing with God and abiding in the love of God through Jesus Christ—that's grace.

Everyone in the body of Christ is special and important to God—that's grace. Calling yourself names that are contrary to the Word of God is not being true to yourself. The Word of God does not give you names to call yourself and others that are contrary to His Word. The grace to live this life here on earth is in the Word of God. Jesus Christ always spoke God's Word over Himself. Grace says, "I can do all things through Christ who strengthens me" (Philippians 4:13 NKJV). It is in Christ's Words that you have and receive the ability to do what He has asked you to do. Because you believe in Him and His Words, He will give you the power and the anointing—that's grace—as you declare His Word to strengthen you, build you up, and to empower you. However, if you continually operate in the demonic spirits of jealousy, hate, and backbiting, grace will not flow through you to fulfill your calling or purpose in Christ. These and other demonic spirits are from the enemy and are tormenting spirits of the soul.

If you continue to speak and operate in the demonic spirits of jealously, hatred, and backbiting, your words will be ineffective or cancelled out. As a result, your stay in the desert will go into overtime because the dead words you are declaring will keep you dead.

Where dead words are, there is no movement; there is no power or enabling abilities. You must be steadfast and declare God's Word in faith, believing. It takes grace and the anointing power of the Word of God to overcome certain tragic circumstances. Therefore, follow Christ in the new era of grace. He did not condone sins but forgave. That's grace. He spoke healing with His Words. That's grace. He showed love and mercy. That's the word of grace in action when He said to His Father, "Not My will, but Yours, be done" (Luke 22:42 NKJV). After He said that, God gave Him the anointing power of grace to endure the cross. I believe grace is the work of the Holy Spirit, and this grace is one of the words used in the era of the New Covenant operation of the Holy Spirit.

Grace—unmerited favor, love, and mercy—is what is going to bring the harvest of nations into the Kingdom of God, not judgment and condemnation. How can love, goodness, and mercy be biased? We all know we were sinners and already judged without Christ. Therefore, why do we use the righteousness and the blood of Jesus Christ to accuse and condemn?

Use the only solution for sin to save others: Jesus Christ. That's the Good News of the Gospel.

Now, let me explain something to you who are new Believers: God gave you the faith to believe His Word. Romans 12:3 (NKJV) says, "God has dealt to each one a measure of faith." Jesus Christ gave us the gift of grace that saves us, our spirit-man, from our sins. He even demonstrated how this grace should function in His Believers by defying Old Covenant rules of works to please God, who Himself gave us the gift of grace. Ephesians 2:8 (NKJV) says, "For by grace you have been saved through faith, and that not of yourselves; it is the gift of God." The Holy Spirit empowered us (Act 1:8, 2:4) to be witnesses to spread and share that humanity now has eternal life because of Christ's blood and to also communicate with God in a heavenly language, tongues, using our newborn spirit. You do not need His permission or an appointment to speak in tongues or in the spirit to your Father God. This is separate from when the Holy Spirit uses a Believer publicly, according to His will for the benefit of all, to reveal one or more of His nine supernatural, spiritual gifts to man. These gifts are weapons placed in the Body of Christ for everyone's benefit. This is not for an individual to become a superstar because the Holy Spirit uses him or her to reveal, show, or manifest one or more of these nine spiritual gifts. For example: the gift of working of miracles belongs to the Holy Spirit, not the individual it is being revealed to or being operated through. First Corinthians 12:8–10 lists the names of the miraculous, supernatural gifts of His Holy Spirit. These gifts are the word of wisdom, the word of knowledge, faith, gifts of healings, workings of miracles, prophecy, discerning of spirits, different kinds of tongues, the interpretation of tongues.

Remember, all the above supernatural, miraculous gifts can operate through any Believer as the Holy Spirit wills as these are His gifts, not yours. This is different from speaking in your heavenly language [unknown tongue] in your daily prayer time or when praying with other Believers in tongues. God the Father, God the Son [the Word/Jesus], and God the Holy Spirit are not independent of each other. They gave us New Covenant Believer gifts, and they too are not independent of one another. Therefore, when you hear others speaking or teaching against faith, believing in God's Word, the gift of grace: forgiveness, mercy, love, favor that we receive through Jesus Christ, and the gift of speaking in tongues, the Holy Spirit's language, and the Holy Spirit's nine supernatural gifts, it is not the Bible.

Prayer and Why Be Filled with the Holy Spirit?

In the Old Testament, the tabernacle had the altar of incense in front of the veil (Exodus 26:31–33) which parted the first room, the Holy Place, from the second room, the Most Holy Place. The burning of the incense contents were sweet spices. These special ingredients in the incense were ordered by the Lord. The smoke rising to heaven from this altar of incense is symbolic of New Testament Believer's prayers rising to Heaven (Exodus 30:1–37).

You must have a prayer life, and it must be consistent. That means praying God's Word and in the spirit daily. "But you beloved, building yourselves up on your most holy faith, praying in the Holy Spirit" (Jude 1:20 NKJV). Do not wait until you have been Born-Again for twenty years to start praying in the spirit. In that space of time, you would have missed out on what the Holy Spirit would have accomplished through you. Remember that being filled with the Holy Spirit is one of Jesus Christ's requirements. "And being assembled together with them, He commanded them not to depart from Jerusalem, but to wait on the promise of the Father" (Acts 1:4 NKJV). He asked you to be empowered or to fill your spirit with His Holy Spirit's presence. Imagine your spirit is an empty gas tank and you went to the gas station and filled it up with gasoline. Jesus Christ said, "But you shall receive power when the Holy Spirit has come upon you; and you shall be witnesses to Me in Jerusalem, and in all Judea and Samaria, [your state, city, or country] and to the end of the earth" (Acts 1:8 NKJV).

People tend to write their own policies and principles on Born-Again Believer's living. It is imperative that you follow God's manual, not man's. Read the Bible for yourself and receive His instructions. Why would you follow someone who can not or will not follow the instructions in the Bible? Why read a map when you refuse to follow the directions? For too long, God's Sons and Daughters have been following a man-made manual instead of God's Word. The instructions in the Bible on being filled with the Holy Spirit are clear. Why go to a doctor that prescribes the wrong medication? Ingesting wrong medication can kill you. Sunday after Sunday, Believer's in Christ Jesus go a to church where the pastor preaches a watered-down version of the scriptures. It is watered down because the Holy Spirit has not been allowed in. Who is directing your service? "Therefore he who rejects this does not reject man, but God, who has also given us His Holy Spirit" (1 Thessalonians 4:8 NKJV).

I can read books and gain intellectual knowledge. When I go to church, I go to gain revealed knowledge of the Word of God through the speaker. "Every word we speak was taught to us by God's Spirit, not by human wisdom. And this same Spirit helps us teach spiritual things to spiritual people" (1 Corinthians 2:13 CEV). Why listen to natural, humanistic, intellectual teaching from a person who desires a paycheck week after week but can not hear from the Spirit of God. This person may be Born-Again but the teacher, the guide, the helper, the instructor, the revealer of truth, the counselor, and the director is absent because this person's spiritual gas tank is empty. "But the helper, the Holy Spirit, whom the Father will send in My name, He will teach you all things, and bring to your remembrance all things that I have said to you" (John 14:26 NKJV). A sinner can read the Bible, and it is effective because it is the Word of God. However, the effect and the anointing are two different things. The Holy Spirit comes with the anointing to destroy bondages or demons when spoken through a Holy Spirit–filled person. "Not by might nor by power, but by My Spirit, say the Lord of hosts" (Zechariah 4:6 NKJV). It's not by the eloquence of a speaker; it is the

Holy Spirit's fire and power on the spoken Word that brings deliverance. Remember, Born-Again Believers are not automatically filled with the Holy Spirit.

Being Born Again is the work of the Holy Spirit to bring you to God because of Jesus Christ, who made this possible. The Holy Spirit is the one who convicts you of sin. Jesus Christ said, "He will convict the world of sin, and of righteousness, and of judgment: of sin because they do not believe in Me" (John 16:8–9 NKJV). Jesus Christ is the one who saved you. However, you will have no spiritual power to live the Born-Again, saved life without being filled with the Holy Spirit. This is much like a newborn baby that is left to feed itself. Under normal circumstances this does not happen because a mother feeds and cares for her newborn. God's spiritual newborns are often left without His Holy Spirit to train, guide, direct, counsel, and teach their spirits that are now alive in His kingdom.

Now when the apostles who were at Jerusalem heard that Samaria had received the word of God, they sent Peter and John to them, who, when they had come down, prayed for them that they might receive the Holy Spirit. For as yet He had not fallen upon none of them. They had only been baptized [birth spiritually or born again] in the name of the Lord Jesus. Then they laid hands on them, and they received the Holy Spirit (Acts 8:14–17 NKJV).

God the Father, God the Son—Jesus, and God the Holy Spirit work as a team. You should not ask for the gift of salvation and refuse to ask for the gift of the infilling of Holy Spirit. "If you then being evil, know how to give good gifts to your children, how much more will your Heavenly Father give the Holy Spirit [the evidence of speaking in other tongues] to those who ask Him!" (Luke 11:13 NKJV). (1 Corinthians 14:2 NKJV): "For he who speaks in a tongue does not speak to men but to God." When you get filled with Holy Spirit, the evidence or what you or someone else can hear is the physical display of that infilling, the speaking in tongues or talking in a spiritual language. If I fill up a cup with coffee, you can see the evidence of that infilling when I spill the coffee on the ground, the same way that speaking in a heavenly language is your evidence or sign of being filled with the Holy Spirit. Praying in the spirit is one form of communicating to God.

In Luke 4:18 (NKJV), Jesus Christ said, "The Spirit of the Lord is upon Me, Because He [God] has anointed Me [Jesus Christ] To preach the gospel to the poor. " Everyone who proclaims the gospel should be saying the same thing as Jesus Christ. The Holy Spirit's power must anoint you to preach or teach the gospel, to heal the brokenhearted, to set the captives free, to open prison doors, to bring healing to the blind, and to bring freedom to the oppressed and depressed.

If the Holy Spirit is not allowed in certain ministries, then God is not allowed and the operation of the nine supernatural, miraculous, power gifts of the Spirit in Believers is nonexistent. If this were true, then 1 Corinthians 12:1–14 would have to be thrown out of the Bible, just as some ministries have thrown the Holy Spirit out.

The Holy Spirit is in every page of the Holy Bible because He wrote the Book through holy men of God. However, some church members make comments such as, "The pastor says we do not speak in tongues in our church." Whose church is it? Is Jesus Christ not the head of the church? Did Christ die for mankind's sin? In the upper room, every Believer—yes, every Believer—none was left out, every Believer was filled with the Holy Spirit. Tongues of fire (a symbol of the Holy Spirit) sat upon each Believer, and they were filled with the Holy Spirit with the evidence of speaking in tongues. They became bold with the power of the Holy Spirit to proclaim the Gospel. No wonder some Sons and Daughters of God have no power to share the Gospel.

They go to church Sunday after Sunday, yet their neighbors perish and may go to Hell because they never shared the Gospel or handed them any form of literature with the Gospel message.

This is a story of a Follower of Jesus Christ whose neighbor went to Hell. When he reached Hell, his tongue was so dry it stuck to the roof of his mouth. "Oh! If I could only get a drop of water!" he cried as he looked toward Heaven. As he did, he saw his Born-Again neighbor, who had never once told him about Hell, drinking Kool-Aid. God, forgive our complacency. "And it shall come to pass at that time that I will search Jerusalem with lamps, and punish the men who settled in complacency" (Zephaniah 1:12 NKJV). Is this true of the New Testament church members too? You need this power, your helper, to go into your Jerusalem and to the uttermost part of the world. Send someone with the power of the Holy Spirit if you can not go. Remember, this is only a story. The spirits of persons in Hell can not see into Heaven. Spirits do not have physical eyes. That would be double torment. They have spiritual eyes. They can still use their imaginations. Please note that Born-Again Believers are the Church of Jesus Christ, not a physical church building.

How then shall they call on Him in whom they have not believed? And how shall they believe in Him of whom they have not heard? And how shall they hear without a preacher? And how shall they preach unless they are sent? As it is written, "how beautiful are the feet of those who preach the gospel of peace, who bring glad tidings of good things!" (Romans 10:14–15 NKJV)

Some people do not have any knowledge of the Holy Spirit for one reason or another. This is true in this passage:

Paul, having passed through the upper regions came to Ephesus. And finding some disciples he said to them, "Did you receive the Holy Spirit when you believed?" So they said to him, "We have not so much as heard whether there is a Holy Spirit?" And when Paul laid hands on them, the Holy Spirit came upon them, and they spoke with tongues and prophesied (Acts 19:1–2, 6 NKJV).

You can receive the Holy Spirit after you receive Christ as your Savior and Lord. That's the only prerequisite. When you begin to speak in your heavenly language, do not expect to speak in a language you know. Do not expect tongues of fire to fall on your physical body. This only happened on the day of Pentecost with the first Believers who were filled with the Holy Spirit. You do not have to have hands laid on you either, but this can be done. You do not have to tarry or wait for days. Jesus Christ did not tell you to do that. You are not one of the original 120 in Acts 1:4, 15 who He asked to wait in Jerusalem until the promise of the Father came, which was the Holy Spirit.

Emotional displays such as falling down and foaming at the mouth like a frog is not necessary. Note that I made a distinction, *emotional*. It is not acting out and performing that is going to make you receive the Holy Spirit. It is asking and receiving. The Holy Spirit is a gentleman, not an emotional mascot who works up emotions. In the upper room, the 120 appeared drunk to the people because there was a manifestation of the anointed presence of the Holy Spirit in Acts 2.

Your body or flesh may respond to His presence. You may cry or show other emotions. It does not have to be "worked up."

This tongue [heavenly language or spirit language] should not sound like any language you know or speak. Pray the following prayer to receive the Holy Spirit:

Dear Heavenly Father, I ask you to fill me with the Holy Spirit with the sign, evidence, or proof of me being filled by speaking in tongues. In the name of Jesus Christ, amen!

Move your lips and start speaking. The Holy Spirit will give you the words, tongues, language, or utterance as the Bible calls it. However, He will not move your tongue for you. The language will come out of your voice because you acted in faith, believing. Everyone in a church congregation should speak in tongues and be praying in the spirit daily, even the children. This will help minimize carnal and fleshly behaviors of Believers who are given to strife, jealousy, gossip, backbiting, and selfishness, and being easily offended. They will live their lives out of their spirit and not out of their egotistic flesh.

"While Peter was still speaking these words, the Holy Spirit fell upon all those who heard the word…because the gift of the Holy Spirit had been poured out on the Gentiles also. For they heard them speak with tongues and magnify God" (Acts 10:44–46 NKJV).

My final reason why a Born-Again Believer should be filled with the Holy Spirit is because it is vital to pray in the spirit and intercede for others in order to stop Satan's agenda. He would love to keep praying in tongues out of churches to keep them weak and anemic, with no fire and power. You can not fight demonic spirits in the flesh. It is very evident today that spiritual warfare prayers or intercessory prayers must be done in this satanic-plagued world we live in. The body of Christ must intercede for the persecuted church and all forms of satanic strongholds in the world. Once again, this scripture speaks for itself. "For we do not wrestle against flesh and blood, but against principalities, against powers, against the rulers of the darkness of this age, against spiritual host of wickedness in heavenly places" (Ephesians 6:12 NKJV).

The main agenda of Satan is to keep the body of Christ occupied doing things in the natural so that they won't have time to pray and intercede in the spirit for others and for God's will to be done on earth.

Go into all the world and preach the gospel to every creature. He who believes and is baptized will be saved; but he who does not believe will be condemned. And these signs will follow those who believe: In My name they will cast out demons; *please note that the sign, speaking with new tongues, will follow those who* **believe. Speaking with new tongues is also one of the signs that shows that you are a Believer**. They will take up serpents [or devils] and if they drink anything deadly, it will by no means hurt them; they will lay hands on the sick and they will recover (Mark 16:15–18 NKJV).

Get plenty of exercise in praying in the spirit as God is Spirit and you too are a spirit. You will build up your spiritual muscles and become stronger in your spiritual life. Communicating with God in the spirit will bypass your soul/mind, just like you bypass the streets and traffic lights when you drive on the expressway or freeway in your city, if this applies to you. When you travel to Mexico or France, it may be advisable to communicate with the natives in their known language. When you communicate with God in your spirit language, your thoughts from your mind can not spy on the conversation, nor can they influence or manipulate your words. Therefore, relax. Only believe and exercise your tongue when praying in the spirit/tongues.

When you exercise your physical body, you can relax, knowing that your body will be transformed. You also do mind exercises when you study and meditate. Therefore, there is no need for you to get frustrated in figuring out what you are doing. Do the same while praying in the spirit/tongues. The Holy Spirit will help you to pray God's perfect will on earth. This scripture needs to be repeated: "But you, beloved, building yourselves up on your most holy faith, praying in the Holy Spirit" (Jude 1:20 NKJV). I want to clearly define what I mean by *pray and intercede.*

There are several types of prayers in the Bible. Intercessory prayer is one of them. The languages used to pray the intercessory prayer are in the spirit/tongues or with the understanding (known language). Intercession with the Word of God (known language) is declaring back to God His Word in preferably known situations. Jesus Christ is the High Priest of our confession. He is the Advocate and Representative of our confessions, which should be the same words that God says about us. Jesus Christ speaks grace/favor to God about us when we declare His promises back to Him. He intercedes and goes to God on our behalf with our prayers. "Therefore He is also able to save to the uttermost those who come to God through Him, since He always lives to make intercession for them" (Hebrews 7:25 NKJV). "Who is even at the right hand of God, who also makes intercession for us" (Romans 8:34b NKJV).

Christ is our greatest intercessor and the best example of one because He laid down His life for mankind by dying for us. Being an intercessor is laying down your life for others. This is the greatest love. John 15:13 (NKJV) states, "Greater love has no one than this, than to lay down one's life for his friends," which is being that bridge that others will be able to cross to connect to God. You are the one who lays down your life in prayer, enabling others to get to God. You, the intercessor, represents

Jesus Christ on earth. Without you, there would be *no* connection to God. You are not only being the gap, you are the crossroad that God uses in this earth realm to save, redeem, bless, deliver, heal, and in addition, to bring the love, life, knowledge, and Word of God as if you were Jesus Christ Himself: "and raised us up together and made us sit together in the heavenly places in Christ Jesus" (Ephesians 2:6 NKJV).

We, the Believers, are in Christ spiritually. An intercessor is in the middle, God is on one side, and man is on the other side. The intercessor's prayers reach for the man's hand and pulls that person, people, or nation into God's territory, pulling them out of darkness. We are Christ's legal representatives in the earthly realm. This is legal because the sinless, undefiled blood of Christ is on us. The blood that God accepted makes us Jesus Christ's representatives who carry out His assignments on earth and on His behalf. Colossians 2:10 (NKJV) states: "And you are complete in Him, who is the Head of all principality and power." Therefore, as a Believer, you are seated in the position of Christ's representative on earth. A Believer may be aware of the effects of Satan's destruction and pray with the understanding, but the Holy Spirit knows how to annihilate his plans. Allow the Holy Spirit to use your spirit to pray because He knows where Satan and His entourage are staking out. Ephesians 6:12 (NKJV) states, "For we do not wrestle against flesh and blood, but against principalities, against powers, against the rulers of the darkness of this age, against spiritual hosts of wickedness in heavenly places." (atmosphere, second heaven).

Praying in tongues releases the Holy Spirit to move in with "aircraft fighter explosives" to demolish and crush the enemy. Praying in the spirit uses your spirit, with the help of the Holy Spirit, to reveal and spoil the plans of every evil force of darkness. Praying in the spirit allows the Holy Spirit to do battle in the realm of the spirit on your behalf. Jesus Christ won the battle over spiritual death, Hell, and the grave, but man must continue to enforce the victory won by Jesus Christ, using intercessors in the earthly realm, until people, nations, and the earth are released from the Kingdom of Darkness. Romans 8:26–27 (NKJV) states, "Likewise the Spirit also helps in our weaknesses. For we do not know what we should pray for as we ought, but the Spirit Himself makes intercession [pray through us, using our spirit to pray on earth God's perfect will] for us with groanings which cannot be uttered. Now He who searches the hearts knows what the mind of the Spirit is, because He makes intercession for the saints according to the will of God." Intercessory prayer pulls the veil of blindness from man's eyesight and stops the adversary. It releases man from Satan's prison legally. After Jesus Christ speaks to the Father about your prayer according to His will, God then tells the Holy Spirit what He desires to happen in the earth. The Born-Again man has dominion in the earth, received through Jesus Christ.

The Holy Spirit then gives man's spirit the utterance, "words," tongues/spirit language. He helps your spirit to pray God's perfect will in the earth realm. The Holy Spirit, our Divine Helper, uses our prayers in the spirit to give man a divine "prison break" because He can go past demons, principalities, and rulers of darkness, releasing man from Satan's handcuffs and strongholds. This bound-up, eternally dead prisoner/man sitting on death row is now released into God's freedom of everlasting life. He is now able to walk this earth as a man in Christ Jesus, under His umbrella of protection when He receives Him.

An intercessor praying in tongues does not have to travel to a foreign land to intercede for that nation. Their dominion in the earth given by Jesus Christ is released through intercession or with the Word of God.

God is not in charge of the earth. He gave that responsibility to man/Adam. Adam/man regained it through Jesus Christ. Therefore, God will not trespass onto man's property or earth.

He is going to have you/man pray to Him for whatever you need in the earth, and that is through intercessory prayer, which is man praying to God on behalf of another in the earth. First Timothy 2:1 (NKJV) states, "Therefore I exhort first of all that supplications, prayers, intercessions, and giving of thanks be made for all men." That means the rich, poor, wicked, and good. Therefore, every Born-Again Believer should be an intercessor. This important prayer is required of all the saved, Believers, to give of themselves to others. Jesus Christ came to earth as Man to give of Himself to you/man. We, as Born-Again Believers, are in Jesus Christ and He is in us. Therefore, He requires us to give of ourselves in prayer for the unsaved world, like He did. Whether through individual or corporate prayer, He requires that we not leave people of the earth to be destroyed by Satan and his demonic army and powers. Our prayer can stop him and demolish his agenda to destroy mankind. Second Corinthians 10:4 (NKJV) states, "For the weapons of our warfare are not carnal (flesh) but mighty in God for pulling down strongholds."

Paga is the Hebrew word for intercession, which is to impinge by accident or violence, to mediate, meet, to bring a situation up to God, to entreat, to plead for another. (This can be done with the understanding, known language, and the Word of God.)

Daka in Hebrew is not pleading, as a mediator and going before God directly (with the Word of God). It is intercession in the spirit about the unknown: The Father knows what the spirit is saying; to *daka* in the spirit is to crumble, it's crushing, bruising, destroying, oppressing, beating and dashing to pieces.

An intercessor's prayer, which is praying on behalf of others, should involve having the Word of God, the name of Jesus Christ, the Holy Spirit's presence, power, anointing, and "language" in the spirit. "Not by might nor by power, but by My Spirit," says the Lord of hosts (Zechariah 4:6 NKJV).

The Reason for Intercessory Prayer

You have made him to have dominion over the works of Your hands; You have put all things under his feet (Psalm 8:6 NKJV).

The heaven, even the heavens, are the Lord's; But the earth He has given to the children of men (Psalm 115: 16 NKJV).

Therefore pray the Lord of the harvest to send out laborers into His harvest (Matthew 9:38 NKJV).

Nor is there any mediator between us, Who may lay his hand on us both (Job 9:33 NKJV).

So I sort for a man among them who would make a wall, and standing in the gap before Me on behalf of the land, that I should not destroy it; but I found no one (Ezekiel 22:30 NKJV).

If My people who are called by My name (Born Again Believers) will humble themselves, and pray and seek My face, and turn from their wicked ways, then will I hear from heaven, and will forgive their sin and heal their land (II Chronicles 7:14 NKJV).

And He bore the sins of many, and made intercession for the transgressors (Isaiah 53:12b NKJV).

Suggested Ways to Do Intercessory Prayer Meetings

Praying for others should be done by individuals at least once a week, but preferably everyday for no less than one to two hours per individual session. Allow time for praise, thanksgiving, songs, and worship before and after intercession. Keep this to approximately ten to twenty minutes before, if praise and worship are included in the prayers.

Give this time to laying down your life in prayer for others. After reading the prayer items and the scriptures chosen in the known language, pray only in the spirit. It is best to keep the agenda with the scriptures written down so that each prayer item will not have to keep changing. You can add or subtract prayers and scripture verses as manifestations of what you are praying about takes place. Keep intercessory prayer agenda/rooster typed, especially if you are in a group or a leader; others may need to read from it also. Everyone should be in agreement with what is being interceded about, and it must be scripturally based. Intercessory prayer is also doing spiritual warfare, where the Holy Spirit uses your spirit to pray into the earth the perfect will of God, unknown to Satan and his demons.

When praying in the spirit, you are demolishing evil strongholds and pulling off satanic blindfolds of deceptive mindsets from people. In addition, you are storming and dismantling evil and wicked fortresses, territories, principalities, powers of darkness, and every plan and plot of wickedness in the world system. Prayers could concern your family members, school, job, country, local and world leaders, all forms of perversions and lifestyle in the world, weather, satanic or anti-God laws and legislations, judicial/courts, law officers, military, terrorism, injustices to mankind, racism, the peace of Jerusalem, and so on.

Do not give up on prayer because praying on behalf of others in a dark, evil world is the only answer to demolishing darkness. Some people like to pray in their known language after declaring the Word of God. This is fine, but your intellect in the soul can only take you so far. Remember, you are not praying against flesh and blood [man]. You are dealing with wicked and demonic spirits, who are in control of this world's systems, and mindsets. Your spirit needs to handle strange, unexplained, and unknown endeavors. You declare the Word of God into the situation and then pray about it in the spirit. That is why these kinds of prayers are called spiritual warfare. Your spirit language must do the praying, not your mind and thoughts from your soul, which is limited to intellectual wisdom and understanding.

You are a three-part being—spirit, soul, and body. You must now rely upon the supernatural ability of the Holy Spirit, who now prays through you. He is dealing with wicked spirits using your spirit language that He gave you. God has given the earth to men to rule. The heavens belong to God (Psalms 115:16). Demons and Satan are evil spirits that are in charge of this world's system, which was given to them by the first man, Adam. The Born-Again man is a spirit and soul in a body and, therefore, physically limited in the spirit world of Satan and demons. God can not do anything for man in the earthly realm, legally, without man's permission or spiritual prayers. Therefore, He gets His permission legally from a Born-Again man/Christian who regained dominion of the earth through Jesus Christ spiritually. That man or woman prays and declares God's Word in the earth, and it is returned to Him. God's will can then be done in the earth as it is done in Heaven. "So shall My word be that goes forth from My mouth; it will not return to Me void, But it shall accomplish what I please, And it shall prosper in the thing for which I sent it" (Isaiah 55:11 NKJV).

However, communication between God and the Born-Again, spirit-filled Christian bypasses Satan when he prays in the spirit. I have discussed this before, but I believe the Holy Spirit wants you to understand the importance of prayer and intercessory prayer in the spirit. Every move of God on the earth to intervene on behalf of mankind begins with prayer and intercession.

Prayer and intercessory prayer are the highest office of man in the kingdom of God. Service and works are to be done and there are rewards for these. It was intercessory prayer that brought Jesus Christ to earth. Two of the intercessors, Anna and Simeon, are recorded in Luke 2. It was intercessory prayer that brought the Israelites out of Babylonian bondage, through Daniel's prayers and intercession (Daniel 9:3–19). It was Abraham's intercession for Sodom that saved his nephew Lot (Genesis 18). Jesus Christ's Intercession for Believers while on earth (John 17:1, 26) is still relevant today. His job right now as High Priest in the Kingdom of Heaven is also intercessory prayer and mediator for His Believers. Hebrews 7:25 (NKJV) states, "Therefore He is also able to save to the uttermost those who come to God through Him, since He always lives to make intercession for them."

In the Old Covenant, which was symbolic of what was to come in the New Covenant or a replica of what is already in Heaven, the Altar of Incense was the place where incense was burnt in the tabernacle, as previously mentioned. God gave instructions as to the kinds of special sweet spices He wanted to make this incense (Exodus 30:1-37).

In the New Covenant, God also gave us the special ingredients to include in our prayers to Him, which are the following: (1) Bring Him His Words in faith believing (Hebrews 11:6); (2) Pray to God in the name of His Son Jesus Christ (John 15:16); (3) Pray also in the Holy Spirit, a language given to your spirit [tongues]. "Praying always with all prayer and supplication in the [Holy] Spirit" (every Christian should be interceding in the spirit) (Ephesians 6:18a NKJV). Praying in the spirit means, praying in an unknown tongue.

This will, without ceasing, rises up to God as sweet incense. We must abide by God's ingredients, not only in intercessory prayer, but also in all other prayers or they will be cast to the ground unanswered. Aaron's sons used unholy spices to burn incenses in the Old Covenant Tabernacle and they both died (Exodus 30:1–38; Leviticus 10:1–4).

The Importance of Intercessory Prayer and Praying in the Spirit

Intercessory prayer, praying on behalf of others, is an important part of the Body of Christ/ Church. It should not be left to a few ladies or mothers of the church who gather in the church basement. Every Christian should be interceding for others, especially in the spirit [unknown tongues/heavenly language]. Your personal prayer in the spirit is not operating in the nine supernatural, gifts of the spirit spoken about by Paul (1 Corinthians 12:10), which includes the following: (1) *different kinds of tongues* (2) *the interpretation of tongues.* Of the nine supernatural gifts, these two were given to the New Testament or to the New Covenant Believers with the coming of the Holy Spirit. After Jesus Christ returned to Heaven, the Holy Spirit's presence is now able to live in Born-Again Believers' spirits who invite His presence into their spirits.

Also, like the nine supernatural, miracle-working gifts, these two different kinds of tongues and the interpretation of tongues can be given by the Holy Spirit to a person whenever the Holy Spirit wants to operate in them for the benefit of the people. Remember, you are a spirit. A Holy Spirit–filled, Born-Again spirit can talk to and connect with the Spirit of God. Many Believers confuse the two supernatural gifts of the Holy Spirit with their private praying in their heavenly language or unknown tongues. Their understanding is that speaking in tongues, which is your heavenly language, is only used as a manifestation of the gift of the Holy Spirit. Remember, you can operate in the two supernatural, manifested gifts of the Holy Spirit, *different kinds of tongues* and *the interpretation of tongues,* because you can speak with tongues or in the spirit, that is known tongues such as English or unknown tongues which is your spirit language.

Do not allow the God-given gift of praying in the spirit to offend you. The only one that wants you to shut up is Satan. He will try to silence you because he does not understand your communication. Furthermore, he knows you are using your "ammunition," the Holy Spirit operation, against him. You do not understand what you are praying about, but you may ask the Holy Spirit to give you revealed knowledge. The Bible says, "For he who speaks in a tongue does not speak to men but to God, for no one understands him; however, in the spirit he speaks mysteries" (1 Corinthians 14:2 NKJV). If there is a revelation of the gift of prophecy given in tongues, usually publicly using the gift of different kinds of tongues, there should be the companion gift of interpretation of tongues, meaning the tongues comes from the Holy Spirit, not your spirit. It is God's Holy Spirit *speaking* from or in your spirit. It is the Holy Spirit talking to His people, not your spirit talking. The platform the Holy Spirit uses to speak through is you, but He gives the Words. Prophecy is given by the Spirit of God to edify, exhort, and to comfort His people (1 Corinthians 14:2).

You should not receive salvation and neglect to receive the infilling or baptism with the Holy Spirit. Baptism in/with the Holy Spirit may be a different or new word to you, but it is biblical. In Acts 19:2, Paul asked the disciples in Ephesus, "Did you receive the Holy Spirit when you believed?" To be baptized means to be immersed in, into, or with something as an outward show of an inward witness, evidence, sign or proof. It is the signpost declaring what happened in your spirit-man, as physical eyes are limited in their ability to confirm a spiritual transformation. The word *baptism* is used to advertise, announce, or declare the change that has taken place in your life. According to the Bible, there are different baptisms (Hebrews 6:2). In Acts 19:3–5, the disciples told Paul they were baptized into John's baptism. Do not be concerned about this baptism, because John the Baptist was sent to convert the Jews from Judaism (which was the legalism of keeping the law of Moses), and keeping the law of good works to gain salvation. They now had to repent of this, be baptized in water by John, and receive the way of salvation through Jesus Christ the Messiah, the Sent One who would fulfill Moses's laws of sin and penalties and, instead, forgive mankind's sin. This baptism showed their repentance or change. Read John 1.

Then, there is the baptism into Christ. This is receiving Christ, the Messiah, as your Lord and Savior, confessing with your mouth that He is the Son of the Living God, and that He died and shed His blood to give you eternal life. This requires your spirit-man to be reborn or created brand-new. The baptism into Christ is accomplished by the Holy Spirit in the unsaved person's spirit. This is not the same as the baptism in or with the infilling of the Holy Spirit or receiving the Holy Spirit with the evidence of speaking in tongues, as discussed earlier in the chapter.

Lastly, water baptism is where one is immersed in water as an outward sign that they have died to the world and the devil and have risen into the things of God. It is an outward show of an inward change. This is done after Salvation. In this immersion, your whole body goes under the water of the sea, a river, or a pool. Being sprinkled with water is not being baptized with water. "Therefore we were buried with Him through baptism into death, that just as Christ was raised from the dead by the glory of the Father, even so we also should walk in newness of life" (Romans 6:4 NKJV).

Let's continue with prayer and the Holy Spirit infilling. You need His power to live in this satanic-riddled world. Your spirit will get stronger and stronger in spiritual things as you pray in the spirit. "But you, beloved, building yourselves up on your most holy faith, praying in the Holy Spirit" (Jude 1:20 NKJV). The Holy Spirit power will increase in your spirit and give you supernatural endurance, stamina, anointing, boldness, and refreshing in your soul and body. In addition, it will give you capabilities and abilities—the grace to run the race to the finish.

Praying in the spirit/intercession will ignite and keep the fire of the Holy Spirit's presence in your spirit burning, which will have you still standing in the ring after round 12 when everyone is waiting for you to fall over. You will still be "fighting the good fight of faith" (1 Timothy 6:12). God will reveal to you and train you for the gifts and callings that He has purposed for your life. The Holy Spirit will show you His plans and purpose as you pray in the spirit. He will share secrets and mysteries about you. He knows you better than you know yourself or anyone else. He made you in His image and likeness. However, complaining and murmuring, which are sins in the soul, will make you anxious, depressed, tired, and weak. In other words, it will drain your "spiritual battery." Satan can now tempt you to get into his "pigsty" of the flesh by not praying, interceding, decreeing, declaring, prophesying, confessing, or reading God's Word. In other words, it is simply not being God's watchman and intercessor, which is every Born-Again Believer's responsibility. Jesus's disciples were curious—they often saw Jesus Christ praying. This was His lifestyle. He often withdrew Himself from them to pray—many times all night. This relationship with God seemed to be very important to Him. The disciples desired this kind of communication and fellowship Jesus had with God. Therefore, they asked Him to teach them to pray. Jesus responded to their request by teaching them the Lord's Prayer (Luke 11:2–4). He understood the strength and power of prayer and He wanted His disciples to understand it also. In fact, on the eve of His crucifixion, when He was agonizing in prayer in the Garden of Gethsemane, He did not ask His disciples to guard Him with weapons or swords. He asked them to watch and pray with Him. *Jesus said to them, "My soul is exceedingly sorrowful, even to death, Stay here and watch with Me"* (Matthew 26:38 NKJV). "The effective fervent prayer of a righteous man avails much" (James 5:16 NKJV).

Watch and Pray

Jesus Christ sent the Holy Spirit to earth in this era, time, and period of grace. Believers who invite His presence into their Born-Again spirits can now pray in a spirit language or in unknown tongues as previously mentioned. All Born-Again Believers should be praying in tongues, which means not only do you have the Holy Spirit with you, but you also have Him in your spirit. Your spirit has been made alive, reborn by the blood of Jesus Christ, and is no longer separated from God. The Holy Spirit's presence can now live within your spirit because it is now sinless and holy. If you have not done so already, you can become a spirit-filled intercessor and God's spiritual watchman in the earth. Interceding in tongues or in your spiritual language will allow the Holy Spirit to pray divine secrets through you. You will be the watchman and intercessor that the Holy Spirit can use to pray divine mysteries, purposes, and plans for yourself and others. Satan can not be aware of these because he does not know what you are saying. You will also be declaring, decreeing, prophesying, and praying God's covenant promises into the earth.

God had revealed through the Old Testament prophets that a Savior was to be born. Anna, a prophetess and an intercessor, along with Simeon, did not close their eyes until they saw Him coming in the Temple (Luke chapter 2). Jesus Christ is an Intercessor with a purpose, to see that every covenant and promise that God made with man are fulfilled and manifested in their lives and are not stopped by the enemy, Satan. Jesus said, "I will build my church and the gates of hades [hell] shall not prevail against it" (Matt. 16:18b NKJV).

He asked us to, "Therefore pray the Lord of the harvest to send laborers into His harvest" (Matthew 9 :38 N KJV). Watchmen are intercessors that are never silent. They pray, as led by the Holy Spirit, God's will throughout the earth, night and day. These watchmen and intercessors, who are praying in the spirit, are the spiritual spies whose prayers allows the Holy Spirit to go into Satanic territorial regions with closed-up fortified walls where there are principalities, wicked spirits, including anti-Christ spirits, bondages, spiritual blindness to God's truth, and evil mindsets. Do not fall asleep like the disciples did on the eve of Jesus's Crucifixion. Instead of watching and praying, they fell asleep. Jesus Christ came to the disciples and asked Peter, "What? Could you not watch, and pray with Me for one hour?" (Matthew 26:40 NKJV) Be that watchman that intercedes in unknown tongues. "For we do not wrestle against flesh and blood," (Ephesians 6:12a NKJV).

Be that watchman who intercedes for your family, neighbor, city, and country. Pray your children and grandchildren will live their lives as virtuous and excellent men and women of God in spirit, soul, and body. Be the watchman who intercedes for what you have spoken out to come to pass.

Do not be like the spies, except for Joshua and Caleb, in Joshua chapter 2, who came back to the camp after spying out the enemy's land and gave Moses an evil report concerning the giants in the land. The negative images and thoughts in their minds kept them from entering the promised land. As prayer watchmen and intercessors, God wants you to decree, declare, and prophesy His Word into the earthly realm, but you must not then turn around and declare Satan's negative words. This is sin and it nullifies the decreed Word of God and your intercession.

Simeon and Anna, who was a widow of about eighty-four years old, fasted and prayed night and day in the temple. They were both intercessors and watchmen who waited in prayer for the coming of the promised Messiah (Luke 2: 22–39). They did not stop praying and start speaking negative when years past and their prayers were still not fulfilled, nor did they stop being watchmen and intercessors. They watched and prayed with a purpose. They continued to pray until they saw their Messiah being carried by his mother through the Temple door.

Adam was placed by God to be a keeper/ watchman in the Garden of Eden. He stood back, "folded his arms," and allowed Satan to infiltrate his house, the earth, by telling his wife lies (Genesis, chapter 3).

Declare God's Word over your household and be that watchman and intercessor who will see God/Jesus Christ's Promised Words manifest in your family, your neighborhood, country, government, and the leaders of nations all over the world.

This is the time and season to watch and pray night and day. Then you will see Jesus Christ, not coming through a temple door as a baby, like the watchmen and intercessors Anna and Simeon saw, who were watching for Christ appearance into the earth (Luke 2:22–39), but you will be interceding and watching for His return on the clouds of Heaven *in the sky. He comes* with power and great glory (Matthew 24:30).

For he who speaks in tongues does not speak to men but to God, for no one understands him; however, in the spirit he speaks mysteries (2 Corinthians 14:2 NKJV).

Then will appear the sign of the Son of Man in heaven. And then all the people of the earth will mourn when they see the Son of Man coming on the cloud of heaven, with power and great glory (Matthew 24:30 NIV).

The Covenant Blessings of the Tenth

You may say to yourself, "My power and the strength of my hands have produced this wealth for me." But remember the Lord your God, for it is He who gives you the ability (power physically, mentally, legally, morally, financially) to produce wealth…" (Deuteronomy 8:17–18 NIV).

God sent His Son to redeem not only those born in the nation of Israel, but also the Gentile Born-Again Believers who are now adopted into Jesus Christ, Sonship with God. Believers engrafted are heirs, *beneficiaries* to God and joint heirs with Christ (Romans 8:17, Romans 11). "So also Abraham believed God, and it was credited to him as righteousness" (Galatians 3:6 NIV). What was credited to Abram? His belief in God's promises to give him an heir and many descendants. This belief in God's promise was called faith. "Understand, then, that those who have faith are children of Abraham. Scripture foresaw that God would justify (declare innocent or guiltless, acquit) the Gentiles by faith, *like Abram*, and announced the gospel (good news concerning Jesus Christ coming to earth to save man from Satan, redeeming him back to God) in advance to Abraham, "All nations will be blessed through you" (Galatians 3:7–8 NIV). God told Abram that he would be the father of many nations because he believed God. "No longer shall your name be Abram, but Abraham; for I have made you a father of many nations [*ethnic families*]: nations" (Genesis 17:5 NKJV). When you believe God, it is called faith/trust/confidence/ evidence. We, as Believers, must be righteous like Abraham by believing God and His Son Jesus Christ.

"Then He brought him outside and said, 'Look now toward heaven, and count the stars if you are able to number them.' And He said to him, 'So shall your descendants [*that's you and I*] be'" (Genesis 15:5 NKJV). "Then He said, 'Take now your son Isaac, whom you love, and go to the land of Moriah, and offer Him there as a burnt offering on one of the mountains of which I shall tell you'" (Genesis 22:2 NKJV). Then the angel said, "Abraham, Abraham." "Do not lay your hand on the lad... for now I know that you fear (reverential fear) God" (Genesis 22: 11–12 NKJV). "By Myself, I have sworn, says the Lord, because you have done this thing, and have not withheld your son, your only son—blessing I will bless you and multiplying I will multiply your descendants, as the stars of the heaven and as the sand which is on the seashore" (Genesis 22:16–17 NKJV).

Note Abraham gave his all by offering his only son Isaac, which is symbolic of God giving His all by offering His only Son, Jesus Christ. So also Abraham believed God, and it was credited to him as righteousness [declared justified never sinned, innocent, holy, guiltless, without sin, acquitted] (Galatians 3:6 NIV). Jesus Christ paid off that credit with His precious blood at the cross. "Understand, then, that those who have faith" (put their trust, belief in God) have the same Father God like Abraham (Galatians 3:7 NIV). "Scripture foresaw that God would justify (make righteous) the Gentiles: [*none-Jewish Christians*] by *their* faith" in His Son, Jesus Christ (Galatians 3:8 NIV).

"So those who rely on faith are blessed along with Abraham, the man of faith" (Galatians 3:9 NIV). Therefore, your faith and trust in God saved your life from eternal damnation, [eternal death] which was caused by an inherited sin nature from the first man, Adam. Giving your life to Him automatically puts you in the place of receiving God's Blessings, which are His divine favor, kindness, mercy, love, and divine gifts He has placed in you. Abraham could not out give God's Kindness. God gave of His only Son as a sacrificial offering of His love and kindness to Mankind. Abraham was appreciative to God, especially when God gave him the abilities, capabilities, power, favor, or blessing to win the battle he fought to rescue his nephew Lot (Genesis 14). Abraham knew none of this was possible without God's divine blessings on his life. Therefore, he trusted Him and held on to the same faith he had in Him to save when he held the knife to sacrifice his only son, Isaac, like God asked him to.

This righteous man, Abraham, whom God was pleased with because of his faith, belief, and trust in Him, was previously met coming from battle by the Priest of Salem/Peace Melchizedek, which means, King of Righteousness. He had a covenant meal with Abraham, who at that time was called Abram. The meal was similar to a communion meal and Melchizedek blessed him. Abram brought the tenth [tithe] of his wealth to this High Priest as an offering of worship and thanksgiving to God, whom he was in covenant with and who gave him the power to increase in wealth.

The word *covenant* does not only denote ceremonial blood sacrifices as mentioned in Genesis 15:1–19, where God's presence passed through the bloody animal pieces. Abraham was perhaps familiar with this custom of cutting a covenant, *Karat Birit*, because God used it to confirm a promised spoken, covenant word or oath to him. God made a cut (*karat* in Hebrew), a blood covenant with Abraham. He may have known about this kind of covenant by coming from ritualistic countries such as Mesopotamia and cities such as Ur of the Chaldeans that worshipped idol gods at the time. Signs are also used to confirm covenant, for example a rainbow, which showed God's covenant with Noah (Genesis 9:2–15).

Covenant means an oath-bound promise by one party to another. *Birit*, the Hebrew word for covenant, means "binding relationship between two parties," and that binding relationship was spoken by God in Genesis 12:1–3 (NIV) to Abram: "Go from your country, your people and your father's household to the land I will show you. I will make you into a great nation, and I will bless you; I will make your name great, and you will be a blessing. I will bless those who bless you, and whoever curses you I will curse; and all peoples on earth will be blessed through you."

Other covenants that God made with Abraham are: Genesis 17:1–14, a name change from Abram to Abraham, Sarai to Sarah, the covenant of circumcision, and Genesis 22:15–18, a covenant of blessings to his offspring, including the Messiah, Jesus Christ, and every Believer, which God made with Abraham for his obedience in being willing to sacrifice Isaac, his son.

Wherever God appeared to Abram/Abraham, he built an altar unto the Lord as a marker of God's presence that appeared to him (Genesis 12:7, 8, Genesis 13:4, 18). In Genesis 22:9–13, He sacrificed a burnt offering, a ram that God provided on the altar he built, instead of his son Isaac.

Abram gave his covenant tithe to his High Priest, Melchizedek, who was a type of Christ, Messiah. The tithe is a sign showing covenant relationship. Covenant relationships use signs to perpetuate covenant remembrance. For example, our Lord Jesus Christ asked us, who know Him, to partake of a covenant ceremony, called communion to keep in remembrance His death, burial, resurrection, ascension and seating at the right hand of the Father God. "Then Melchizedek King of Salem brought out bread and wine; he was the priest of God Most High. And he blessed him and said: Blessed be Abram of God Most High, Possessor [*Owner*] of heaven and earth; And blessed be God Most High, Who has delivered your enemies into your hand. And he [*Abram*] gave him a tithe of all" (Genesis 14:18–20 NKJV).

Whenever you are in covenant with someone, what belongs to you also belongs to them. What is yours is theirs. What threatens you also threatens them. Whoever blesses you also blesses them. Whoever curses you also curses them. The bread, in this ceremony, symbolizes or foreshadows the body of Jesus Christ and the wine, the blood of Christ who was to come, which declared the New Covenant of everlasting life for Mankind. God's covenant with Jesus to set mankind free from sin was revealed when Jesus Christ offered Himself up as a sacrifice and shed His sinless blood on a wooden, lifted up altar called a cross. A covenant is more than a contract, an agreement, or a treaty. It has greater divine spiritual significance. Covenant with God now means He is responsible and is in charge of every aspect of your life, spirit, soul, and body as a Born-Again Believer. His Son Jesus Christ regained Lordship as the Giver, Owner, Lord of your life. He legally recovered you with His own blood. His legal Word declared, "Without the shedding of blood there is no remission, [*pardon, forgiveness* of sin]" (Hebrews 9:22b NKJV). Due to His shed blood, the Greater One, in the form of His Holy Spirit's presence, resides, lives, and is now housed in you. He is in charge of blessing, healing, delivering, and providing. He will never leave you, nor forsake you, unlike some human marriages. Divine covenant with God can never fail you. This Covenant comes with everlasting life in it. Covenant, however, in some countries such as the USA, can not be compared with the Covenant of primitive times that Abraham lived in, as its powerful bond cannot be broken. Abraham's Covenant with God could not be broken by either party. This covenant was called a Blood Covenant. In this modern society, the only other institution that I can have some readers relate to is a God-ordained marriage, between a man and a woman. This institution is temporal until one or both parties die or it ends in divorce. All God ordained covenant marriages have divine spiritual significance.

God's covenant with the Man-Christ Jesus is an everlasting, blood covenant; it comes with eternal promises to Christ's Covenant Church of Believers. Christ-ordaining communion ceremonies are due to His Blood Covenant relationship with us when He agreed with God's request to shed His blood to save Mankind. That was a covenant act that Jesus entered into with God. When Jesus and God did this, the whole family of Believers came under God's covering or family. For example, a husband, wife, and children can be protected under the same health insurance. They are of the same connection, league, or family, and they share the same last name.

Did Abraham understand covenant? More importantly, blood covenant? In Genesis 15:2 (NIV), Abram said, "Sovereign Lord, what can you give me since I remain childless…?" God told him: Your offspring will be as the stars in the sky, I will give you this land to possess (Genesis

15:5–7) Still Abram's question: Genesis 15:8 (NIV) "Sovereign Lord, how can I know that I will gain possession of it?" God credited Abram with righteousness in verse 6 because He believed Him. However, God had to use covenant evidence or a sign to which primitive people in Abram's time could relate to. They did not draw up contracts and place signatures. An agreement was called a covenant, and Abram related to this transaction due to the society he lived in. God did not answer Him with a spiritual sign. He used what Abram could relate to—A Blood Covenant. At God's request, animals were brought and cut in half. Then God's presence passed through the pieces. The smoke represented God's presence. Genesis 15:17–18 (NIV) states, "When the sun had set and darkness had fallen, a smoking firepot with a blazing torch appeared and passed between the pieces. On that day the Lord made a covenant with Abram…" God used a symbol or a sign that was used in certain cultures, societies, ethnicities, and nations to thoroughly convince Abram that He spoke the truth and His promises would come to pass.

When a primitive culture entered into a blood covenant using animal sacrifices, but failed to honor or keep that covenant, there were severe implications. What happened to the animals would happen to the lying party. God entered into covenant with Abram and God cannot lie. In the scriptures, Genesis 14, Melchizedek blessed Abram and Abram brought the portion that belonged to God as evidence or witness of their covenant relationship. In a covenant relationship, both parties are expected to bring a share. Abram was not supposed to keep all the spoil or any of his increase to himself, as he now has a covenant Partner. We all can relate to this in a marriage. For example, your paycheck is not only for your well-being, but it is to be shared with the person you are one with.

Believers are one with God because of Christ Jesus. Melchizedek, King of Salem, now Jerusalem was God's representative or advocate during Abram's time and was also the King of Righteousness who worked in God's service, order, or government as a priest of the Most High God. Therefore, Abram already had a relationship with God through his priest Melchizedek. Can you relate to this kind of relationship in your own family? For example, you eat dinner with your own family and not your neighbor's. This is similar to Abram and the King of Righteousness having a covenant or communion meal. This means they were bonded and sealed together, and now both parties were one in their relationship or union in God's righteousness. What was Abram's possession and connection was also God's possession and connection. The bread, wine, and the tithe [tenth] are used in covenant worship ceremonies as evidence of covenant unions or connections.

Jesus Christ is now the Believer's Eternal Savior of our righteous Born-Again life. He gave us His robe of righteousness to wear because of the New Covenant in His blood. We now have a righteous spirit in His image or likeness and are one with Him, Christ. In the Old Covenant, God put Abraham's righteousness on a layaway plan before Christ came. However, in the New Covenant, Christ paid the full price with His Covenant Blood for Mankind to have His righteousness. Believers now have an immediate covenant relationship upon receiving Him. He now treats His Believers special. When they need protection, He provides it. When they need food, clothing, and shelter, He provides it. He provides healing when they are sick, and He provides deliverance in spirit, soul, and body.

A husband is expected to care for his wife like a queen and vice versa because they are in a covenant relationship. Unbelievers, sinners, or those who are not Born-Again, meaning Jesus Christ is not the Lord and Savior of their lives, cannot partake of this Communion of the bread, wine, and tithing [tenth] because they have no covenant relationship or connection with God through Jesus Christ, the Messiah. Melchizedek's high priestly office, according to God's Word, never died. It was passed on, transferred to Jesus Christ, who was crucified, but His Father, a covenant-keeping God resurrected Him from Hell as He had promised to do. God's covenant promise to Abraham was, "I will surely bless you and…Your descendants will take possession of the cities of their enemies, and through your offspring all nations on earth will be blessed, because you have obeyed me" (Genesis 22:17 NIV). Abraham believed and obeyed God and found favor with Him. This covenant relationship and connection between these two parties are still alive in those Born-Again Believers who now believe God and obtained righteousness through Christ His Son, who has blessed them with salvation.

Jesus Christ is High Priest to both God and Man in His Heavenly Temple. We, as Believers, are priests unto God and as we bring Him our tithes and offerings, Christ does the High Priestly duty of blessing us with added blessings: supernatural, spiritual, physical, and materially so that we can become a blessing in the earth, both to ourselves and others. God told Abraham that all nations of the earth will be blessed through his offspring because he obeyed God. One of his offspring was Jesus Christ, who came from Abraham's lineage.

God used Abraham's earthly lineage to bring forth Jesus Christ, "The Seed" of Himself, which He sowed to save man's eternal life in the earth realm. Jesus Christ came from God the Holy Spirit, not from Abraham's biological body. God blessed Abraham, not only with spiritual blessings, but also with financial blessings, health, and long life. Therefore, the tenth [tithe] did not belong to Abraham who represented righteous man in the earth. The High Priest, Jesus Christ, is still receiving the tithe that belongs to God, like Melchizedek received it from Abram. The tenth [tithe] is the part that is brought to God by believers who have a covenant relationship with Him. Bringing the tithe to God via the High Priest, Jesus Christ, and remembering Him with the communion meal are because of the Believer's relationship and fellowship with Him and the Father God. Even though God is your Father and Jesus Christ is your Elder Brother, you must activate God's plan to bless you with overflowing material blessings as you bring Him your tithes and offerings, like Abraham.

"The Lord has sworn and will not change his mind: 'You are a priest forever, in the order of Melchizedek'" (Psalms 110: 4 NIV).

A. The Messiah: High Priest of The Most High God.

The Messiah: King of Righteousness over the Kingdom and people of God.

B. Melchizedek: King of Righteousness over Salem/ Jerusalem and people of God.

Melchizedek: High Priest of the Most High God.

Melchizedek and The Messiah: Yeshua/Savior were both KINGS and HIGH PRIESTS.

Other chief rulers/priests.

The following were never kings only priests:

Levitical priests

Aaronic high priest

Zadokite priests-Blue Letter Bible

The MESSIAH - Christ is King and Priest after the order of Melchizedek-Priesthood-

God was specific about the Messiah's Priesthood order or line of Priesthood.

The Word of God calls, Jesus Christ' church and Body of Believers, kings and priests in Revelations 1:6 KJV:

"And hath made us kings and priests unto God and His Father; to him [be] glory and dominion for ever and ever. Amen."

God uses tithes and offerings as His supernatural portal [window] and His divine permission to get involved in believers' affairs in the earth. Therefore, Satan cannot accuse God of being an illegal trespasser on earth. God uses the "passport" of our tithes and offerings to return blessings which are unlimited, and these blessings are not just limited to finances. For example, Abraham also gave offerings. He built several altars and gave sacrificial offerings. He built an altar to offer his son, Isaac, as a sacrifice to God. Jesus Christ also offered Himself on a lifted-up altar called a cross on behalf of mankind's sin.

God supernaturally prospered Abraham when he cut covenant (*karat birit*) with God and brought his tithe and gave his offerings. His possessions increased, he was protected, he had servants, and he became wealthy in lands, cattle, gold, and silver. His offspring brought their tithes and offerings to God and they also prospered. Abraham honored and worshiped the Lord his God who gave him the power or ability to get wealth by proving that the tithe [tenth] belonged to Him. This was special to Abraham because he chose to set apart or sanctify the first part of his increase to God. To him, it was not a sacrifice like paying taxes to a government that demands it. In this case, it is a burdensome debt that is owed and if not paid, one's life will be made miserable with penalties or imprisonment. Under the Old Covenant Law of Moses, the Command to forgive sins had to be paid with sacrificial animals and grain. Tithing was also a Command under the era of Mosaic Law. Under the New Covenant, tithing is giving/bringing the tenth of your increase not to the church, but to God. It is not a demand or even a command anymore. It is a wonderful opportunity in which Jesus Christ allows His church body of Believers to participate. Providing for His earthly Kingdom Work of preaching His Word, Jesus Christ, throughout the earth costs finances. He could have used angels, but He chose to partner with Born-Again Believers with whom He is in covenant.

Tithes and offerings are not making payments toward a debt owed to God. In the New Covenant, it is God's covenant way of prospering His covenant body of righteous Believers. It is also for reaching people with the message of the gospel. Jesus Christ already paid off every debt that mankind owed God by bringing sin upon Himself. Bringing the tenth to God, is putting His requested part of the substance of your labor or increase, which is His specified amount into His hands. With this particular seed, you reap not only general blessings such as favor, mercy, healing, provision, and protection which you received when you were saved, but you also receive and exceptional, divine, supernatural, or extraordinary blessings. These are the kind of blessings that Abraham received. God laid it out clearly in Malachi 3:10 (NKJV):

"BRING all the tithes into the storehouse, That there may be food in My house, and try Me now in this," says the Lord of Hosts, "If I will not open for you the windows of Heaven, and pour out for you such blessing that there will not be room enough to receive it."

Abraham gave a tithe or a tenth of what he earned from the battle he fought to free Lot his nephew. Melchizedek, king of Salem, represented the Priest of God Most High, because of his covenant faith relationship with God. Abraham was allowed to bring the amount he wanted to. God honored, respected, blessed and received it. He did not change this limit under the law or after the law of Moses. Jesus Christ also, did not change what God had already established with Abraham. The covenant blessing upon Abraham's tithe, still stands today and on every tithing Jew or Gentile engrafted in God and Abraham's relationship of faith. This covenant relationship of faith believing in God has been inherited by Born-from-Above Believers through Jesus Christ, our now High Priest. "For I am the Lord, I do not change…" Malachi 3:6 (NKJV). Everything belongs to God. We own none of it—not even the earnings from the sweat of your brow. If you planted an apple tree, God owns the tree and the ground it is in, along with the apples it bears. Therefore, He has a right to ask you for the first ten apples that you pick from that tree, before you eat the rest of the crop, just like He gave commandments to Adam and the Messiah, Yeshua.

Doing this is worshiping, thanking, and honoring Him for being your source of everything you receive in life. You are worshiping God when you dedicate your children to Him. You are giving back to God what you have received from Him.

When you make a marriage covenant (between a man and a woman) in the presence of God, you are honoring and putting God first and in that relationship. Tithing the tenth and giving offerings gives God permission and a portal into the earthly realm to return a harvest of blessings. Remember, God must have your permission to bless you financially, and that is through tithes and offerings. He will not force His Will upon man. Bringing the tenth to God is giving you the opportunity to sow a particular seed into God that will yield a particular harvest and blessing. You cannot sow orange seeds and reap apples. You must sow the seed or tenth that God asked of you to reap the return of blessings or harvest from that given seed. God regards and blesses His Words, principles, commands, instructions, and laws. He does not regard or bless disobedience. You can choose to debate His Word in unbelief. He gave everyone free will, but that will was not to violate or rebel against His Will because God honors His Word. God makes requests of man from Genesis to Revelation. He owns man, the air he breathes, the water he drinks, the rain that falls from the sky, the food he eats, and the ground from which it came. God was specific with Moses when He asked Him to build the tabernacle in the wilderness.

God is a God of order, and He is very specific in His transactions with man and man's obedience to Him. Third John 1:2 (NKJV) says, "Beloved, I pray that you may prosper in all things and be in health, just as your soul prospers." The soul of the disobedient cannot prosper. Your job is not your source of life. It is merely a means of earning a paycheck to obtain material goods and services. However, it is God who gives you the power, the supernatural, anointed abilities to prosper you and bring you wealth. You did not receive it in your own strength. Man does not exist in the earth in his own strength. He is dependent on someone, something—the Creator God who made him. God told Adam not to eat from one of the trees in the Garden of Eden. He ate what was God's and ended up with nothing but God's leaves to cover himself.

That which belongs to God is holy unto Him and set apart. Adam and Eve's disobedience brought a curse upon the earth. Everything in it began to die. However, man's obedience can reverse the curse and bring life and God's blessings. One of these ways is through tithes and offerings. Bringing the tenth to God makes a statement in the earth and to God that He is your source. Proverbs 3:9–10 (NIV) states: "Honor the Lord with your wealth, with the firstfruits of all your crops; then your barn will be filled to overflowing, and your vats will brim over with new wine." The covenant of multiplication blessings God first gave to Adam and Eve and later to Abraham and Isaac endures forever. It is the same covenant He has given us. His words never change. The laws of God may not be written on stone now, but God said He will write them in your mind and heart: "But there is a spirit in man, And the breath [inspiration] of the Almighty gives him understanding" (Job 32:8 NKJV).

Pay attention to the truth the Holy Spirit is revealing. He is called "the Spirit of Truth", who is The Holy Spirit. "And I will ask the Father, and He will give you another advocate, [*one who speaks or intercedes on behalf of another*] to help you and be with you forever—The Spirit of Truth. The world cannot accept Him, because it neither sees him nor knows Him, for he lives **with you** and will be **in you**. (John 14:16–17 NIV)." You must consult with Him to rightly divide the Word of Truth (II Timothy 2:15 NKJV), "Do your best to present yourself to God as one approved… a worker who **correctly** handles the Word of Truth. Avoid godless chatter, because those who indulge in it will become more and more ungodly. Their [*ungodly*] teaching will spread like gangrene" (II Timothy 2:15-17). God used His own finger to write, "Two tablets of the covenant law, the tablets of stone inscribed by the finger of God" (Exodus 31:18 NIV).

The three-in-one God, God the Father, God the Son [the Word], and God the Holy Spirit, is the Author and Originator of the Bible, the Word of God, from Genesis to Revelation. God the Holy Spirit breathed into Moses, David, John and all the writers and inspired them to write. This same Author has to reveal to every reader the revelation of what was written. Remember what the Word says: "All Scripture is God-breathed and is useful for teaching, rebuking, correcting and training in righteousness, so that the servant of God may be thoroughly equipped for every good work" (2 Timothy 3:16– 17 NIV).

For the time will come when people will not put up with sound doctrine. Instead, to suite their own desires, they will gather around them a great number of teachers to say what their itching ears want to hear. They will turn their ears away from the truth and turn aside to myths" (2 Timothy 4:3–4 NIV).

God did away with the earthly tabernacle that had housed the Ark of the Covenant, which contained the Ten Commandments. When Jesus Christ ascended to Heaven, He became High Priest in the New Covenant. Therefore, the establishment of the earthly Levitical priests from the line of Aaron under Moses [the law of the Old Covenant], which included the duties of the tabernacle or temple here on earth were no longer needed. These earthly high priests were the mediators, intercessors, and advocates who, along with the other priests, brought the people's tithes, gifts, and offerings to God. "Every high priest is selected from among the people and is appointed to represent the people in matters related to God, to offer gifts and sacrifices for sins" (Hebrew 5:1 NIV). The tithes and offerings were given to maintain the livelihood of the Levitical priests. The daily tasks of the tabernacle were their wages. They devoted their time, lives, and service only to God.

Note that after the people brought their tenth, the priests also brought their tenth to the high priest. They were not allotted any lands to own. They were to be taken care of by the people who brought their tithes and gave their offerings to God. Refer to these scriptures concerning the Levitical priesthood: (Numbers 18, 2 Chronicles 31:4, 10, Malachi 2:7–9). The physical tabernacle or temple was where they served God. All of that has been abolished because the earthly temple was only a shadow of the real temple in Heaven, which is now presided over by God's True High Priest, Mankind and God's Honored Representative. He is God's Son, the Most Majestic and Triumphant Savior, Jesus Christ, who was not after the order of the earthly priests.

This Melchizedik did not trace his descent from Levi *of Aaron's line of priesthood under the Law of Moses, Old Covenant*. Yet he collected a tenth from Abraham and blessed him who had the promises of Jesus Christ and birthing a great ethnic group or nation of righteous Believers in God through His Son. And without doubt, the lesser is blessed by the greater (Hebrew 7:5–6 paraphrased).

The ORDER OF Melchizedek (Hebrew for King of Righteousness), Priest of God Most High, resembled the Son of God who was, "Without father or mother, without genealogy (genes, DNA, chromosomes) without beginning of days or end of life, resembling the Son of God, he remains a Priest forever" (Hebrews 7:3 NIV). Please carefully note the word FOREVER. God ordained, appointed, and called Jesus Christ, who is sinless and spotless, to be a High Priest forever. He was also made Manager, Steward, Mediator, and Intercessor over God's House after the order or government of Melchizedek. He is not after the order of Aaron or the line of Levites in the Old Covenant. This was a temporary order in the earth that God used to portray and display a shadow of things in Heaven and things to come.

Melchizedek was not a given name, it was a title meaning: King of Righteousness and King of Peace and Priest of the Most High God.

Melchizedek was Shem, Noah's Son who was related to Abram/Abraham and also his priest, pastor, teacher. Therefore Abram was under the teachings of Shem, whose life spanned from before the flood. This was the person that Abraham would bring his covenant tenth to, or tithe. Melchizedek was 800 years old about this time when Abram brought the tenth. The people did not know who Melchizedek mother and father was, because he was a very old priest. The Patriarchs Abraham, Isaac, Jacob/Israel, King David, King Solomon to the birth of Jesus the Messiah were born in the line and order of the King of Righteousness and High Priest Melchizedek.

Psalms 110:4 "The Lord has sworn and will not change His mind: "You (Jesus Christ) are a priest forever, in the order of Melchizedek." (Exerts from Rabbi Isaac Assemble of called out Believers teachings on Melchizedek).

Aaron was not under the order of the King of Righteousness and High Priest unto The Most High God and the Davidic line of kings and priests that the Messiah was born into. Aaron was a high priest under the law of Moses, or Mosaic Law which was not forever. The priesthood of Levites under Aaron and the tabernacle they served were only a foreshadow of the Heavenly Tabernacle and Priesthood of Jesus Christ.

Abraham was under the blood covenant promises of God to him and to his descendants. God chose not to break His oaths and promises He made because He cannot lie. Remember God went through the bloody animal pieces as these: smoke, fire, and torch. This blood covenant cannot be nullified by God. It had to be passed on to another King of Righteousness and High Priest of The Most High God: Jesus Christ. Hebrews 7:28:28 NIV states: "For the law appoints men as high priests in all their weakness but the (word of the) oath, which came after the law, appointed, the Son, who has been made perfect for evermore."

Abrahamic Promises and Covenants:

1. Genesis 1 2:1-3: God promised to bless Abram and his descendants, make his name great, bless those who bless him and curse whoever curses him.

2. Genesis 15:2-5: God promised to give Abram an heir, the genealogy of which Jesus was from.

3. Genesis 15:6: Abram and his lineage were counted as righteous because he believed and was obedient to God.

4. Genesis 15. The Lord cut a blood covenant {karat-birit} with Abram evidenced by moving through bloody animals pieces as smoke etc., symbolic of the making of a blood covenant where there is intermingling.

5. Genesis 17. God made an everlasting covenant with Abraham's descendants to give them the land of Canaan. Covenant of Circumcision: signs of covenant promises in the flesh and covenant name change: Abram to Abraham and Sarai to Sarah.

Who is God's House? Jesus Christ, you, I, and all Born-Again Believers in Christ who are made sinless and spotless because of our High Priest who became a man, sacrificed Himself, and died in our place once and for all. Through this relationship we are now called sons of God, kings, and priests under the New Covenant, High Priestly order of God. He stated that Jesus Christ will follow the High Priestly order of Melchizedek, who was King of Righteousness. Now, Jesus Christ is the King of RIGHTEOUSNESS.

We are God's righteous people due to our covenant, or being in league or alliance, with Jesus Christ. He is High Priest forever in God's Heavenly line and in the earthly, ancestral line with the Abrahamic Covenant, where God made or cut a Covenant with Abraham. Remember your relationship with God is a covenant relationship and He is a covenant-keeping God.

Jesus Christ made a covenant with God to redeem Mankind with His own flesh. Cutting into the flesh and shedding the blood is a sign of covenant. For example, there are many symbols that cultures use to show a covenant marriage. However, in the Western world, wearing a ring on the second finger of the left hand is the evidence or sign of marriage between a man and a woman. This shows that two people are in covenant relationship with each other.

Jesus Christ wears the scars and the nail prints in His Hands and in His feet. This shows that He cut covenant with God for man to become Born Again and have eternal life with Him. He is the Covenant Husband that never leaves or forsakes His Covenant Bride, the Church of His Believers. Born-Again Believers are all in a covenant relationship with God, Jesus Christ, and the Holy Spirit. It is not a covenant that is temporal, such as a marriage, which can end in divorce. It is permanent—signed and sealed in and with the Blood of Jesus Christ. Christ fulfilled all of God's requirements to be High Priest. He now presides over Believers' prayers and confessions of God's Word, gifts of offerings and tithes [tenth], just as the earthly priests did.

Whenever you communicate with God, you can never bypass God and man's High Priest-Jesus Christ. He goes to God on your behalf. Everything you need from God comes to you IN the name of Jesus

Christ, who is your mediator. Believers have been given the name of Jesus Christ as their covenant name, due to their covenant relationship with Jesus Christ. Jesus Christ is in the middle of every conversation you have with God. God does not see you as an individual. He knows you because of your Covenant relationship with Christ. Every word that comes out of your mouth, spoken to God, represents the Word of Jesus Christ and His presence. It is as if Jesus Christ Himself is speaking. Because of covenant, you have been given authority to speak to Him [God] in His Son's name. Remind the devil of your covenant marriage with Jesus Christ and that you have been given His name.

In a family, the wife and children are given the last name of the husband and father, because they are of the same covenant family, league, relation, and bond. A husband has authority to speak on behalf of his wife and vice versa, without their physical presence because of covenant relationship.

Abraham brought the tenth to Melchizedek, the High Priest of the Most High God, who resembles the Son of God (Hebrews 7: 1–3). However, you may say, "But wait, that was then." Let's see if God still receives the covenant tenth that Abraham instituted due to covenant relationship. Does God still require it from Believers, who are now in His House, Government, or Kingdom?

How were the blessings Abraham received from Melchizedek, 430 years before Moses incorporated tithing into the Law, still relevant today? Hebrew 7:7 (NIV) states, "And without doubt, the lesser is blessed by the greater." When in covenant with God, He is the Greater that invokes the blessings.

How are the Blessings of obedience to God as it is written in Deuteronomy 28:1–15 enforced and maintained in all of our lives? Should Believers who are heirs of God and joint heirs with Jesus Christ be automatically and equally blessed, while still living in disobedience by not giving of the tenth of their increase, which belongs to God?

Abraham used this method of tithing the tenth of what God increased Him with to show that He will forever put God in remembrance of His covenant Words TO BLESS and multiply him. Abraham and the nations of the earth that live by faith believe and receive God and His Son Jesus Christ in their lives. Covenant demands evidence to prove covenant relationships. Every time you give the tenth [tithe] of your paycheck, you are reminding God of His covenant to bless and prosper you. "Do not be deceived: God cannot be mocked. A man reaps what he sows" (Galatians 6:7 NIV). "For I AM the Lord, I do not change" (Malachi 3:6 NKJV). In Malachi 3:8, God tells the people that they have robbed Him in tithes and offerings. Note the scripture does not say tithes only or offerings only. It states both tithes and offerings. Therefore, if you bring the tithes and not the offering or the offering and not the tithes, you are still robbing God. Here is where God makes an exception: You bring all the tithes (here He left off offering) into the storehouse, that there may be food in My house (Malachi 3:10). Note, you bring, not give, the tenth of your increase. You bring the tithe because it is not yours; it does not belong to you. Therefore, you bring to God what is His. If you do not, whether Old or New Testament, you will be stealing.

The offering is to be given because that is yours to give or not to give. If you lived in the Old Covenant, you would bring to the storehouse or the temple grain, food, or animals which are meat. Even though you bring your tithes to your local church building, spiritually, you are God's dwelling, tabernacle, building, temple, or church. You are bringing it to God's "storehouse," which may be a physical building, where the Body of Believers assemble together to worship.

The tithe, in these passages, is mainly monetary gain and the tenth of the monetary gain is called the tithe. Bringing the tenth to God is a witness, sign, and testimony of your faith and trust in Him, who is your creator and provider. The whole of your increase belongs to God; all that you receive belongs to Him. However, He shares it with you and by you giving Him back the portion He asks for, He can bless your obedience. You prosper when God blesses your obedience by giving Him a tenth of your income. That's the portion He asks for. God doesn't want your money. The earth belongs to Him. He wants your obedience.

The first man, Adam, was disobedient. God told him not to eat of the fruit of one specific tree in the Garden of Eden. He disobeyed and his blessings were cut off. His son, Cain, was disobedient by bringing the offering that he wanted to bring to God, instead of what He asked of him.

In contrast, Abraham was obedient when he offered up his son as a sacrificial offering to God because it is what He asked of him. There was another Man called Jesus Christ who offered up Himself as a sacrifice for mankind because it is what God asked of Him. The Greater is able to bless the lesser when they are obedient. God's relationship, as well as His Son Jesus Christ's relationship with a Born-Again Believer is covenant. Believers cannot relate to Them outside of covenant. The Bible or the Word of God and all of its promises are law and Covenant Words to Christ's Body. God, in Genesis 9: 9–17, established covenant between Noah, every living creature, and the earth not to destroy it again with water. He made evidence of His promise visible by putting a rainbow in the sky to remind Him of His promise.

What does Jesus Christ say about tithing [tenth] in the New Testament? Matthew 23:23 (NLT), "What sorrows awaits you teachers of religious law and you Pharisees. Hypocrites! For you are careful to tithe even the tiniest income from your herb gardens, but you ignore the more important aspect of the law—justice, mercy, and faith. YOU SHOULD TITHE, YES, but do not neglect the more important things" God said when you bring the tithes (Malachi 3:10– 11), He will open the windows of Heaven. This implies that if you do not bring the tenth, you will not have access to an open Heaven; the windows will remain closed, and blessings will not be poured out. Therefore, even when you give offerings and not the tenth, you may receive a return on your giving according to the measure you gave to man because your return will come through or from men. However, the blessings come through an open window, and that's from bringing the tenth to God. Remember even when the tenth from your monetary gain is brought to an institution, which may be a physical building, the tenth from a $50 earning = $5 tithe. This goes to your spiritual and physical church, storehouse, or treasury. God then breathes upon it in order to maintain the blessing and covenant of blessings He spoke to our forefathers.

Everything God breathes on springs up with multiplied life. However, it must be done His way. In order for Him to maintain the blessings in the life of the Levitical priests who tended to the temple, the tenth had to be brought to the temple by the people. The priests also had to bring their tenth to the high priest. Spiritually, you are now God's priests in His Heavenly Temple. For Him to maintain the open windows of overflow blessings in your life here in the earth and in your storehouse, or house, you have to give Him permission or an access in the earth to do so. Again, God cannot operate in your life apart from His Word. Obeying His Word and acting on His promises concerning tithes and offerings gives Him the legal right to bless you. Otherwise, Satan will accuse Him of violating His own Legal Word. God cannot lie. Therefore, His system to bless and prosper you in receiving wealth, riches, and prosperity is via tithes and offerings. He cannot violate His Word concerning these. His promises to increase and bless you are clearly written in these covenant promises to you, His Born-Again Believer. This involves bringing your tenth, which is what belongs to Him first. "But seek first the Kingdom of God and His righteousness, and all these things shall be added to you" (Matthew 6:33 NKJV).

Remember, He has rules you must live by in His Kingdom. The blessing on the tithe [tenth] is God's divine grace, abilities, and capabilities to get you wealth. You must bring His portion first, the tenth, because He is the One who gives you the power to get wealth.

You, as parents, give your child tasks or duties in your house. You give them their tasks in the house to keep it clean and functioning at their level of contribution to the household. In the same manner, God gave the Born-Again Believer tasks to function in His Kingdom or Government and to bring the tenth into His Kingdom. Believers make up the Kingdom/storehouse of God and we obey His Government, just like your children in your physical house. High Priest to God and man forever, in the same order as the High Priest Melchizedek who took the tenth from Abraham. "This man, however, did not trace His descent from Levi, (*the tribe of Aaron and earthly high priests, these priests were temporary and foretold what was to come in Heaven*) yet he collected a tenth from Abraham and blessed him who had the promises. (*Jesus Christ and High Priest and Head of the Church of God is still collecting your tithes and offerings in the Kingdom of God*). And without a doubt the lesser is blessed by the greater" (Hebrews 7:6–7 NIV).

"I will pour out a blessing so great you won't have enough room to take it in! Try it! Put me to the test" (Malachi 3:10b)! Note that this is the blessing for your obedience in tithing, which are good health, prosperity, longevity, favor, open doors, and protection.

God will shield you and divert the enemy.

"Your crops will be abundant, for I will guard them from insects and disease. Your grapes will not fall from the vine before they are ripe" (Malachi 3:11 NLT).

"What sorrow awaits you Pharisees! For you are careful to tithe even the tiniest income from your herb gardens, but you ignore justice and the love of God. You should tithe, yes, but do not neglect the more important things" (Luke 11:42 NLT). Jesus Christ said these words:

"Woe to you, scribes and Pharisees, hypocrites! For you pay tithe of mint and anise and cummin, and have neglected the weightier matters of the law: justice and mercy and faith. These you ought to have done, without leaving the others undone" (Matthews 23:23 NKJV).

It is best to give offerings as regularly as the tenth. The offering amount is according to the amount you may choose, or God may give you a specific amount to give. To increase the amount of return, the giving should be increased accordingly. The return on this giving will be coming from people. This is the law of giving and receiving, sowing and reaping. For example, if you give a smile you will reap a smile. God honors His Word on seed, time, and harvest, sowing and reaping, and this should not be neglected. It is knitted with the tithes. It is tithes and offering, not tithes or offerings. If you give offerings, you will need God's rain to pour out and water your offering seed that you planted in the ground of others. If God's windows are not opened over your offering, and, according to God's Word, to bring the tithe and offering, this may mean you have not been tithing.

In the passage above, I mentioned that God said bring the tithes to the storehouse. The offerings are your giving/planting seeds in order to reap a multiplied harvest. The tithes are brought to God's storehouse. The physical church is symbolic of a place where your spirit is fed spiritually. Remember not to kill your returned blessing with soul wounds, which are unforgiveness and unrepented sins. Sins traumatize and injure the soul. Remember, the blood of Jesus Christ cleanses, washes away, and heals sins of every kind. Remain cheerful, thankful, and appreciative in your declaration from your lips. As the Bible says, "The tongue has the power of life and death" (Proverbs 18:21 NIV).

Repent if you failed in the above areas to put God first, make money your idol, or have robbed God of the tenth of your increase. Remember to put God first in all areas of your life. You can never get away with robbing from God; it's an open door for Satan to rob from you. Negative attacks from Satan will eat up your harvests.

"Give, and it will be given to you: good measure, press down, shaken together, and running over **will be put into your bosom**. For with the same measure that you use, it will be measured back to you" (Luke 6:38 NKJV).

"…He who sows sparingly will also reap sparingly, and he who sows bountifully will also reap bountifully. So let each one give as he purposes in his heart, not grudgingly or of necessity; for God loves a cheerful giver" (2 Corinthians 9:6–7 NKJV).

"I fast twice a week and give a tenth of all I get" (Luke 11:42 NIV). Remember the covenant blessings of the tenth spans generations.

It does not fade out with the change of dispensations. The following is God talking to Abram thousands of years ago: "Then He brought him outside and said look now towards heaven, and count the stars if you are able to number them." And He said to him, "So shall your descendants be" (Genesis 15:5 NKJV). Abraham's descendants are still alive and growing, both the geneological descendants: his Jewish lineage and the spiritual ones through Christ Jesus.

God came into covenant with Abram (as he was known before God changed his name to Abraham). Abram came into covenant with God when God walked through bloody, cut animal pieces. God was depicted as the smoke moving through the cut animals. When He did that, Abram knew He had to keep His Word of giving him a son, as the act entered into was a covenant symbol. If God did not keep His Word to Abram, what happened to the animals would happen to Him. God did not allow Abram to walk through the animal parts also, as He cannot lie. He put Abram to sleep. (See Genesis 15:7-18). In a covenant relationship, tithing is a covenant act. Abraham, an Old Testament Believer and tither, brought his tithe to the then High Priest, Melchizedek-King of Righteousness and Peace. The New Testament Believer and tither is still bringing the tithe to the present High Priest, Jesus Christ, King of Righteousness and Peace. In the life of a Follower/ Disciple of Christ, tithing and communion show covenant-building relationships in action, till Christ Jesus returns for His Church.

Communion shows covenant relationship. Jesus demonstrated this by breaking bread and drinking wine with His disciples before offering all of Himself to God and the world. They were to share this covenant agreement symbolically. Jesus' body was the bread and His shed blood was the wine in the cup. Melchizedek did this with His disciple Abraham hundreds of years before Jesus did. Abraham presented his pastor and God's High Priest, Melchizedek, with a tenth of his increase, signifying that God helped him to get wealth. In a covenant relationship, the increase is shared when two are in an agreement. One party cannot keep 100% because two are in the agreed covenant relationship. God never breaks covenant relationship. The tenth does not have to be money. Leviticus 27:30 NIV states, "A tenth of everything from the land, whether grain from the soil or fruit from the trees, belongs to the Lord; it is holy to the Lord." There are still fruits, grains, and trees in the land and on the earth today. God still requires His covenant portion of everyone's increase in the earth. If you sell what was planted and received the money, a tenth is God's. The land was created by God, not an individual. The crops came from His earth.

The New Covenant /Testament Church

The New Will and Testament Church of The Lord Jesus Christ did not only start in the Gospels: Matthew, Mark, Luke, and John. They were collectively a bridge from the Old order of worshiping God, which was doing works or physical performance, to the New Covenant order of worshiping God in the Spirit, which Jesus Christ the Messiah introduced. The New covenant worship was fully established in Acts after the coming of the Holy Spirit. In the Old Covenant, the Spirit of God's anointing would come upon a person for service. In the New Covenant, the Holy Spirit's anointed presence is now in and with the spirits of the Believers. "Yet a time is coming and has come when the true worshipers will worship the Father in the Spirit and in truth." (John 4:23 NIV). Jesus hanged on a cross at Calvary and His covenant blood was shed to do away with sin. In other words, the shedding of Jesus' blood abolished sin I John 1:7).

Luke 22:20 (NKJV) states, "This cup is the new covenant/ testament in My blood which is shed for you." The New Testament Believers are now able to remind Jesus of His promises in His Will/ the Bible as they symbolically eat bread that represents His body and drink grape/juice from the cup, that represents His blood. Communion respects covenant; it shows honor that can never be broken, dismissed or hidden. Whenever you take communion, it shows that you are in covenant agreement or a marriage relationship. To explain, there is intimacy; strangers are not welcomed. Therefore, it is not focused on a community relationship. It is personal, individualized with someone else. The communion meal the High Priest Melchizedek officiated with Abram meant they made covenant or they were already in covenant. This same blood covenant relationship was transferred to Jesus Christ's Priesthood and his covenant Believers, which is a branch of Melchizedek's Priesthood.

Aaron was not a king of righteousness. He officiated as high priest over animal blood sacrifices that could only cover sin for a year. These sacrifices could not remove sin because they were weak, carnal, and fleshly. Aaron's order of priesthood ended because Jesus' blood sacrifice was of the Spirit of God which remitted sin forever.

The priesthood of Aaron from the tribe of Levi was supported from the people's tithes and offerings. The priests had no other job but to care for the work of the tabernacle/temple, which was a foreshadow of today's Heavenly Tabernacle and Priesthood of Jesus Christ.

God's Blessings come from tithing the covenant, tenth. In Malachi 3:10 (NIV), God said, "Bring the whole tithe into the storehouse that there may be food in my house. Test me in this, says the Lord Almighty, and see if I will not throw open the floodgates of heaven and pour out such blessing that there will not be enough room to store it." Believers are blessed when they are obedient to bring God His tenth/tithes that He asked for. Jesus stood before God with His own sacrificial blood, which God required and asked for. Jesus obeyed and God blessed Him and gave Him the name above every name. "Therefore God exalted Him to the highest place and gave Him the name that is above every name" (Philippians 2:9 NIV).

The giving of offerings is for the prospering or increase of the Believer. Luke 6:38 (NIV) states, "Give and it shall be given to you. A good measure, pressed down, shaken together and running over, will be poured into your lap. For with the measure you use, it will be measured to you."

The priests of Aaron's priesthood were not of the order of Melchizedek and they were not given the title, *Kings of Righteousness*. They were not under the Abrahamic and Davidic set of priesthood, which was the heritage of Judah, that brought forth Jesus Christ. However, Judah's brother was Levi and their father Jacob/Israel (Matthew 1:1-2). Aaron's priesthood was under the Levitical order, set, and tribe and therefore, had a different assignment under God and Moses.

Regardless of the nation, Believers in Jesus Christ were born into the New Covenant era. First Peter 2:9 states, "But you are a chosen people, a royal priesthood, a holy nation, God's special possession, that you may declare the praises of Him who called you out of darkness into His wonderful light."

Believers in Jesus Christ are now one Holy Nation in the New Covenant that started with Noah, his son Shem, who was Melchizedek, King of Jerusalem and Righteousness and Priest of The Most High God, and his family member and disciple Abraham, in the Old Covenant that spanned to Jesus Christ: King of Righteousness and High Priest of The Most High God and His Body of Believers who are and being engrafted legally as New Blood Covenant royal kings and priests.

God the Father, Jesus the Word and the Holy Spirit Relationship are Blood Covenant with a Born-Again Believer. Believers must study The Blood Covenant, as this is the foundation of a Believer's relationship with Christ Jesus. The Bible: Old and New Testaments are Covenant Books written by The Holy Spirit's Inspiration to Believers.

2 Timothy 3:16 NKJV "All Scripture is given by the Inspiration of God, and is profitable for doctrine for reproof, for correction, for instruction in righteousness."

Jesus made that possible because of His redemptive blood that was shed at the cross to adopt Believers into His Covenant Son- Ship with God. The Adoption Paper that God received from Jesus was due to His shed blood and Their Binding Everlasting Covenant Agreement, that cannot be changed. To put Jesus to death for our Sin, Adam/Mankind Sin.

John 3:16 "For God so loved the world that He gave His only begotten Son, that whoever believes in Him should not perish but have eternal life."

Tithing the tenth, giving offerings and taking communion are due to Believer's Covenant Relationship and written promises with God through Jesus Christ.

God's blessings are given when the instructions from His Word are heeded and we are obedient. It is pleasing to God when we exercise, act on His Word which is Faith.

Hebrews 11:6 NKJV "But without faith (acting, believing God's Word) it is impossible to please Him, which is sin or committing one's personal acts of disobedience against God's Word."

Satan is an opportunist, to not obey God's Word or Rules,'Laws is satan's legal open access to kill, steal and destroy you, a son of God, that doesn't tithe or give offerings.

Please study: The Blood Covenant in order to exactly understand our covenant relationship with God and also to understand covenant acts such as tithing the tithe/tenth, receiving communion, God's Word and declaring His promises given to all Believers in Christ Jesus.

Praise and Worship

Praise and worship to God can take on several forms, but the main expression of these forms is song and music, among other expressions of adoration. The Lord is Holy, and He is seated on the throne. The whole earth is full of His glory and divine presence. Everything that exists in the earth belongs to Him. We stand in awe of Him. My prayer is that we will always stand in awe of who Jesus Christ and the Father God is, and never be controlled or manipulated by some man's poor estimation of Him. I also pray that we will never fall short of praising and worshiping Him with our lives because of the fear of man. Praise to God is not about us. It is about the reverence, glory, and exaltation that we should give Him in worship and adoration. We need Him. God does not need us. Our next breath comes from Him. The air we breathe, which we cannot live without, comes from Him. He gave us everything that is good. The only thing we can give back to Him is our praise and worship.

We should never be ashamed to lift our voices and our hands to magnify Him in total appreciation of the Almighty God. Our lives should be to praise and worship Him at all times because there is no one like Him—not our money, not our cars, not our families, our husband or wife, our career, profession, business, or homes. The whole earth is created in praise and worship of Him. There is nothing that can compare to Him, the Creator God. Who is like Him? He is great in everything. No one can avoid worshiping God, not even Satan. "Then Jesus [Christ] said to him, 'Away with you, Satan! For it is written, 'You shall worship the Lord your God, and Him only you shall serve" (Matthew 4:10 NKJV).

In Heaven, around God's throne, there are the four living creatures that do not rest day or night, saying,

"Holy, holy, holy Lord God Almighty, Who was and is and is to come!" Whenever the living creatures give glory and honor and thanks to Him who sits on the throne, who lives for ever and ever, the twenty-four elders fall down before Him who sits on the throne and worship Him who lives forever and ever, and cast their crowns before the throne, saying: "You are worthy, O Lord to receive glory and honor and power; for You created all things, And by Your will they exist and were created" (Revelation 4:8–11 NKJV).

No one can esteem God better than you. No one can do that for you. The musicians can not do it. The song can not do it. Your praise and worship should be to glorify Him from your spirit. An expression of who He is to you and you to Him can only be revealed to your spirit by the Spirit of God.

Is God your Father? Is Jesus your Lord? It's not what He can do for you, such as receiving healing, deliverance, or obtaining a new job. You sing because He is your owner and your Lord. The music, dance, and song assist us with this knowledge and appreciation when we engage in praise and worship. We also give glory to God because He is our Father and because we know that we are His children. Praise and worship are forms of adoration to God. Therefore, never go to God without praising and worshiping Him for who He is in private and in public. It's an insult when you refuse to adore Him, especially before others.

"Make a joyful shout to the Lord, all you lands! Serve the Lord with gladness; Come before His presence with singing. Know that the Lord, He is God; It is He who has made us, and not we ourselves; We are His people and the sheep of His pasture. Enter into His gates with thanksgiving, And into His courts with praise. Be thankful to Him, and bless His name" (Psalm 100:1–4 NKJV).

It's not about how the flesh feels. It's about honor, respect, and reverence to a Holy God. He gave you a will, that belongs to you. You can do whatever you want with it. You have a choice. However, your life belongs to Him, God! He is God, whether you acknowledge Him or not. He wants you to know who He is. He wants you to know that He loves you and you love Him. He delights in you and you in Him. Do not be afraid to praise and worship Him. "Bless the Lord, O my soul; And all that is within me, bless His Holy Name!" (Psalm 103:1 NKJV)

Say, "I renounce the lies and accusations of the enemy: feeling afraid of God, fear of man, feelings of rejection and that I am not good enough." Stop performing for people, or even for God. Throw off that garment of heaviness: worry, anger, bitterness, self-hate, shame, and guilt of past involvements, lack of self-confidence, depression, feelings of inadequacy, and dwelling on man's opinion of you instead of God's opinion of you. On a daily basis, tell God before entering into prayer, praise, and worship, "Your will be done in my life" (Matthew 6:10).

Forgive those who trespass against you or have wronged you (Matthew 6:12). Ask God to forgive you for those whom you have trespassed or wronged. If you do not remember or if you are not aware of any wrongdoing, ask the Holy Spirit to reveal to you the person that you may have wronged and follow His instructions. Unforgiveness will block your prayers.

Say, "Father God, I am made in your image, and I am the apple of Your eye. You love me and I love You. You are smiling over me. I am in Your arms. Therefore, I am free to praise and worship You! I am Your beautiful daughter or handsome son! In the name of Jesus! You hear that devil? I pour the blood of Jesus Christ in my soul and wash away every sin that is hindering my time of praise and worship with You."

Put some praise music on and dance your socks off or praise Him with the joy of your lips. You are now confusing the enemy. He is killing himself. Those spirits of bitterness and strife fell dead. Transform your soul, mind, will, emotions, with your praise and worship. Move your soul from glory to glory! Go right into God's anointed presence and atmosphere of peace, rest, joy, love, and refreshing with thanksgiving. Do not just stay in the outer court of your flesh. Go right into the Holy of Holies where God's throne is, where He "embraces" you—your spirit. Welcome the Holy Spirit and ask Him to escort you right into "God's presence." You can now sing in your heavenly language. Sing to the King of Kings!

Remember, no authentic husband stays outside the bedroom and blows kisses to his wife. He is expected to enter and embrace his wife, or I believe he won't be married very long.

You are also expected to enter God's courts with praise and worship. Be respectful of Him. Honor His Majesty's Glory and the anointed power of the Holy Spirit. You honor Him with your praise and worship. Never get so familiar with God that you develop a stiff neck, a proud, stubborn look, folded arms, and an unwillingness to bow down, lay prostrate before Him, or lift up holy hands to glorify the King of Glory. When you glorify Him, His manifested presence, that can be felt and sensed, comes down into the atmosphere of worship and adoration. His presence brings healing, anointing, and other supernatural gifts, benefits, and blessings.

As a parent, in the natural, you freely bless your children who respect and honor you. They, in turn, receive God's blessing because they show honor, respect, and appreciation for you as a parent. Ephesian 6:2–3 (NKJV) states, "Honor your father and mother. that it may be well with you and you may live long on the earth." God is not only Father and Mother to us, He is everything. He is the creator of your life. You give Him honor in your praise and worship unto Him.

As a Born-Again Believer, our spirits are already in God's presence. So we should get used to praising and worshiping the Most High God with outstretched hands now, here on earth, because that is one of many activities we will be doing throughout eternity.

The meaning of Praise:

The word *praise* in the Hebrew language: *Yadah* means "to give thanks, laud, praise." Root word *Yads*: hand, hold out the hand, extend the hand.

Meaning of worship:

The word *worship* in the Hebrew language is *Shachah* - portrays the act of bowing down in homage before a superior ruler, to bow down, to fall down to stoop, crouch.

Who Is Jesus Christ (Yeshua)? What Was His Purpose on Earth?

1. **JESUS (YESHUA) IS THE CHRIST, SON OF THE LIVING GOD:**

Suddenly a voice came from heaven, saying, 'This is My Beloved Son, in whom I am well pleased'" (Matthew 3:17 NKJV).

"Simon Peter answered and said, 'You are the Christ, the Son of the living God'" (Matthew 16:16 NKJV).

2. **JESUS (YESHUA):**

Savior:
"For to this end we both labor and suffer reproach, because we trust in the living God, who is the Savior of all men, especially of those who believe" (1 Timothy 4:10 NKJV).

Messiah, the same meaning as Christ or the Anointed One:
The woman said to Him, "I know that Messiah is coming" (who is called Christ); "When He comes, He will tell us all things." Jesus [Christ] said to her, "I who speak to you am He" (John 4:25–26 NKJV).

3. THE KING THAT HAS COME TO EARTH AND WILL RETURN:

"He will be great, and will be called the Son of the Most High; and the Lord God will give Him the throne of His Father David. And He will reign over the house of Jacob forever, and of His Kingdom there will be no end" (Luke 1:32–33 NKJV).

"Where is He who has been born King of the Jews? For we have seen His star in the East and have come to worship Him" (Matthew 2:2 NKJV).

"I am the Alpha and the Omega, the Beginning and the End," says the Lord, "who is and who was and who is to come, the Almighty" (Revelation 1:8 NKJV).

4. CHRIST MEANS ANOINTED ONE: THE HOLY SPIRIT'S POWER IN HIM TO SAVE, HEAL, AND DELIVER:

"But Jesus kept silent. And the high priest answered and said to Him, 'I put you under oath by the living God: Tell us if You are the Christ, the Son of God!'" (Matthew 26:63 NKJV)

"How God anointed Jesus of Nazareth with the Holy Spirit and with power, who went about doing good and healing all who were oppressed by the devil, for God was with Him" (Acts 10:38 NKJV).

"And Jesus [Christ] went about all Galilee, teaching in the synagogues, preaching the gospel of the kingdom, and healing all kinds of sickness and all kinds of diseases among the people" (Matthew 4:23 NKJV).

5. HE WAS A PROPHET:

For Moses truly said to the fathers, "The Lord God will raise up for you a Prophet like me from your brethren. Him you shall hear in all things, whatever He says to you" (Acts 3:22 NKJV).

Then those men, when they had seen the sign that Jesus (Christ) did, said, "This is truly the Prophet who is to come into the world" (John 6:14 NKJV).

6. HE WAS A TEACHER OR RABBI:

And when they found Him on the other side of the sea, they said to Him, "Rabbi, when did You come here?" (John 6:25 NKJV).

This man came to Jesus (Yeshua) by night and said to Him, "Rabbi, we know that You are a Teacher come from God" (John 3:2 NKJV).

7. HE CAME TO EARTH TO DO THE WILL OF GOD:

Jesus (Christ) said, For I have come down from heaven, not to do My own will, but the will of Him who sent Me (John 6:38 NKJV).

8. HE GIVES ETERNAL LIFE:

Jesus (Christ) said, I come that they might have life, and that they may have it more abundantly. And I give them eternal life, and they shall never perish; neither shall anyone snatch them out of my hand (John 10:10b, 28 NKJV).

9. JESUS CAME TO FULFILL THE LAW OF MOSES (MATTHEW 5:17):

"For the law was given through Moses, but grace and truth came through Jesus Christ" (John 1:17 NKJV).

We have all benefited from the rich blessings He brought us - one gracious blessing after another.

"For the law was given through Moses, God's unfailing love and faithfulness came through Jesus Christ" (John 1:17NLT).

10. JOHN THE BAPTIST BORE WITNESS AND TESTIMONY OF JESUS CHRIST BEING THE SON OF GOD AND THE LAMB OF GOD (JOHN 1:34 AND 36):

The next day John saw Jesus coming toward him, and said, "Behold! The Lamb of God who takes away the sin of the world!" (John 1:29 NKJV)

Jesus Christ rose from the dead

The tomb is empty:

For as yet they did not know the Scripture, (Psalm 16:10) that He must rise again from the dead (John 20:9 NKJV).

Jesus Christ seen alive from the dead

Jesus came and stood in the midst, and said to them, "Peace be with you." When He had said this, He showed them His hands and His side. Then the disciples were glad when they saw the Lord (John 20: 19b–20 NKJV).

Jesus Christ gave Thomas His disciple, proof that He had come back from the dead

Jesus said to him, "Thomas, because you have seen Me, you have believed. Blessed are those who have not seen and yet have believed" (John 20:29 NKJV).

Jesus Christ's (Yeshua) Statement

Luke 4:18 (NKJV)

THE SPIRIT OF THE LORD IS UPON ME, BECAUSE HE HAS ANOINTED ME:

To preach the gospel to the poor:

Tell people the Good News of His coming to earth to save them from eternal death or separation from God: "Most assuredly, I say to you, he who believes in Me has everlasting life" (John 6:47 NKJV).

To heal the brokenhearted, the sick, those who are sorrowful and in need of comfort. Jesus (Christ) said, "Come to me, all you Who labor and are heavy laden, and I will give you rest" (Matthew 11:28 NKJV).

To proclaim freedom to those who are bound to Satan's bondages, to deliver them from all forms of addictions, perverted lifestyles, demonic curses, and the spirit of homosexuality (Leviticus 18:22 NKJV) states, "You shall not lie with a male as with a woman. It is an abomination": [*filthy, detest utterly*], and also (Leviticus 20:13 NKJV) "If a man lies with a male as he lies with a woman, both of them have committed an abomination. They shall surely be put to death. Their blood shall be upon them." Jesus Christ came to earth to proclaim freedom to those who are bound by all perverted, evil spirits and by witchcraft, the occult, incest, fornication, and adultery. Proverbs 6:32 (NKJV) states, "Whoever commits adultery with a woman lacks understanding. He who does so destroys his own soul." Jesus Christ the Son of God, came to earth as a man like us, but without sin—to save and set us free from every sin. Jesus Christ was fully man without Satan's sin and fully God who knew no sin. He, however, did not live in the earth as God, but as Man and functioned as God's divine, anointed, set-apart, consecrated Man. He came to deliver every man, woman, boy, and girl from Satan's destructive weapons. He uses these weapons to destroy us by using sickness and disease of the body and of the soul such as homosexuality, masturbation, murder, suicide, and pornography. "He (Jesus Christ, who went to the cross and shed His blood) has delivered us from the power of darkness and conveyed us into the kingdom of the Son of His love" (Colossians 1:13 NKJV). Take My yoke upon you and learn from Me, for I am gentle and lowly in heart, and you will find rest for your souls. For My yoke is easy and My burden is light" (Matthew 11:29 NKJV).

To give sight to those who are physically and spiritually blinded by the powers of darkness, or of Satan and his deceptions, those who are unable to see the truth about Jesus Christ due to being separated from God and being under Satan's control.

"The whole world lies under the sway of the wicked one" (1 John 5:19b NKJV).

To set at liberty those who are oppressed, those who are emotionally and mentally depressed by Satan or who have a negative mindset about God. Satan has these people and their minds captivated or in bondage to his way of thinking. "Whose minds the god of this age Satan has blinded, who do not believe, lest the light of the gospel of the glory of Christ, who is the image of God, should shine on them" (2 Corinthians 4:4 NKJV).

The following are not inclusions in Jesus's statement from Luke 4:18. "To seek and to save that which was lost" (Luke 19:10b NKJV).

To forgive sins:

"But that you may know that the Son of Man has power on earth to forgive sins" (Mark 2:10 NKJV).

Jesus Christ came to forgive sin. The world, under a satanic system, can influence nations and the people in that society to murder the unborn. Herod was the king who ordered the killing of babies in the Bible after he found out about Jesus Christ's birth. "And he sent forth and put to death all the male children who were in Bethlehem and in all the districts, from two years and under" (Matthew 2:16 NKJV). Society may choose to murder their unborn by telling people that the unborn child is not a human. "Woe to him who builds a town with bloodshed, who establishes a city by iniquity!" (Habakkuk 2:12 NKJV).

The world system, under Satan, cannot give human life. The same murdering spirit of Herod is still alive today in the earthly realm because Satan was the spirit that inspired that King to murder babies. A body is formed in the womb of a woman, but life comes from God, the giver of life. Therefore, if the creator of life says we should not kill another human life, it is a command whether that human life is inside the womb or outside the womb. In Deuteronomy 5:17 (NKJV), God said, "You shall not murder."

If mankind, society, or the government chooses to disobey this command, it is called sin, and this sin is murder. Abortion is the name society uses, but God calls it murder. In Jeremiah 1:5 (NKJV), God said, "Before [note the word *before*] I [God] formed you in the womb I knew you; Before you were born I sanctified [or set apart] you; I ordained you a prophet to the nations." Society did not know you before you were born. Man's spirit does not originate from a physical egg and a sperm at conception. The spirit of that conception comes from God, the giver of life. The image of that man's spirit was created before conception.

Here is an example of a spirit and a body in a womb, which was conceived by the Holy Spirit: The angel Gabriel said to Mary, "You will conceive in your womb [or be pregnant with] and bring forth a

Son, and shall call His name Jesus" (Yeshua-Savior) (Luke 1:31 NKJV). This angel knew everything about the person that would be in Mary's womb. Jesus Christ said, "A body You [God] have prepared for me" (Hebrews 10:5b NKJV).

Examples of pregnancies that were spoken about before conception include as follows:

"Do not be afraid, Zacharias, for your prayer is heard; and your wife Elizabeth will bear you a son, and you shall call his name John" (Luke 1:13 NKJV).

"And the Lord said to Abraham, Why did Sarah laugh, saying, 'shall I surely bear a child, since I am old?' Is anything too hard for the Lord? At the appointed time I will return to you, according to the time of life, and Sarah shall have a son" (Genesis 18:13–14 NKJV).

WOMEN WHO FEARED GOD, RATHER THAN THEIR GOVERNMENT:

The midwives of Egypt:

Then the king of Egypt spoke to the Hebrew midwives…and said, "When you do the duties of a midwife for the Hebrew women, and see them on the birthstools, if it is a son, then you shall kill him; but, if it is a daughter, then she shall live." But the midwives feared God, and did not do as the king of Egypt commanded them, but saved the male children alive. Therefore, God dealt well with the midwives, and the people multiplied and grew very mighty (Exodus 1:15– 17, 20 NKJV).

The mother of Moses:

So Pharaoh commanded all his people saying, "Every son who is born you shall cast into the river, and every daughter you shall save alive" (Exodus 1:22 NKJV).

So, the woman [Moses's mother] conceived and bore a son. And when she saw that he was a beautiful child, she hid him three months (Exodus 2:2 NKJV).

If you had abortions, repent. Attached to abortions are other dark spirits of the soul because of this sin that you also must renounce. These are guilt, depression, shame, blame, grief over the lost life, and condemnation, where the accuser, Satan, accuses you of murder and harasses you with tormenting thoughts. Therefore, as a Born-Again Believer, murdering the unborn is not just a casual bodily procedure like having a tooth extraction; it is disobeying God's command not to murder, which is sin. This act will not go away by burying the memories in the subconscious of your mind. That's a life from God and a wrong was committed against that life given by God.

You need to release yourself from that sin committed against another life with forgiveness, repentance, and the blood of Jesus Christ. You must cleanse your soul and heal the wound and injury in it that the sin of abortion caused. You may get away from man with this sin, but not from God. Jesus said, "For nothing is secret that will not be revealed, nor anything hidden that will not be known and come to light" (Luke 8:17 NKJV).

And God said to Cain, "What have you done? The voice of your brother's blood cries out to Me from the ground" (Genesis 4:10 NKJV).

And the blood of Jesus Christ His Son cleanses us from all sin. If we confess our sins, He is faithful and just to forgive us our sins and to cleanse (the blood of Jesus Christ) us from all unrighteousness (1 John 1:7b, 9 NKJV).

If you have had an abortion or participated in an abortion in any way, pray this prayer:

Dear Father in Heaven, I forgive myself, and others for having this abortion/s or participating in it in any form. I now believe that "children are a heritage from the Lord, The fruit of the womb is a reward" (Psalm

127:3 NKJV). I renounce and repent of this evil that I have done. Your Word says, I shall not murder (Matthew 5:21). I also renounce all the lies of the enemy, and I render inoperative the spirit of depression, fear, guilt, and condemnation in my soul from Satan. Psalm 23:4b (NKJV) says, "I will fear no evil" or (name any of the above soul sins, e.g., depression) that has/ have attached itself to me. Revelation 12:11 (NKJV) states, "And they overcame him [Satan] by the blood of the Lamb and by the word of their testimony." I curse every dark spirit of guilt due to having this/these abortion/s from the roots and wash all these sins of fear, hurt, depression, betrayal, unsound mind, and confusion because of listening to Satan's lies and not Your Word, God. Wash, cleanse, and heal my mind, will, emotions, and body with the blood of the Lamb, Jesus Christ. I command every voice of accusation, judgment, guilt, and fault from Satan to dry up, wither, and die; and I cast them into the depths of the sea and bind them there, never to return to me. You will not torment me any longer, devil. Jesus Christ took my sins away and cast them into the sea of forgetfulness. "For You have cast all my sins behind Your back" (Isaiah 38:17b NKJV). I believe my baby's/babies' spirit/s is/are in heaven with the Lord! Jesus Christ said, "Even so it is not the will of Your Father who is in heaven that one of these little ones should perish" (Matthew 18:14 NKJV). I thank you, Father God, that you have raised my soul out of this place of darkness with the power of your Holy Spirit's anointing presence that has healed my soul. The cross of Jesus Christ, His blood, and His resurrection from death, Hell, and the grave have raised me up out of the bondage of this sin. In Jesus Christ's name, I pray, amen!

Now, the same Spirit that raised Christ from the grave, lives in you. Thank God for raising your soul with the same anointing power of the Holy Spirit that raised Jesus out of Hell (Romans 8:11). Now help and inform others to avoid the pitfalls and baggage that comes with having an abortion. Jesus Christ sent Paul to the people to "open their eyes, in order to turn them from darkness to light, and from the power of Satan to God, that they may receive forgiveness of sins and an inheritance among those who are sanctified by faith in Me," [*Jesus Christ*] (Acts 26:18 NKJV).

Featured Facts from the Bible

The following account of Lazarus and the Rich Man shows that man's existence does not end with physical death. The rich man's existence after his death shows how his spirit and soul still functioned in Hell, where he went after his physical death or after his earthly body died.

People are eternal spirits. When they die, their spirits do not cease to exist. Do not let Satan deceive you into thinking that you or your spirit go into nothingness or disappears when you die.

Your spirit and soul are eternal, the real you. Your spirit is from God, who is eternal. Therefore, you are also eternal. You are a spirit, you possess a soul, and you have a body or a house. "Then the dust will return to the earth as it was, And the spirit will return to God who gave it" (Ecclesiastes 12:7 NKJV). When Jesus Christ returns, the bodies in the dust of the earth, meaning the dead, will be resurrected and returned to their owners.

Jesus Christ already has a resurrected body. He already rose from the dead. Christians, when Christ returns, will receive glorified and resurrected bodies also. First Corinthians 15:52 (CEV) states, "Not every one of us will die, but we all will be changed. It will happen suddenly, quicker than the blink of an eye. At the sound of the last trumpet the dead will be raised. We will all be changed, so that we will never again die [or decay]." The bodies that we now have on earth are temporary. They are weak, frail, and can die. These temporary bodies one day will be changed into eternal bodies that will never die. John 5:28–29 (CEV) states, "Don't be surprised! The time will come when all the dead will hear the voice of the Son of Man, and they will come out of their graves. Everyone who has done good things will rise to life, but everyone who has done evil things will rise and be condemned." They will be doomed to eternal, spiritual death or Hell.

Lazarus and the Rich Man

There was a certain rich man who was clothed in purple and fine linen and fared sumptuously every day. But there was a certain beggar named Lazarus, full of sores, who was laid at his gate, desiring to be fed with the crumbs which fell from the rich man's table. Moreover the dogs came and licked his sores. So it was that the beggar died and was carried by the angels to Abraham's bosom. The rich man also died and was buried. And being in torments in Hades [or Hell], he lifted up his eyes and saw Abraham afar off, and Lazarus in his bosom. Then he cried and said, "Father Abraham, have mercy on me, and send Lazarus that he may dip the tip of his finger in water and cool my tongue for I am tormented in this flame." But Abraham said, "Son, remember that in your lifetime you received your good things, and likewise Lazarus evil things; but now he is comforted and you are tormented. And besides all this, between us and you there is a great gulf fixed, so that those who want to pass from here to you cannot, nor can those from there pass to us." Then he said, "I beg you therefore, father, that you would send him to my father's house, for I have five brothers that he may testify to them, lest they also come to this place of torment." Abraham said to him, "They have Moses and the prophets; let them hear them." And he said, "No, Father Abraham, but if one goes to them from the dead, they will repent." But he said to him, "If they do not hear Moses and the prophets, neither will they be persuaded though one rise from the dead" (Luke 16:19–31 NKJV).

Note in the account of Lazarus and the rich man, the senses of taste, touch, sight, smell, and hearing are not only limited to this earthly realm, before the physical man dies. They still operate in Hell as spiritual senses. Your soul, which consists of your mind: thoughts/ memory/imagination, emotions, and will is your "inner" consciousness. It never dies.

The Soul of Man

The gateway into the soul is through the five physical senses. Do not allow Satan to influence your actions in the following described areas, as it will affect your soul if done repeatedly. "Why are you cast down, O my soul? And why are you disquieted within me? Hope in God; For I shall yet praise Him, the help of my countenance and my God" (Psalm 42:11 NKJV). Your soul is also eternal like your spirit. If there are evil spirits, e.g., of depression, lies, and jealousy, which are demonic influences in any compartment of the soul, it is called sin. These dark spirits make your soul sick, mentioned in the title "Soul Restoration" and other parts of this book. Ask God to heal your soul, as God's love is light shining from your spirit into it. He does not want darkness from the devil to be in your soul.

Matthew 26:27–28 (NKJV) states, "Then He took the cup, and gave thanks, and gave it to them, saying, 'Drink from it, all of you. For this is My blood of the new covenant, which is shed for many for the remission of sins.'" Communion is also one of the Believers' weapons to heal emotional trauma, such as heartache, pain, and sorrow. Do it as often as you can, daily if possible. Combine it with your other spiritual weapons such as praying in your understanding, praying in the spirit, the Word of God, the name of Jesus, the blood of Jesus, Anointing oil, etc. Repent, forgive others and yourself, and spiritually wash the sins from your soul with the blood of Jesus Christ. First John 1:7b states, "…the blood of Jesus Christ His Son cleanses us from all sin." His blood not only cleanses your soul of sin, it purges and heals your soul. A healed soul has been raised up out of darkness and is no longer controlled by sin-inducing, demonic spirits. The Word of God and the presence of the Holy Spirit, which is in your spirit, can now fill your soul. Roman 8:11 states (NKJV), "But if the Spirit of Him who raised Jesus from the dead dwells in you. He who raised Christ from the dead will give life to your mortal bodies [soul] through His Spirit who dwells in you [your spirit]." Bind and cast these sins operating in your soul out in the name of Jesus Christ. Throw them in the depths of the sea and bind them there never to return to you. He has given you authority to use his name that is above every name.

Go through any area or compartment of your soul below that is bound by any sin you may have identified. Confessing the Word will then be much more effective in your life, as Satan and his demons use sin as their invitation into the soul of man to kill.

Emotions.

This is the conscious, emotional or "feeling" part of you. It is awake and aware. According to what you feed it, the soul can be influenced negatively with spirits of sadness, depression, oppression, meanness, and a host of other perverted, demonic spirits. Praise, worship, and laughter are healing remedies for the spirit of heaviness in this area of the soul.

Image/Imagination.

Your spirit-man is the part of you that identifies with God. The nature that God creates in your spirit is also from God. Therefore, imagination or eye of the mind is also how you picture yourself based on what the Word of God says about you. This picture can be distorted by listening to the lies of Satan or by what you focus on, negatively or positively. The imagination involves thoughts that are framed or formed in the mind or soul. If the picture frame does not line up with what God's Word tells us, we are to cast it down or discard it (2 Corinthians 10:5). Imagination lives forever.

Intellect/personality/intelligence.

What God has gifted you with that can be trained or developed? What has God given you that makes you different from anyone else? The plan and purpose that God made you for can be destroyed, killed, or stolen, if you allow it. This part of your soul needs to be guarded very carefully with the Word of God. Definition: Intellect/ reasoning, personality/character/reputation, intelligence/ability to learn.

Will.

The will is influenced by choice. You can use your will to operate in any area of your soul. It is the "command post" of your soul. The place where a man's free will ceases to operate is in Hell. The only operator of your will in the earth is you. God, Satan, and people can only influence your will. This area of man's soul can choose to accept or reject eternal life given by God as his final destiny.

Memory.

Recall of good or bad experiences, negative or positive events and information that can be conscious or subconscious. Subconscious memories, which may be past involvement that are still affecting your behavior/soul negatively such as being in the occult, psychic reading, horoscope, witchcraft, evil spirit transfer from articles, objects worn, family history of drug dealing, gangbanging, gambling, incest, all kinds of abuse, prolong grief, and every familiar spirit. Do not continue to let the devil condemn you of the past in the memories of your mind. Replaying those sinful memories will allow Satan to hold you as his captive. Tear down every dead memory of the mind and allow Jesus Christ and His blood to heal it. Allow Him to wash away those sinful and bad memories that traumatized and wounded your soul.

Mind.

Thought/thinking/reasoning/perception/conscious/unconscious/subconscious. The saved mind should seek to know God in all of these compartments.

They should all line up, having the same knowledge of God. You can change the old, satanic nature of your thoughts by programming them with the Word of God and meditating on it. Meditation gives the mind the power, or the anointing power of the Holy Spirit, to believe God's Word. Believing will cause action on your part, which can be doing, decreeing, or confessing. Acting on the Word of God, however you received it, is faith. Hebrews 11:6 (NKJV) states, "But without faith it is impossible to please Him." "Now the just shall live by faith [or the Word of God]" (Hebrews 10:38) (Joshua 1:8, Hebrews 4:12, 2 Corinthians 10:5).

It is every person's responsibility to keep watch over all compartments of their own souls/ mind and guard it and cultivate it with God's Word. Adam was told to tend, meaning to cultivate and keep, the garden of Eden (Genesis 2:15), but he allowed Satan to enter and deceive.

Do not allow Satan to enter your soul/ mind, because he will enter and cultivate or plant weeds of deceitful, and wicked words that are not of God. Satan uses these sins to give you a sick, dark mind and body. The mind is the center of thought, intellect, sanity, memory, opinion, intention, and motive in the area of your soul.

You must get rid of sinful, negative thoughts that you allow in your mind with the blood of Jesus Christ: "To Him who loved us and washed us from our sins in his own blood" (Revelation 1:5b NKJV). Use the blood of Christ to wash any sin seeds that Satan planted in your soul, along with speaking the Word of God, which is spirit and life (John 6:63). Second Timothy 1:7 (NKJV) states, "God has not given us a spirit of fear, but of power and of love and of a *sound mind*." Use this scripture and others to renounce and curse all the roots of fear, intimidation, lack of confidence, shyness, doubt, unbelief, failure, poverty, and a host of others. Then, the power of the Holy Spirit will raise your soul up out of the darkness in your mind. Command them to dry up and die. Bind them, cast them out, and command them to go into the depths of the sea in the name of Yeshua, Jesus Christ.

Keep [guard] your heart [soul] with all diligence [watchfulness]. For out of it springs the issues of life [instructions from God for your life] (Proverbs 4:23 NKJV).

For the Word of God is living and powerful, and sharper than any two-edged sword, piercing even the division of the soul and spirit, and joints and marrow, and is a discerner of the thoughts and intent of the heart (Hebrews 4:12 NKJV).

Deception is the *only* weapon that Satan has to use against mankind: suggestive thoughts of the mind and imagination. He influences one to speak and act upon those thoughts. "Then the serpent said to the woman, "You will not surely die. For God knows that in the day you eat of it your eyes will be opened, and you will be like God, knowing good and evil" (Genesis 3:4–5 NKJV). Eve, in Genesis 3:6, acted on suggestive, imaginative words that had no truth to it. The only thing that the fruit from the tree could do was to make her belly full or ache if she ate too much of it. She saw (imagined: "Lust of her eyes") "the tree was good for food" pleasant to (her) eyes, a tree desirable to make one (her) wise. After the serpent's deceptive suggestions were made, Eve then acted upon his words. Jesus Christ said, "My sheep hear my voice, and I know them, and they follow me" (John 10:27 NKJV).

The spirit of deception must be cast down. If one believes Satan's lies, the picture that is formed in the imagination is going to be a lie. Rebuke Satan's deceiving lies and every high thing (of this mind controlling/lying spirit) *"that exalts itself against the knowledge of God, bringing every thought into captivity to the obedience of Christ"* (2 Corinthians 10:5 NKJV).

Satan's words are not based on truth, but on one's unrealistic imagination. The mind submitted to the words of Satan can become anti-God or anti-Christ. It can even declare that there is a creator other than God, there is no God, and that the human race came from the animal kingdom. Only Satan, the god of lies, could put these blinders/lies in man's mind. "We are certain we come from God and the rest of the world is under the power of the devil" (1 John 5:19 CEV). Be in control of your mind and body with the Word of God and do not follow after Satan's deceptions and be destroyed. Proverbs 10:9 (NKJV) states, "He who walks with integrity walks securely, But he who perverts his ways [with perverted, evil lies, wickedness, filthy abominable thoughts, lifestyle because Satan is all of these] will be known."

Do not love the world or the things in the world. If anyone loves the world, the love of the Father is not in him. For all that is in the world—the *lust of the flesh* [strong craving/desires of the body], the *lust of the eye* (strong craving/desires of the mind, thought, imagination/false pictures, impressions in the mind outside of the will of God), and the pride of life—(what is idolized or worshiped, false, fake, unreal man-made gods or mind images) is not of the Father but is of the world" (Satan) (1 John 2:15–16 NKJV).

Worship of idols, statues, pictures, or man-made images are not of God. They are not living and are lifeless. There is no power or authority in them that is of God. Evil powers of Satan and his demons can operate through these objects.

Therefore, renounce, destroy, and get rid of these items and materials that evil spirits may possess. You must never bow down or pray to statues and images.

All throughout this book, I have explained that man is made in the image of God who is Spirit. He is not in a pretty statue hanging on a wall, in sticks, stones, wood, worldly possessions, people, animals, money, or a job. You enjoy the beautiful world God created and the things in it, but He wants you to worship Him, the Eternal Almighty God only. The spirit of God is in Born-Again man's spirit, those who received Jesus Christ/Yeshua as their Lord and Savior.

Greater is He that is in you [the spirit of Jesus Christ] than he that [the devil or things] is in the world (1 John 4:4 KJV).

The idols of the nations are silver and gold, The work of men's hands. They have mouths, but they do not speak; Eyes they have, but they do not see; They have ears, but they do not hear; Nor is there any breath in their mouths. Those who make them are like them; So is everyone who trusts in them (Psalm 135:15–18 NKJV).

Religions and Organizations

Christ is the Head of His Church, which is also called the Body of Christ. Every righteous, Born-Again person is in Christ Jesus and makes up the membership in His body. "And He put all things under His feet, and gave Him to be the head over all things to the church, which is His body" (Ephesians 1:22–23 NKJV). This congregation of Believers are holy unto the Almighty, their Father. His presence dwells in them; they are the temple of the Holy Spirit. "Do you not know that you are the temple of God and that the Spirit of God dwells in you?" (1 Corinthians 3:16 NKJV). God is no longer behind a veil, in a man-made tabernacle or temple, on top of a box called the Ark of the Covenant as He was in Old Covenant days, where He dwelt among the people. Jesus Christ's coming to earth implemented the New Covenant where God's Spirit and man's spirit do not have to be separated because of man's sin nature from Adam. The Spirit of God, the Holy Spirit's presence, now dwells in the Born-Again spirit. The Believer's purpose in going to a building is to assemble, worship, and fellowship with other Believers because they have the same Savior. Christ is the founder of His church, which is His Body of Born-Again Believers, who received Him as their Savior because of His shed blood. Man-made religion is not founded on Jesus Christ's blood, but in man's handed-down historical traditions or cultural beliefs. You are not a Baptist, a Catholic, or a Presbyterian, which is the name of the building or the organized assembly. You are a member of Jesus Christ's body of Believers on earth when you received Jesus Christ. You should follow only after His scriptural doctrines that are founded on God the Father, God the Son [who is Jesus Christ], and God the Holy Spirit.

If you do not have a Bible that is about God the Father, God the Son/Word/ Jesus Christ, and God the Holy Spirit, get one so you can read it for yourself. Become filled with the Holy Spirit, your Helper from God, who will teach you His Word. The whole earth is asking, "When will the redeemed in Christ's Church become a united Body in Christ instead of fragmented member parts, so that the earth can be redeemed from mankind's curse that it is still under?" It too is awaiting the return of the Savior. Christ already declared His body complete in Him in Colossians 2:10, with no fragments, and His Word never changes. "For we know that the whole creation groans and labors with birth pangs together until now" (Romans 8:22 NKJV).

Organized, man-made religions are not founded on the truth of who Jesus Christ is. He is God who came to earth as a man, shed His blood, and died on a cross. His body was placed in a tomb, His Spirit went into Hell for Adam's/mankind's sin, and was taken out of Hell and the grave by God His Father. God then gave Him a resurrected body that can never die again. He is now seated at the right hand of God, His Father.

Man-made, counterfeit religions, which have been placed in the minds of men by Satan, can never claim to have done what Jesus Christ did. Christians, Born-Again Believers in Jesus Christ, now remember Him and what He did by partaking in communion together. This is represented by the cup at communion, which is symbolic of the blood of Jesus Christ and the broken bread, the body of Jesus Christ. This relationship is built on better terms and conditions, which is love. Christ, being the Head of His body of Believers, brings oneness and closeness into this relationship. Before His sacrifice, mankind was under constant punishment for sin. Now, the shed blood of Christ gives forgiveness from Adam's sin nature and when we sin individually. Therefore, organized religion is not about what was done for them. It is about man's performance, works, rituals, and self-effort to accomplish the unrealistic. It is man climbing up a ladder and never reaching the top. He is always striving, but never attaining because his religion may have thousands, if not millions of gods to please.

A relationship with Christ is not about giving a statue some fruit, which it cannot eat. It is knowing that we are the healed, the wealthy, the blessed, and the eternally forgiven. We do not have to be mean and hateful anymore because the satanic nature in us died and returned to Hell. We are now resurrected in peace, joy, love, and kindness. We do not have to be "wanna be gods." We are gods, made in God's image. John 10:34b and Psalms 82:6 (NKJV) states, "You are gods."

The cup of blessing which we bless, is it not the communion of the blood of Christ? The bread which we break, is it not the communion of the body of Christ? For we, though many, are one bread and one body; for we all partake of that one bread (1 Corinthians 10:16–17 NKJV).

The Spirit of Man Versus the Soul of Man

The spirit of a Born-Again Believer in Jesus Christ receives what is called the nature of the Spirit of God into his/her spirit after becoming a Believer in Christ, much like the fruit on a mango tree will be mangoes and not oranges. Therefore, the mango tree produces mango fruit that belongs to the mango tree. Believers/Christians say that God is righteous and that they are His righteousness. God is Truth and Goodness. These are all attributes or the nature of God. Out of those God attributes come (Galatians 5:22 NKJV), "Love, joy, goodness, long-suffering, kindness, faithfulness, gentleness, self-control," which Christians receive because they are now born from God.

When I give someone some money, that money is now that person's property. A Believer now has to learn how to live out of his God-given spirit and eat those fruits, of love, joy, etc., instead of the soul's fruit of lies, hate, and worry. To do that, the Believer has to nourish the "fruit" of his spirit—love, joy, peace, kindness, etc.—with the Word of God. Remember, the soul is carnal or worldly and has been under Satan's influence and training for all that person's life. In order for a Christian's spirit to receive the food of the Word of God, it has to pass through the soul —mind/thought, reasoning, intellect, will, and emotion of this man. For example, when you eat, in order for the food to get to your stomach, it has to first go into your mouth. Your body is going to now depend on what is placed into your mouth. The nutrition your body receives comes from the nutrition your body digests. As a Born-Again Believer, your spirit depends upon the truth of God's Word placed in it. You now have to feed/water the fruit in your spirit or the nature you received from God with His Word on love, peace, joy, faith/faithfulness, self-control, kindness, long-suffering/patience, goodness, and gentleness in order to bear more fruit. Remember, you are not a soul; you are a spirit. You have a soul in a body. Your spirit must be able to dominate your mind or thinking in the mental/soul realm with the Word of God or scriptures. You feed your spirit on the Word of God, which is now your spirit's diet. This will also nourish your soul. Change starts from the inside of your spirit, where the Word of God you have meditated on is. Then your mind will start to change and conform to those words. If not, the "junk words" Satan feeds your soul will take over, leaving your spirit empty. This will cause you to gravitate to the old nature, which is cursing and arguing. Remember, you are now who Jesus Christ is: love, peace, joy, and kindness. You are not the nature or attributes from your soul; you have them, but you are not them.

You are not an emotion from your soul. You have emotions/feelings. Satan can rule your emotions with spirits of heaviness, sadness, anger, and fear, which are his nature, if you do not meditate on love, joy, kindness, gentleness, peace, and goodness. Find scriptures in the Word of God that matches the fruit that you want to increase/improve in your Born-Again spirit and meditate on them, which should be the Fruit of the Spirit. For peace, Isaiah 26:3 (NKJV) states, "You will keep him in perfect peace, Whose mind is stayed on You, Because he trusts in You." Instead of meditating on the mean nature of Satan that you once possessed, meditate on God's Word and your life will be less stressful. You are a spirit, and whatever the Word of God says your spirit is, that is what you are. In your soul you possess a will/choice, imagination, memory, personality/intellect. Your spirit must rule these with the Word of God. Meditate also on scriptures to increase/improve the fruit of your spirit in faithfulness, long-suffering, and self-control. Your soul/body will become less irritated, touchy, sensitive, offended, nervous, fretful, selfish, to the negatives of life.

Do not allow these spirits to operate in your soul; these are sins that will pull you deeper and deeper into their torments and spirits of darkness.

They may end up controlling your soul and body with addictions and ungodly habits or desires. Become more grateful, a praiser, and a worshiper. You will become pleasant, kind, thankful, peaceful, patient, loving, forgiving, faithful, and trusting.

Remember to get your soul healed if you have been operating in any form of sin. Sin wounds the soul and gives Satan a foothold to cause your mind or body sickness. You will have to repent of your actions, words, and deeds done in the soul, whether it is gossip or backbiting.

Confessing scriptures may have a more difficult fight in an evil soul. You gave Satan and demons the right or authority to devour you by engaging in these sins. Therefore, when you cast his spirits out, they do not have to leave. Get the evil out of your soul that you have entertained first with repenting and forgiving others if this applies. "Nor do they put new wine into old wineskins, or else the wineskins break, the wine is spilled and the wineskin are ruined. But they put new wine into new wineskins, and both are preserved" (Matthew 9:17 NKJV).

You may wonder why your healing and prosperity scriptures are not being easily and immediately fulfilled in your life. You may need to ask God to *first* "wash me thoroughly from my inequity, And cleanse me from my sin" (Psalm 51:2 NKJV). "You gave your mouth to evil, And your tongue frames deceit. You sit and speak against your brother; You slander your own mother's son. These things you have done, and I have kept silent; You thought that I was altogether like you; But I will rebuke you…" (Psalm 50:19–21 NKJV).

Whether someone did you evil or you did evil, repent, change, and forgive. Dark spirits can not stay in a healed soul. Apply the blood of Jesus Christ to that sin in your soul. Then ask the Holy Spirit to replace hate with love. Bind the spirit of hate and cast it out.

Meditate on the following scripture and others like these for your spirit-man to grow in the Word of God. This will also heal your soul as you meditate on these: peace, love, joy, and goodness.

Do not sorrow, for the *joy* of the Lord is your strength (Nehemiah 8:10 NKJV).

And on her tongue is the law of **kindness** (Proverbs 31:26 NKJV).

Love your enemies, bless those who curse you, do **good** to those who hate you, and pray for those who spitefully use you and persecute you (Matthew 5:44 NKJV).

To speak no evil of no one, to be **peaceable**, **gentle**, showing all humility to all men (Titus 3:2 NKJV).

He who is **faithful** in what is least is faithful also in much; and he who is unjust in what is least is also \in much (Luke16:10 NKJV).

Strengthened with all might, according to all glorious power, for all **patience** and **long suffering** with *joy* (Colossians 1:11 NKJV).

Whoever has no rule over (**self-control**) over his own spirit /(soul) is like a city broken down, without walls (Proverbs 25:28 NKJV).

He who is slow to anger is better than the mighty, And he who **rules** (**has self-control over**) his spirit/(soul) than he who takes a city (Proverbs 16:32 NKJV).

Lust! Taking Fire to Your Bosom!

Perverted, lustful desires are sins of the soul and flesh. The meaning of lust in the *Webster Dictionary* is "a strong sexual desire, a strong desire for power; feel an intense desire." A Believer should not "play" with this fire. Remember, as it has already been mentioned, the "cleaning up" of one's soul has to involve that person. In the chapter on "Deception," I dealt with 1 John 2:16 regarding the lust of the flesh, lust of the eye, and the pride of life. Here, I am dealing specifically with perverted, lustful, sexual desires.

As with all lustful desires, you will need to cleanse the body and soul by repenting of lust sins and by forgiving yourself and others of these sins if this is an issue. Then, use the blood of Jesus Christ to cleanse and heal the soul of these sins. Ask the Holy Spirit to raise you up out of this demonic darkness and then kick/cast that lustful spirit out of your soul in the name of Jesus Christ. Born-Again Believers have been given authority to use His name to cast out demons and devils. Satan can also deceive this person into thinking that this perverted spirit is their natural flesh reaction, but in reality, the flesh is reacting to what was already in the soul. A Son or Daughter of God should not allow a perverted, lust spirit to take up residence in their soul. A person who has a lust spirit may become attracted to another person who also has a perverted, lust spirit. Involving yourself with sins of lust gives Satan access to your soul, not your Born-Again spirit.

Lust sins in any part of the soul—mind, thought, imagination, memory, character, will/ desire emotion/feeling may give Satan legal rights and an open door to tempt one to fall into these sins of perverted lust simply by meditating on it. Jesus Christ said in Matthew 5:28 (NKJV), "But I say to you that whoever looks at a woman to lust for her has already committed adultery with her in his heart (soul)" [in the mind, thoughts, memories].

He also said "Casting down arguments (those reasonings, thoughts, images, idols) and every high thing that exalts itself against the knowledge of God, bringing every thought into captivity to the obedience of Christ" (2 Corinthians 10:5a NKJV). This could also be old files and records of your past, perverted lifestyle and sins that need to be destroyed in every compartment of your soul: mind, will, emotion, etc. Leviticus 17:11 (NKJV): "For the life of the flesh is in the blood, and I have given it to you upon the altar to make atonement [Old Testament uses the word "atonement", New Testament uses Jesus Christ's blood to cleanse/wash away soul sins] for your souls; for it is the blood that makes atonement/cover for your soul." For Born-Again Believers, Jesus's shed blood cleanses the soul, not covers it.

Jesus Christ's blood is the only blood that can get rid of and take away sins. Tell the devil your past record has been cleared by the blood of Jesus Christ. That file cabinet is empty. The album, tape, and CD are blank. Whenever the devil tempts you to return to that vomit—lustful thoughts, in order to use and abuse you, tell him there is no replay button on any of these devices. That was one of the reasons why Jesus Christ shed His blood. He knew the thief only wants to kill, steal, and destroy mankind (John 10:10).

Lust does not have to be sexual. It can be lust for food, alcohol, drugs, and all sorts of perversions. Lust in the soul can lead to idolatry: the worship of false, fictitious beliefs, made-up mental demonic lies, images, that may be sexual and perverted that have no foundation in truth. These are sins of the soul that need to be cleansed with the blood of Jesus Christ. If you never repented of these sins, do it. Remember, God already forgave you of all sins spiritually. However, your soul is not Born Again and therefore, needs to repent or change its mind, will, and emotions toward those sins. This is accomplished by meditating on the Word of God, which brings about change. Also, have the power of the Holy Spirit raise your soul out of this destruction in the name of Jesus Christ. God did His part when you became Born Again by removing the sin of mankind/Adam. If lust/ sex sins have been an addiction, you need to do a soul cleansing with the blood of Jesus Christ. His blood heals, delivers, and will set your soul and body free from every bondage, not just at Calvary's Cross, but during your lifetime.

When an alcoholic becomes Born Again, he goes into his/her liquor cabinet and pours the alcohol down the drain. As far as God is concerned, you are no longer an alcoholic. He has no spiritual record of it. However, your soul and your flesh will be tempted to take a drink if you keep the alcohol in the liquor cabinet. The mind/ memory needs to be renewed with the Word of God, but first, wash the lust sins from the soul with the cleansing, healing/ delivering blood of Jesus Christ.

Satan will tempt you to pull out those pictures and images in the memory of your mind. He will remind you of the "good old days." Tell him, God has forgotten them, so you can not remember what he is talking about. God has no account of your sins' past, present, or future. In the book of Ruth chapter 2, Ruth went to find fallen barley grain in the field of Boaz, a landowner, after the reapers found favor with her. He was kind and respectful to her because she was kind to her mother-in-law, Naomi, who was his deceased brother's wife. Boaz's brother had moved to the country of Moab with his wife, Naomi and their two sons. Naomi returned to Bethlehem with Ruth because her husband and their two sons, one of whom was Ruth's husband, died. In Ruth 2:12 (NKJV), Boaz said to Ruth, "The Lord repay your work, and a full reward be given you by the Lord God of Israel, under whose wings you have come for refuge."

"And now, my daughter, do not fear I will do for you all that you request, for all the people of my town know that you are a virtuous woman" Ruth 3:11(NKJV).

Virtuous means moral excellence in soul: mind, thought, motive, will, and emotion. Being virtuous should be a Christian's lifestyle in soul and body. Christians should want to please God morally. Lust sins in the soul and flesh may lead to an immoral life or unholy attractions. Satan's deception labels lust for love, which becomes provocative/tempting and seductive. *Webster's Dictionary* defines seductive as: to seduce into sexual intercourse. A person that allows him/herself to become deceived by these demonic spirits may become selfish by turning their back on the truth of God's Words that they once embraced. However, there is no sin so deep that Jesus Christ cleansing and forgiving blood cannot redeem you from because of His love for you.

In the Old Testament, it was a close relative's responsibility to redeem what belonged to a deceased or poor blood relative (Ruth 2:20, Lev. 25:25, 48–49). Noami told Ruth to ask Boaz to purchase his deceased brother's field. Along with that purchase, he would be redeeming all that had belonged to the deceased owner to preserve the family name (Ruth 4:4:10). Boaz redeemed his deceased brother's property and with that purchase, he also redeemed his deceased nephew's wife Ruth, whom he married.

Jesus Christ purchased and redeemed each of us, who were dead because of sin. He redeemed us, not with money, but purchased us with His own sacrificial blood. That's true, deep, indescribable love!

He who covers his sins will not prosper, But whoever confesses and forsakes them will have mercy (Proverbs 28:13 NKJV).

Can a man/*woman* take fire to his/her bosom, And his/her clothes not be burned? Can one walk on hot coals, And his/*her* feet not be seared? (Proverbs 6:27–28 NKJV)

Whoever commits adultery with a woman lacks understanding; He who does so destroys his own soul (Proverbs 6:32 NKJV).

The Brazen Altar in the Old Testament and the Altar of the Cross in the New Testament

The Altar of Burnt Sacrifice or Offering called a Brazen Altar or Bronze Altar was a place of slaughter upon which sin offerings or blood sacrifices were done. The lives of animals were sentenced to die upon the Brazen Altar, in exchange for a person or a nation having sinned. The Brazen Altar was located in the Courtyard of the Wilderness Tabernacle. Here the people of God brought their animals to be sacrificed. These sacrificial offerings were brought to the priests, who slaughtered the animals to atone or cover sin. Only the death of a perfect, innocent substitute could appease God's wrath on sin. God, who is the righteous judge must render judgment on sin. This is how God reconciled man for having sinned in Old Testament times. He allowed the sacrificing of animals and the blood shed to bear the penalty of that person's sin every time he or she sins and yearly for the nation. To rebel and disobey God was a deadly, serious sin.

The cross of Jesus, was a lifted up Altar made out of wood from a tree. This was the place where He was put to death for the sin of mankind. The Brazen Altar of the Old Covenant was made out of acacia wood, which was symbolic and a foreshadowing of the Cross of Jesus. To cut a divine blood covenant or (*karat birit* in Hebrew) is more than an agreement. It is a binding, irrevocable promise or decision, that may not be altered. That was the covenant blood sacrifice that Jesus entered into with God. This kind of covenant goes into effect when the sacrificed animal or person dies, shedding blood. Hebrew 9:22 (NKJV) says, "Without the shedding of blood there is no remission of sin." Jesus allowed our sin to put Him to death. Whenever man disobeys God, that sin must be judged with death, but only an innocent, sinless substitute could be used to forgive and dismiss this death sentence. The binding, irrevocable promise of Jesus to God to take on man's sin was displayed on a lifted up altar called a cross. Jesus Christ was the perfect sacrifice. Therefore, there is no further need for any other sacrifice for sin. Hebrews 10:10 (NIV) "...We have been made holy through the sacrifice of the body of Jesus Christ once and for all." Now we have eternal redemption from sin.

The Brazen Altar that innocent animals were sacrificed on was not capable of redeeming mankind. Only another man's sinless, innocent blood that cried out mercy for the sinner and not judgement could redeem mankind. "Not the blood of goats and calves, but with His (Jesus') on blood. He entered the Most Holy Place once and for all, having obtained eternal redemption" (Hebrews 9:12 NKJV).

The Altar of the cross upon which Jesus was sacrificed, made it possible for God and Jesus to make Covenant. "You have come Jesus, the one who meditates the new covenant between God and people, and sprinkled the blood, which speaks better of forgiveness instead of crying out vengeance like the blood of Abel" (Hebrews 12:24 NLT). Jesus's sacrifice and the blood He shed on the Altar of the cross speaks and cries out for better things which are: salvation, mercy, love, grace, healing, forgiveness, protection, and provision for everyone.

The Lord's Coming for His Followers

My friends, we want you to understand how it will be for those followers who have already died. Then you will not grieve over them and be like people who don't have any hope. We believe that Jesus died and was raised to life. We also believe that when God brings Jesus Christ back again, He will bring with Him all who had faith in Jesus before they died. Our Lord Jesus told us that when He comes, we won't go up to meet Him ahead of His followers who have already died. With a loud command with the shout of the chief angel and a blast of God's trumpet, the Lord will return from heaven. Then those who had faith in Christ before they died will be raised to life. Next, all of us who are still alive will be taken up into the clouds together with them to meet the Lord in the sky. From that time on we will all be with the Lord forever. Encourage each other with these words...I do not need to write you about the time or date when all this will happen. You surely know that the Lord's return will be as a thief coming at night. People will think they are safe and secure. But destruction will suddenly strike them like the pains of a woman about to give birth. And they won't escape. My dear friends, you don't live in darkness, and so that day won't surprise you as a thief (1 Thessalonians 4:13–18, 5:14 CEV).

Evil in the Earth: How Did This Come About?

Satan was originally Lucifer in heaven. He was an angel who rebelled against God and was kicked out of heaven. According to Luke 10:18 (NKJV), "Jesus [Christ] said, 'I saw Satan fall like lightning from heaven.'" Isaiah 14:12–15 (NKJV) gives an account of Lucifer's fall:

How you are fallen from heaven, O Lucifer, son of the morning! How you are cut to the ground, You who weakened the nations! For you have said in your heart: "I will ascend into heaven, I will exalt my throne above the stars of God; I will also sit on the mount of the congregation On the farthest sides of the north; I will ascend above the heights of the clouds; I will be like the Most High." Yet you shall be brought down to Sheol *or Hell* to the lowest depths of the Pit.

Satan's Purpose on Earth

Satan is a thief. His primary purpose on earth, as Jesus Christ states, is to kill you, steal from you, and destroy you (John 10:10 paraphrased). He wants to wrongly influence your purpose and the reasons you were placed here in the earth by God. He hates man with a deep, deep hatred. He goes about looking for people to devour according to Job 2:3 (NKJV), which states, "And the Lord said to Satan, 'From where do you come?' Satan answered the Lord and said, 'From going to and fro on the earth, and from walking back and forth in it.'" "Be on your guard and stay awake. Your enemy, the devil, is like a roaring lion [meaning he is a hungry prowler] sneaking around to find someone to attack. But you must resist the devil and stay strong in your faith" (1 Peter 5:8 CEV) by believing in God and believing His Word.

Remember, Satan is the manager of this earth. This management job and position was handed over to him by Adam. God is not the manager, but He is the owner of the earth. Satan, being the manager, is the reason why the operation of the world is so chaotic, unjust, cruel, wicked, evil, and unfair. However, a Believer's prayer can override Satan's management because through Jesus Christ, they (the Born-Again, spirit-filled, praying-in-tongues Believers) can regain power, authority, and dominion over the satanic powers that rule the earth.

"We know that we are of God, and the whole world lies under the sway of the wicked one [Satan]" (1 John 5:19 NKJV). We are in Him who is true, His Son Jesus Christ. This is the true God and eternal life.

Hell

This is a real place, *reserved* for the devil and his fallen angels. "Then He will also say to those on the left hand, 'Depart from Me, you cursed, into the everlasting fire prepared for the devil and his angels'" (Matthew 25:41 NKJV). Satan and his fallen angels are in the world plotting destruction, evil, and wickedness. They are not in Hell yet. Satan can be described as the following:

Satan is the prince of the power of the air [atmosphere above the earth] (Ephesians 2:2).

Jesus Christ said, "Satan is the ruler of this world" [world systems] (John 12:31, John 14:30, John 16:11 NKJV).

"The god of this age [present world]" (2 Corinthians 4:4 NKJV).

"Leader of: host of wickedness, principalities, ruler of the darkness of this age" (Ephesians 6:12 NKJV).

The father of lies and a murderer (John 8:44 NKJV).

The serpent of old, which deceives the whole world (Revelation 12:9 NKJV).

Tempter of mankind (Matthew 4:3, 1 Thessalonians 3:5 NKJV).

Ruler of demons (Matthew 9:34, 12:24, Mark 3:22, Luke 11:15 NKJV).

Enemy (Matthew 13:39 NKJV).

Wicked one (Matthew 13:38 NKJV).

An accuser (Revelation 12:10 NKJV).

Adversary (1 Peter 5:8 NKJV).

Can appear as "an angel of light" to deceive (2 Corinthians 11:14 NKJV).

Leader of demons to inflict diseases, bondages, and possesses people (Matthew 17:14–18, Luke 13:18–32, Luke 22:3 NKJV).

This is what the angel said that was returning to earth with the answer to Daniel's prayer request: "But the prince of the kingdom of Persia withstood me twenty-one days; and behold, Michael, [that is God's archangel, or God's warring angel] one of the chief princes, came to help me" (Daniel 10:13 NKJV). There was a demonic spirit called a principality in the atmosphere influencing the rulership over the country of Persia.

Hell is a place prepared for Satan and his fallen angels or demons. "And the angels who did not keep their proper domain, but left their own abode, He has reserved in everlasting chains under darkness for the judgment of the great day" (Jude 1:6 NKJV). "For if God did not spare the angels who sinned, but cast them down to Hell and delivered them into chains of darkness, to be reserved for judgment" (2 Peter 2:4 NKJV). These are angels (not Satan's fallen group) that are already in Hell. However, the spirits of those who reject or refuse to receive Jesus Christ will go to Hell after they die. The final destination for anyone not written in the Book of Life is the Lake of Fire and Brimstone. The final destination for Satan and his demons, is the Lake of Fire and Brimstone. The final destination for Death, Hades, or Hell is the Lake of Fire and Brimstone forever and all of the above will be cast into it (Revelation 20: 14–15 NKJV).

A View Into Hell

Hell is centered in the heart of the earth. The earth opened up and swallowed the men that rebelled against Moses. "And the earth opened its mouth and swallowed them up, with their households… So they and all those with them went down alive into the pit; the earth closed over them" (Numbers 16:32–33 NKJV). Hell, also called Sheol or the pit, is described as a hole, a dungeon, or a place for the departed who have chosen the way of evil. These are the ones whose physical bodies perished, but their spirits are still alive in Hell, a place where the Spirit of God is not. Among hell occupants are: Hate bitterness, anger, blasphemy, and terror, which are evil, wicked spirits.

Hell has compartments. God speaks of Satan, "Yet you shall be brought down to Sheol, To the lowest depths of the Pit" (Isaiah 14:15 NKJV). This prison, as it is also called, cannot be compared to any prison in the entire world. Jonah prayed to God from a great "fish's" belly that swallowed him and said, "The earth with its bars closed behind me" (Jonah 2:6 NKJV). "As prisoners are gathered in the pit, And will be shut up in the prison" (Isaiah 24:22 NKJV). "Her house is the way to hell, Descending to the chambers of death" (Proverbs 7:27 NKJV). Hell is a prison with chambers and gates. "Will they go down to the gates of Sheol [or Hell]?" (Job 17:16 NKJV). Jesus Christ also said, "The gates of Hell shall not prevail against it [the church]" (Matthew 16:18b KJV). "I shall go to the gates of Sheol" (Isaiah 38:10a KJV).

There is only pain, trouble, and sorrow in Hell. Psalm 116:3–4 (NKJV) states, "The pains of death surrounded me, And the pangs [distresses] or grief of Sheol laid hold of me; I found trouble and sorrow."

Hell's fire is never quenched. It is a pit with everlasting, raging fire. Jesus Christ said, "If your hand causes you to sin, cut it off. It is better for you to enter into life maimed, rather than having two hands, to go to Hell, into the fire that shall never quenched—where their worm does not die" (Mark 9:43–44a NKJV). This is so severe. Jesus Christ gave three different examples and repeated, "where their worm does not die and the fire is not quenched." "And those who forsake the Lord shall be consumed" (Isaiah 1:28 NKJV). "In flaming fire taking vengeance on those who do not know God, and on those who do not obey the gospel of our Lord Jesus Christ. These shall be punished with everlasting destruction from the presence of the Lord and from the glory of His power" (2 Thessalonians 1:8–9 NKJV).

David states in Psalm 86:12–13 (NKJV), "I will praise You, O Lord my God, with all my heart, And I will glorify Your name forevermore. For great is Your mercy towards me, And You have delivered my soul from the depths of Sheol." "Death cannot praise You; Those who go down to the pit cannot hope for Your truth. The living, the living man, he shall praise You" (Isaiah 38:18–19 NKJV).

The Word of God is not preached in Hell. It is surrounded by and full of cruelty and wickedness. "When the waves of death surrounded me, The floods of ungodliness made me afraid. The sorrows of Sheol surrounded me; The snares of death confronted me" (2 Samuel 22:5 NKJV).

Life is no more. It does not exist in Hell because God is not there. "I shall not see Yah, The Lord in the land of the living; I shall observe man no more among the inhabitants of the world. My life span is gone" (Isaiah 38:11–12 NKJV). "You have laid me in the lowest pit, In darkness, in the depths" (Psalm 88:6 NKJV). There is no rest for the wicked (Isaiah 57:21) nor is there any water, not even a drop. Zechariah 9:11 calls Hell the waterless pit. The thirst for water is forever. When the rich man in

Luke 16 died and went to Hell, he begged for a drop of water from the tip of Lazarus the beggar's finger.

Torment ascends forever and ever. The screams of tormented, lost spirits continue forever and ever. They have no rest day or night. There is no peace or quietness for the wicked. Isaiah 38 states that in Hell the eyes fail for looking upward; there is mourning, oppression, and bitterness of soul. Hell is the pit of corruption.

This is indeed a place of everlasting torment where there is no lovingkindness nor is there any declaring of God's faithfulness in this land of destruction; His righteousness is not in the land of forgetfulness (Psalm 88:10–12). "There will be weeping and gnashing of teeth" (Matthew 8:12 NKJV). "So it will be at the end of the age. The angels will come forth, separate the wicked from among the just, and cast them into the furnace of fire. There will be wailing and gashing of teeth" (Matthew 13:49–50 NKJV). "If your right eye causes you to sin, pluck it out and cast it from you; for it is more profitable for you that one of your members perish, than for the whole body to be cast into hell" (Matthew 5:29 NKJV).

Hell is an eternal place of damnation. God paid a great, great, price to keep man out of there. He gave up everything in order that man would not have to choose to go there.

Jesus Christ, God's Son, experienced for you the burning, roasting fire of Hell, the worms that never die, the pitch darkness, the torment, fear, agony, and thirst so that you would not have to experience it, and furthermore, He came out of it victoriously for your sake.

If you have read this book and you still have not made the decision to give your life to Christ, call upon the name of the Lord while there is still the opportunity to do so on earth to deliver your spirit and soul from going to Hell.

Jesus Christ said, "I am He who lives, and was dead, and behold, I am alive forevermore. Amen. And I have the keys of Hades/Hell and Death" (Revelation 1:18 NKJV). Jesus Christ has the keys of Hades/

Hell and Death. Satan no longer has the power to separate you from God, which is being spiritually dead and going to Hell. Now you have a choice.

Who will you choose, Jesus Christ or Satan?

Jesus Christ wants you to roar and cheer with exceeding gladness when He returns to earth. The Lord Jesus Christ said, "Surely I am coming quickly" (Revelation 22:20b NKJV).

And this gospel of the kingdom will be preached in all the world as a witness to all the nations, and then the end will come (Matthew 24:14 NKJV).

Telling Others the Good News, Your Mandate from Jesus Christ!

Jesus Christ's purpose in your life, the Born-Again Believer, is to save people from perishing in Hell because of mankind's sin nature. Believers are responsible for telling others about what God has to offer them through the work of His Son Jesus Christ. This includes His death, burial, resurrection, ascension back to Heaven, and seating at the right hand of God. This victory redeems them from spiritual death and Hell's destruction because Jesus took their place and received their death penalty instead. Therefore, as a believer, you are confident that your salvation is already secure in Christ and you are Heaven-bound. However, do not be complacent and so preoccupied with daily activities of life that you forget to go into all the world and preach the Gospel/Good News of Jesus Christ to others as He commanded. For instance, a person who drives a bus picks up passengers in order to take them to their destination. A bus driver is not expected to drive into town without picking up any passengers. As a believer, you must not "drive" into Heaven with an "empty passenger bus." My advice to believers is, do not spend your time on this earth only thinking about your own eternal salvation. Drive into Heaven with a full passenger bus, filled with people you have led to Christ.

In your lifetime, you will encounter many potential passengers who are Hell-bound. They are flagging you down hoping you will stop and pick them up so that they too can board the Heaven-bound bus you are driving. However, you always give excuses as to why you can never stop to share the gospel, the good news about a savior, who can change their tickets headed to a Hell-bound destination.

Now it is time for you to leave earth and "drive your empty passenger bus" into Heaven. When you have reached Heaven, your final destination, Jesus Christ will look into your passenger vehicle and see that you have no passengers. Before He can say anything, you stretch out your hand and ask for your reward. He looks at it and says to you, "It is not yet time for me to give out rewards to all those who obey My Commands to share My Gospel. Did you?" You say to Him, "I go to church every Sunday, Jesus." He replied, "Devils go to church every Sunday too." You say to yourself, "I did not convince Him." Then you say to Him, "I pay tithes and give offerings." He said, "Devils give tithes and offerings also." He then says to you, "Devils can not share Me with people. Sharing the Good News with others of what I have done for them is My Command to you. Did you tell anyone about Me?" You reply, "No, Savior, I did not tell a soul about You. I was too busy singing in the choir, teaching Sunday school, playing the organ, and being at Bible study on Wednesday nights." "Your service onto My Father is excellent, but you were not faithful in following My command to tell others about Me and the great price I paid for them. Step to my left, Gabriel (the messenger angel) will lead you to the results in your final report card." People of faith that have gone before us can not receive their reward at the end of *their* race until we finish *our* race (Hebrews 11:39 paraphrased). We will all receive our *rewards* at the same time for the Born-Again Believer's works in the earth. Therefore, let us run this race, carrying the baton that has been passed on to us to the finish line.

I told you this story to emphasize the importance of being faithful to obey Jesus Christ's command to "go into all the world and preach the Good News to everyone" (Mark 16:15 NLT). Peaching the Good News brings faith, [trust, truth, belief], which is a work of the Holy Spirit for people's unborn spirit to believe in Jesus Christ to become their Savior and Lord.

And behold, I am coming quickly, and My reward is with Me, to give to everyone according to his work (Revelation 22:12 NKJV).

Glossary

CREATE
Causing what did not exist to exist or bring into being (Colossians 1:16).

MANKIND
The human race or human from the first man, Adam.

HEART
Organ in the body, also used figuratively for the will, feeling, intellect, and the center of anything (according to Strong's Concordance). Center of anything can be called heart location, which is the midst, womb, core of the example—spirit, soul, mind, Hell.

SOUL
The *human* soul is sometimes used interchangeably with the *human* spirit. Both are immortal, but they are different and also different in their functions. Therefore, ask the Holy Spirit to differentiate when you read the Word of God. The soul consists of the mind, will, emotion, memory, intellect, personality, reasoning, thought, purpose, character, and imagination—which is the seat of consciousness, subconsciousness, conscience, or inner man."…For as he thinks in his heart, so is he. "Eat and drink!" he says to you, But his heart is not with you." (Proverbs 23:7 NKJV)"Let not your heart be troubled, you believe in God, believe also in Me" (John 14:1 NKJV). The word *heart* in these scriptures means soul, which has the mind.

THE HUMAN SPIRIT
The life that is within a person's body: the image of God, "the breath of God," the eternal part of man that looks like God, the word spirit of man is referred to as spirit in the Bible.

MIND
The reasoning, thinking part of a man that is in the soul. It is the window into the spiritual and natural world of man. The mind has to be trained to be disciplined in the negatives or the positives of life. "Let this mind be in you which was also in Christ Jesus" (Philippians 2:5 NKJV). Also called the inner man or the heart of man; the conscious and subconscious mind.

SERPENT
A large snake (Genesis 3:1).

SATAN
The chief of demons and evil spirit that tempts one to sin (Matthew 4:3).

JESHUA/YESHUA
The Hebrew name for Jesus, which means Savior

YESHUA
Jehovah/God is Savior/salvation: deliverance, safety, prosperity, liberty, saving, preservation.

GOD
Self-Existent, One Supreme Being, The Most High God: Creator of the heavens, earth, seas and all in them.

CHRIST
The Anointed One, the Messiah Hebrew—*Yeshua Hamashiyach*.

COMMUNION
Identifies Christians with Christ Jesus, by partaking of the bread symbolic of the body of Christ Jesus and the wine/ cup, symbolic of the

blood of our Lord Jesus. Remembering Christ's sacrifice and His birth in the earth, death, burial, resurrection, ascension to Heaven seating by the right hand of the Father God, and return to earth.

GRACE
Undeserved, unmerited favor, mercy, forgiveness, love, goodness, truth, and the supernatural abilities, capabilities, the era of salvation, love, and forgiveness is now in the earth because the Savor Jesus Christ came to pardon Mankind's sin and give salvation to those who receive Him.

RELIGION
False system of worship that is invented in the minds of men. Religions are forms of worship that are endorsed by Satan, not God. God tells man to worship Him only. Deuteronomy 5:6–9. He must not have any other gods/religions. To worship God you must have a relationship with Him: God the Father, God the Son who is the Word of God, who is Jesus Christ and God the Holy Spirit. For this to happen, you must come to Him, God through His Son, Jesus Christ/Yeshua, the Messiah, the Anointed One. The One God has ordained and anointed, by way of His birth, His death on the cross, being in Hell, resurrection from the dead, ascension to Heaven, and is now seated at the right hand of the Father, Almighty God, Creator of heaven and earth.

RESURRECTION
Rising from death to life again.

SALVATION EXPLAINED
The Word of God is Faith, that tells us the reason why it is necessary to get saved. Salvation Prayers should be based on biblical scriptures, for faith and belief in God to be created in the spirit of that man. For example: John 3:16 NKJV, "For God so loves the world, He gave His only Son, that whosoever believes in Him should not perish but have everlasting life."

All Five Fold Ministry Gifts: the pastor, teacher, preacher, apostle, prophet; evangelist should have knowledge of what they mean when an unbelievers is told to just surrender, or repent, these should be declared after receiving Jesus Christ Salvation not before. To repent and surrender is necessary for a sanctified or a set apart life to Christ Jesus. A sinner needs the Savior Christ Jesus first.

The Gospel Scriptures concerning the Good News of Jesus the Savior should be imparted. Jesus the Man and His blood shed on a lifted up cross or a lifted up altar are the only solutions that a sinner has and needs to terminate his sin to the core and send it away. Because the law of God states, "Without the shedding of blood, there is no remission (remitting of sin)."

Romans 5:12 NKJV tells the need for Salvation: "Therefore just as through one man sin entered the world, and death through sin, and thus death spread to all men because all men sinned."

The Holy Spirit is the One who draws or introduces an unbeliever by the preaching of the Word of God to receive Jesus. Therefore a person at any time can say: 'Jesus, I need You.' or ' I believe in You Jesus!

However, the Holy Spirit revelation of Jesus Christ can move through the spoken or written words. it is the Holy Spirit who introduces or reveals Jesus. Because the revelation of Jesus Christ is divine, supernatural, spiritual. A Minister, a friend, parent, teacher may be the vessel used to preach the Gospel- Jesus' Salvation to the hearer.

Surrendering must be scripturally biblical. The surrendering or submitting of a husband/ wife to each other happens after confessing their covenant marriage vows to each other.

Jesus gave an example of how to surrender in Luke 9:23 NKJV "If anyone desires to come after Me, let Him deny himself, and take up his cross and follow Me."

Carrying your cross will not be always easy, but a disciple in Jesus Christ's army learns to persevere with God's help, and to not give up fighting the good fight of faith with the Word of God. Stop by the "water well" to rest and witness to someone, like Jesus did, if you get too tired.

Salvation does not only saves and gives everlasting life. This gift from Jesus: delivers, protects, provides; heals the soul and body -Matt. 8:17. Romans 10:9-10 NKJV "If you confess with your mouth the Lord Jesus and believe in your heart that God has raised Him from the dead, you will be saved. For with the heart one believes unto righteousness and with the mouth confession is made unto salvation."

Confessing is saying the same words that God The Father says about Jesus Christ His Son. They entered into a blood covenant binding relationship and agreement to redeem man, from Satan sin. Jesus shed His own blood upon an altar or cross as His part of the covenant/agreement. He also made a covenant agreement with God which could not be changed to go to hell on behalf of man for man's sin. God The Father and Holy Spirit as a part of Their Covenant Agreement raised Jesus and out of hell after His mission to hell was accomplished.

Receiving Jesus Christ as your Owner and Savior and rejecting, renouncing the lordship of Satan must be accurately declared or spoken.

Confession spoken to receive Jesus Christ is not made to a priest or pastor but to God. Confessing Jesus to be your Lord and Savior are Covenant Words everlasting and binding. Jesus now becomes your Savior and Owner from that moment. All of Heaven and host of Heavenly Angels heard you, also hell and Satan and the Kingdom of darkness.

Preferred scripture: Romans 10:9-10 NKJV

Remember Your Salvation is a Gift: You cannot earn it: By being good or doing good deeds. Salvation is not earned, it is gift freely given, due to God's mercy, favor and grace through Faith or the Word of God and believing it.

Ephesians 2:8-9 NKJV states "For by grace you have been saved through faith and that not of yourselves; it is a gift of God not of works, lest anyone should boast."

John 1:12 NKJV states "But as many as received Him (Jesus Christ) to them He gave the right to be children of God, to those who believe in His name."

You are no longer a child of Satan but a Son of God. You can now call God Father and Jesus Christ Your Elder Brother.

Galatians 3:26 states "For you are all sons of God through faith in Christ Jesus. Through faith in the Word. Who is Jesus Christ, The Son of God."

Matthew 12:31 NKJV "Therefore I say to you, EVERY SIN and BLASPHEMY against the Holy Spirit will not be forgiven men."

Salvation Scriptures to receive Jesus Christ, Yeshua, the Messiah as Savior and Lord, Deliverer and Owner:

John 3:16 Act 4:12 Hebrews 2:3, Roman 5:12, Romans 10:9–10, Roman 5:17, Roman 1:6, John 5:24, John 3:3, Ephesians 2:8–9

Scriptures to be confident of your Salvation:

Ephesians 2:8–9, 2 Corinthians 5:17, 1 Corinthians 5:7, Romans 5:17, Romans 10:9–10, 1 John 1:5–9, Romans 8:12, 2 Corinthians 3:17

Scriptures to receive the infilling of the Holy Spirit with the evidence of speaking in tongues:

John 14: 16–21, 26, Luke 11:9–13, Acts 1:8, Acts 2:4, Act 10:44–46, Act 19:2–6, 1 Corinthians 14:2–4, 4–14

Featured Scriptures from the Bible

Jesus answered and said to him, "Most assuredly, I say to you, unless one is born again [this means the spirit of man is made new through Jesus Christ], He can not see the Kingdom of God. That which is born of the flesh is flesh, and that which is born of the Spirit is spirit" (John 3:3, 6 NKJV).

Nor is there salvation in any other, for there is no other name under heaven given among men by which we must be saved.(Acts 4:12 NKJV).

For God so loved the world that He gave His only begotten Son, that whoever believes in Him should not perish but have everlasting life (John 3:16 NKJV).

Therefore we were buried with Him through baptism into death, that just as Christ was raised from the dead by the glory of the Father, even so we also should walk in newness of life (Romans 6:4 NKJV).

How then shall they call on Him in whom they have not believed? And how shall they believe in Him of whom they have not heard? And how shall they hear without a preacher? And how shall they preach unless they are sent? As it is written: "How beautiful are the feet of those who preach the gospel of peace, Who bring glad tidings of good things!'" (Romans 10:14–15 NKJV)

Salvation Prayer

Dear God: You made me in your image (a spirit). You gave me a soul (mind, will, and emotions) and placed me in a body on the earth. Because Adam (the first man) sinned by refusing to believe and obey Your Word and heeding to Satan (the enemy's) word, all of mankind sinned and became separated from You and received eternal death. Therefore, when I die my spirit would go to the place of eternal punishment - Hell, a place that was prepared for Satan and his angels. However, You sent Jesus Christ, Your Son, as a Man like me but without sin to die on a cross and shed His blood to pardon, and cancel my sin because You said, "Without the shedding of blood, there could be no remission (remitting, cleansing or eradication) of sin" (Hebrews 9:2 NIV). In the Old Testament, the law of Moses required that nearly everything be cleansed with blood. Therefore, Jesus Christ's blood eliminated my sin as He took my punishment. I must now receive Jesus Christ, Your Son, as my Savior/Owner and Lord to receive eternal life. How can I do this? Romans 10:9 (NIV) says "If you declare with your mouth, "Jesus is Lord," and believe in your heart that God raised Him from the dead, you will be Saved. For it is with your heart (spirit/soul) that you believe and are justified (right with God or righteous) and it is with the mouth that you profess/say your faith belief and are saved. Therefore, I say with my mouth and believe in my heart-spirit/soul that Jesus Christ is the Son of the Living God, Who was sent by God to take my place in dying for my sin. He was raised again from death and hell, to eternal life and is now seated in Heavenly places. Therefore, I am raised to eternal life, like Jesus Christ was and

I am now seated with Him in Heavenly realms, according to Ephesians 2:6. I am now saved.

Thank you, Jesus, for my salvation, pardon, healing, deliverance, sound mind, preservation, protection, safekeeping, restoration, emancipation, and redemption from a life of sin. Thank you Father God, I can now call You Father because I am now your son/daughter, just like Jesus. In Jesus Christ's name, Amen!!

About the Author

These books came about through praying for others as an intercessory prayer leader. My decision to join the Prayer Ministry at the church I attended came after I called the ministry prayer line, asking for prayer when my father suddenly passed. The prayer was very impacting, because of God's Words of direction and guidance that was ministered to me by the Holy Spirit. Several years later during a time of prayer and fasting, I heard an audible voice in my spirit while I was thanking God for using me as missionary. The voice said, "No, you are an evangelist." I did not know what an evangelist was, so I went to my dictionary to get the definition. I then attended the Crenshaw Christian Center's ministry school, where the call to ministry was confirmed in a prayer meeting by prophetic words of confirmation given to me—the words were correct, clear, and accurate. I knew the Holy Spirit was speaking through the person, who did not know me. I spent twenty-six years as a prayer leader at my church. It was there that I learned to listen, become aware, know, and to be sensitive to the Holy Spirit's voice as we were instructed to pray in the spirit or (unknown tongues), for the items on the agenda. I became an ordained minister, although I still practice as a registered nurse to some degree after graduating from Kingston School of Nursing over four decades ago.

My previous book was to evangelize or share the Gospel. My intention was to answer my relative's question, "Who Is Jesus Christ?" in a few pages. However, the Holy Spirit told me to keep on writing. This resulted in a 65-page book, which was published in 2007. This second edition, which is an addition to the first book, was started in 2010. These books were solely written by the direct leading of the Holy Spirit. I give all thanks to Him and my prayer partners for making these books possible.

May many lives turn to Jesus Christ. May they come to know their purpose and existence in this earth and to live it to glorify God.

My prayer is that Satan's plans to kill, steal, and destroy the life that God has given everyone be realized and disrupted. Satan does not want you to discover the incredible value God has invested in you, which is to redeem your lost soul from hopelessness, suicidal thoughts, perversion, and despair. He would rather you wonder around this world, trying to find the reason for your existence through riches, success, and relationships instead of through God by receiving Jesus Christ. May this book deliver you from Satan's hellish plans and purpose for your life. Experiencing frustration, discouragement, depression and torment in this world and knowing that Jesus Christ is able to deliver you is far better than waking up in a place called Hell only to experience Satanic torments and Hell's fire. This is a place that Jesus Christ went to for you, so you do not have to go there. God is trying to get your attention! Do not continue to ignore Him! He wants to give you the peace and the purpose for your life that you have been searching for that is only found in knowing His Son, Jesus Christ.

www.ingramcontent.com/pod-product-compliance
Lightning Source LLC
Chambersburg PA
CBHW031412290426
44110CB00011B/346